IBN 'ARABI

This work is dedicated to my teacher, guide, and master, Shaikh Safer Dal Muhib al-Jerrahi.
His soul, in the hands of his Lord, is the gracious governor of the kingdom of his being.

IBN ʿARABI

Divine Governance of the Human
Kingdom
*At-Tadbirat al-ilahiyyah fi islah
al-mamlakat al-insaniyyah*

◆

What the Seeker Needs
Kitab Kunh ma la budda minhu lil-murid

◆

The One Alone
Kitab al-ahadiyyah

by
Hadrat Muhyiddin Ibn ʿArabi al-Hatimi at-Ta'i
Interpreted by
Shaikh Tosun Bayrak al-Jerrahi al-Halveti

My humble thanks to Shaikh Shems Friedlander, Shaikha Jamila Bayrak, Rabia Harris and Zinnur Doganata.They are my companions on the path to the Truth and have all contributed to this work. May Allah be pleased with them and may He not abandon me, this humble servant, to myself.

© 1997 Tosun Bayrak

Printed in Canada

Book Designer
Shems Friedlander

ISBN: 1-887752-05-6

Fons Vitae
Gray Henry, Director
49 Mockingbird Valley Drive
Louisville, KY 40207-1366
USA

www.fonsvitae.com

Contents

TRANSLATOR'S INTRODUCTION

Muhyiddin Ibn 'Arabi is one of the greatest personalities in both Islamic and universal mysticism. Both the Eastern and the Western worlds are in agreement as to his greatness, although they do not necessarily agree as to what sort of greatness it is.

For over seven hundred years the world of Islam has been in controversy about the Shaikh. Many people love, respect and admire him, but there are also those who belittle and curse him.

Farsighted people of refined intelligence have always found treasures in the depths of the vast ocean of his words and have called him "*ash-shaikh al-akbar*" (the greatest of spiritual guides). But narrow-minded people, blinded by fanaticism, who cannot penetrate into his work, have insulted him by calling him "*ash-shaikh al-akfar*" (the greatest of heretics).

Great men have more enemies than friends. Even when our master Muhammad, peace and blessings be upon him, shed his light upon a world buried under the night of ignorance and corruption, only a very few welcomed him. Many, whose eyes were used to darkness, did not see his light—nor did they want to.

Ibn 'Arabi all his life felt the pain of not being understood. Yet the breadth and depth of his wisdom, insight, vision, and knowledge was and is awesome to whomever catches a glimpse of it. Many of his expressions of divine mysteries have never been improved upon. Many important affairs, which he foretold centuries ago, have taken place and continue to take place.

Despite—or because of—the controversy surrounding

him, Ibn 'Arabi has become one of the most important expounders of Sufi wisdom. His influence quickly spread even beyond the Islamic world, entering medieval Europe. In their famous studies, Asin Palacios and Salverda di Grave have pointed out that Dante, in the *Divina Commedia* was often inspired by Ibn 'Arabi's works, deriving from them both the grand design of Hell and Paradise and the image of the beatified young woman as guide to the divine. Through Dante's prestige, these themes permeated old Europe. Today, the Shaikh's influence on the spiritual growth of humanity continues to grow as his works become more and more available in the West.

His words are like waves in an immense sea containing endless secrets. He produced through inspiration perhaps five hundred books. Many of them are short, about the length of a long article. Some, like *Fusus al-Hikam, Mawaqi' an-Nujum*, or *Futuhat al-Makkiyyah*, are books of many volumes that have responded to the questions and yearning of multitudes of seekers since his time. They are wellsprings of wisdom. Yet there is a great deal of thought in these books that cannot be digested by many intelligent people—even scholars—if their intelligence and knowledge are not supported by pure and believing hearts. Nor is this wisdom accessible to theologians who see only the surface and the form of their religion.

In his prime, Ibn 'Arabi was a thin, middle-sized man—well proportioned, with small, delicate hands and feet. His skin was white. His head was small, with a round face, a high forehead and a fine slightly curved nose of medium size. He had eyebrows curved like the crescent moon; he wore a thick white beard.

He was courageous and tenacious, extremely

patient, and very generous with both the material things he owned and the deep wisdom he possessed.

Although not everyone understood him, all were in awe of his spiritual presence. Always gentle, compassionate, and merciful, he viewed everything with love, including his enemies and dangerous animals. He detested violence, even in the punishment of murderers. He wrote, "Although according to religious law the punishment for murder is death, it is better to forgive." He also wrote, "On the Day of Judgment, I will intercede for those who deny me."

One of his contemporaries hated him so much that he would curse him ten times after each of his five daily prayers. When the man died, Ibn 'Arabi went to his funeral. Afterwards he wouldn't eat or drink or see anyone for days. A close friend insisted that the Shaikh come to his house for dinner. He obliged, but neither spoke nor ate, until all of a sudden, he smiled and started eating. When his friend asked him about his recent state, he said, "I vowed to my Lord that I would go into retreat and fast until He forgave that man who hated me so. Now, Allah, in His mercy, has forgiven him, so I can return to the life of this world."

Muhyiddin Abu Bakr Muhammad ibn 'Ali ibn al-'Arabi was born on August 7, 1165 (560H), on the twenty-seventh day of Ramadan, in the city of Murcia in Andalusia. He was a descendant of Hatim at-Ta'i, the legendary model of Arab generosity.

Ibn 'Arabi's father saw the potential in his son early, and when the family moved to the great cultural center of Seville, he had him thoroughly educated. At eight years of age he began to study hadith, Qur'anic commentary, and Qur'anic recitation with the famous teachers of the time. He also studied the literary arts and physical sciences and

associated throughout his youth with many Sufis, including two distinguished female spiritual guides. At a very
tender age he thus became accomplished in both worldly
and religious knowledge. Even his teachers respected the
intelligence and wisdom of this child.

Once his father sent the youthful Muhyiddin to visit
the greatest philosopher of the era, Ibn Rushd (Averroes).
Ibn Rushd was amazed by the supernatural talent and
aptitude of the young man. He received him with respect
and even debated with him. During their interview
Muhyiddin was able to answer questions whose answers
were only known to Ibn Rushd. Ibn Rushd was amazed to
see that this young man knew things, instantly and mirac-
ulously, that he himself had only obtained through years of
study. It was as if the youth were reading his mind. He said
that, having read that such people existed, he was thankful to Allah for bringing him such a being. Still, the great
philosopher, proud of his knowledge, was unable to see his
young guest's true value and continued in his own way.

For his part, Muhyiddin wished to encounter Ibn
Rushd again. In his dreams, though, he saw veils between
himself and the philosopher; he understood this to mean
that there was no way for understanding and agreement to
exist between them. So another meeting never took place.
When Ibn Rushd died in Marrakesh in 1199 (595H), his
body was sent back to Cordoba. Ibn 'Arabi was there, and
he observed with sadness that the transport camel bore on
one side the coffin of Ibn Rushd, and on the other side, as
a counterbalance, the books the philosopher had written.

While Muhyiddin was still a youth, he also made
the extraordinary acquaintance of *Khidr*, a wandering
immortal sent by Allah to assist his special friends. Since

the young man himself was destined to wander for much of his life and had unique access to hidden things, many people came to believe that the cryptic *Khidr* was Ibn 'Arabi's special patron.

In 1201 (598H), when his father and mother had died and his first marriage had concluded, Muhyiddin left Seville, intending to perform his Pilgrimage. He never returned to Spain. The Shaikh's journey eventually included all of North Africa, the Near East, and Anatolia. He visited Marrakesh and Fez in Morocco; Algeria, Tunis, and Egypt; Mecca and Medina on the Arabian peninsula; Syria and Iraq; and the cities of Malatya, Sivas, and Konya of the Seljuk Empire. He traveled, in fact, through the entire Arabic-speaking world.

Before he left on this epic journey, he had a vision in which all the prophets were gathered. The prophet Hud advanced to meet him, and Muhyiddin asked him the reason for such a gathering. Hud replied that the prophets had met together to intercede with Allah on behalf of the great Sufi martyr, Mansur al-Hallaj, who, as punishment for certain critical statements, had been kept apart for centuries from the Prophet Muhammad, peace and blessings be upon him.

In this vision Muhyiddin was also shown his own life—in its entirety, from the beginning to the end. This made him decide to start his travels immediately. His first stop was Marrakesh in Morocco; there a dream directed him on to Fez. In his monumental work, *al-Futuhat al-Makkiyyah* (Meccan Revelations), he relates the dream:

> I saw a treasure under the Divine Throne where the verse, "There is no power nor

strength save in Allah, the High, the Great" is generated. I visited many other treasures under that one, from every corner of which beautiful birds flew out. The most beautiful of them all flew in front of me and gave me greetings. It was revealed to my heart that I should take it as my companion in my travels to the regions of the East. I asked my heart, "Who may this companion be?" I was in Marrakesh at that time. My heart told me, "He is Muhammad al-Hasar in the city of Fez, who begged Allah to bring him to the East. So take him with you as your companion." I was pleased with this, and told the beautiful bird, "Allah willing, you will be my companion." I went to Fez, sought and found him, and asked him, "Have you prayed to Allah for something?"

"Yes," he said. "I begged Him to send me to the cities of the East, and I was told that someone called Muhyiddin would take me there."

I smiled and said, "I am Muhyiddin." We became companions and friends until we reached Egypt, where he died.

During this period of his life, Ibn 'Arabi spent his time fasting, praying, and meditating. The last period of intense worship, which raised him to the level of sainthood took nine months, from Muharram to the end of the month of Ramadan. He neither ate nor drank and was in a continuous state of ecstasy.

In Tunis on their way to Egypt, Ibn 'Arabi and Muhammad al-Hasar had a strange experience. The

Shaikh relates:

On our way, I found a man living in a marsh in a place covered with rushes. I learned that he had lived there for thirty years in seclusion. I stayed with him for three days. He prayed day and night and did strange things. Every morning he went fishing and caught three fish. One he would let go, one was his meal for the whole day, and one he gave to the poor.

As I was about to leave, he asked me where I was going. I told him, "To Egypt." Tears came to his eyes. "Oh!" he said. "My beloved master, my Shaikh, is in Egypt. Please go to him and give him my respects and greetings. Ask him to advise me what to do with myself in this world."

I was amazed. That man had abandoned this world and the worldly. It seemed to me that he did not need any advice about it.

When I went to Egypt, I found his Shaikh living in a palace in complete luxury and wealth. He appeared to be nothing more than a man of the world. When I told him the request of his dervish in Tunis he said, "Go and tell him that he should take the love of this world out of his heart." This also amazed me, coming from him.

On my return to Tunis I found the secluded fisherman and told him what his master had said. He shed tears of blood. "Woe is me! For thirty years I have separated myself from the world and spent my time in worship, but my heart still belongs to the world! While my master lives within the riches of this world, he hasn't a drop of it in his heart, neither its love nor its worries. O Muhyiddin, that is the difference between him and me!"

This story related by Ibn 'Arabi became the essence for many who follow the mystic path. While others withdrew themselves from the world, trying to purify their hearts in caves and cells, Ibn 'Arabi, and other Sufis following his example, wandered the world, viewing the beauties of creation and finding in it the traces of divine power. They used the world as an object of meditation and remembrance of Allah.

Indeed, seclusion is like a hospital for the sick at heart. As one does not stay in a hospital forever, neither is it right to stay in seclusion for more than a short while. Perfecting one's humanity comes through living together socially. At best, seclusion is necessary to clean the mirror of one's heart—which then must be taken out to the world, where the manifestation of divine power reflects on it and brings knowledge of the Creator.

When Ibn 'Arabi came to Egypt, he met most of the scholars, wise men, and sages there. The *qutb*—the chief saint of the time—was also in Egypt. Ibn 'Arabi found him, for he knew that the perfection of his mystical growth depended on divine knowledge manifest in such saints rather than in only praying and fasting and withdrawing from the world. He relates his encounter with the *qutb*:

One day the *qutb* asked to have a feast prepared

for the community of sages in Egypt. We had made a meat dish, which cooked for a long time in large earthenware pots. After the food was brought to the tables, when everyone had taken one mouthful, all the pots broke. Suspecting a divine sign in that strange event, the *qutb* addressed us, saying, "What do you think is the reason for this strange happening?"

Many answered giving physical reasons, and some, theological ones. One comment interested the *qutb*: Someone suggested that the pots were trying to say, "I have been honored by the hands of the friends of Allah who came close to me. That is sufficient for me. If I hadn't destroyed myself I would have risked that the enemies of Allah might cook onions and garlic and leeks in me!"

Then the *qutb* turned to me and said: "O Muhyiddin, what do you think?"

I said, "The pot is telling us, 'May your heart break in a thousand pieces if you put in it the love of others after the love of Allah has entered it!'" The *qutb* smiled and approved and said, "That is exactly what I think."

Thus, spiritual knowledge and the divine wisdom obtained through it bring one close to the truth, enable one to see the inner reality, and grant the ability to take lessons from everything one sees.

Ibn 'Arabi went on to Mecca, where he stayed for several intensely visionary years. Here he encountered his female image of knowledge, the young girl Nizam, "a sage among the sages of the Holy Places," who inspired his famous poetic work *Tarjuman al ashwaq* (The Translator of Ardent Desires). Here, too, he married again: to Fatimah bint Yunus, daughter of the sharif; and fathered a son, 'Imaddudin, who would follow his father and eventually, in 1269 (667H), share his tomb.

In Mecca he also began his monumental work, *al-Futuhat al-Makkiyyah*. The *Futuhat* was a vast compendium of insights and unique symbolic teachings; each of the eight volumes took a calligrapher two years to copy. What it contains is not knowledge obtained from university scholars or written in books, but wisdom revealed from divine sources, discovered through personal experience. When he was writing it, it was as if he were forced to do so against his will. He became feverish and would sweat, even when it was cold. He confessed, "I do not write literature out of my own will and intention, as others do, but I receive such powerful inspiration that it burns my very being. Only writing it down extinguishes the fire."

For instance, he relates in the *Futuhat* an inspiration he received:

> As I was circumambulating the Kaaba I saw a strange person, quite different in appearance from what I was accustomed to seeing among the people. As he walked around the Kaaba he continually recited, "We, like you, are circumambulating this House." I caught up with him and asked him who he was. He said, "I am your ancestor far removed."
>
> "When did you live?"
>
> "I died over forty thousand years ago."

"They say Adam, may Allah's blessing be upon him, was the first man and lived only six thousand years ago."

"Which Adam do you mean? Know that he is only the last of one hundred thousand Adams who came and passed away before him."

(Indeed, modern science has discovered evidence of people who lived hundreds of thousands of years ago. There is no indication in the Holy Qur'an, nor in the hadiths, that man was created seven thousand years ago. This idea came from an interpretation of certain genealogies attached to the Torah.)

The Shaikh relates another such incident that occurred in Mecca:

One Friday, after the congregational prayers, I was circumambulating the Kaaba. I saw a man whose costume and physical appearance were very different from those of everyone else. He seemed to be floating in the crowd, passing in between people without even touching them. It was revealed to me that he was a pure spirit made visible.

I stopped and greeted him and talked to him. His name was Ahmad as-Sabti. I asked him how it was that he was given the privilege of assuming a form and shape and of performing the hajj after having left this world. He said, "I used to work for this world only one day a week, for my sustenance. I spent the rest of my time in worship."

"Which day did you work?" I asked.

"Saturday," he said, "because Allah Most High began the creation on Sunday and ceased working on that day. So I worked the day He ceased work, and received the profit of the six days He worked!"

"Who was the *qutb* when you were in this world?" I asked him. He said that he was. Then he disappeared.

A Meccan friend of mine who was present asked me, "Who was that person who talked to you? I have not seen such a person in Mecca all my life!"

As Hafiz ibn Najjar has said, "Ibn 'Arabi was a *qutb* and knew the other *qutbs* of his time. Furthermore, he knew the *qutbs* of the past and future. Mostly he kept company with the Sufis and spent his time at the Kaaba. That seemed to be his only pleasure."

Despite his deep attraction to the Kaaba, his business in Mecca was temporarily concluded two years later and he resumed his travels. In the year 1204 (601H) Ibn 'Arabi came to Baghdad. He stayed only twelve days. In that brief time he found and wore the cloak that had been left for him fifty years before by the pivotal Sufi teacher, Shaikh Abdul-Qadir al-Jilani, and he met with the wise men and sages of Baghdad. He spent another three years on the road, in Mosul and Egypt, before returning to Mecca in 1207 (604H).

This time he could spend only a year in Mecca before the journey summoned him. He returned to Mosul, proceeded through Malatya and Sivas, and came in 1210

(607H) to Konya, the political and cultural capital of the Western Seljuk Empire. In Konya he is believed to have married the widowed mother of Sadruddin al-Qunawi. Sadruddin was the grandson of the Sultan of Malatya and already a promising Sufi. His intention in this marriage was more than having a good wife; it was also to have as a son Sadruddin, who later became one of his most important disciples.

(The Shaikh's other blood son, and his daughter, were possibly born from this marriage. Sa'duddin, born in Malatya in 1220 (617H), devoted his life to the study of hadith and died in Damascus in 1258 (654H). His beloved daughter Zaynab probably died while still a child.)

Ibn 'Arabi came back to Baghdad in 1211 (608H). Here he encountered another great Sufi shaikh, Shihabuddin 'Umar as Suhrawardi. When they met, they meditated upon each other without saying a word. Suhrawardi's opinion: "Ibn 'Arabi is the ocean of truth. Everything he is and everything he does follows the example of the Prophet. Both his visible self and his inner self reflect and are filled with the light of Muhammad, peace and blessings be upon him."

It was around this time that Ibn 'Arabi's mystical knowledge reached perfection. He was so immersed in the ocean of Truth that his words as well as his inner being became invisible and inconceivable to those who remained on the shore. From 1213 (610H) to 1221 (618H) he moved from Baghdad to Aleppo, back to Mecca, back to Malatya, and again to Aleppo. During this period he increasingly encountered envy and misunderstanding, much of which he attempted to disarm. Yet, he also found supporters in high places: for example, al-Malik az-Zahir, ruler of Aleppo, and al-Malik al-'Adil, ruler of Damascus. When, in 1223 (620H) al-'Adil implored him to settle in his city, he accepted. His wanderings were finally over. Except for a brief visit to Aleppo, he would remain in Damascus for thirty years.

Since the event is said to have occurred in 1223 (620H), it must have been in Damascus that Ibn 'Arabi met a young man who would become another Sufi of universal scope and appeal, Mevlana Jalaluddin Rumi, inspirer of the Mevlevi Sufis, the famous whirling dervishes. (It was still five years before Rumi and his family, now wandering as refugees, would move to Konya, where Ibn 'Arabi's disciple Sadruddin al-Qunawi would later become attached to Jalaluddin as well.)

The adolescent Jalaluddin accompanied his father Baha'uddin (one of the greatest men of knowledge of his time) on a visit to Ibn 'Arabi, who recalled this meeting with pleasure:

> I asked Jalaluddin how old he was and he answered that he was a year younger than *Huda*, Allah the Guide. According to the numerical value of the letters, the word *Huda* adds up to 605. As Jalaluddin said he was a year younger, he meant that he was born in 604 [1207 CE].

As Baha'uddin and young Jalaluddin took their leave, Ibn 'Arabi said, "Amazing, that an ocean is following a small lake!"

Not all of the Shaikh's encounters in Damascus were happy ones. Many of the scholars and theologians there, as elsewhere, envied and hated him—not least because he had the favor of the prince and his highest officials. Their claim, though, was always that his religion was suspect. One scholar who defended him was Kamaluddin ash-Shami. "Those of you who deny him and condemn him and claim not to understand him, come to me!" he offered. "I will speak in your tongue, help you in your difficulties, and eliminate your doubts." It is not clear that his offer was very widely accepted.

In his turn, Ibn 'Arabi was none too fond of the scholars of Damascus, but their opposition to him was not the reason. He disliked them because they sold their knowledge for profit, and that money had become a veil preventing them from seeing the Truth. He hated money, and he hated the people who made money their god.

Someone once gave him an enormously valuable palace as a gift. Immediately after he accepted it, a beggar came and asked him for money. He had none. "O man in need," he said, "I have no possessions except this palace. Please take it, for the love of Allah!" And he gave the beggar the palace.

One day in Damascus he saw an imam—a lover of money, not of Allah—leading a whole congregation of people who also had the love of money in their hearts. He called to them from the door, saying, "I am treading upon the god you worship; he is under my feet!" The congregation left their prayer to curse him and beat him. Some say he died from the wounds he received on this occasion.

He left this world on the night of Friday, November 16, 1240 (638H), the twenty-eighth day of the Arabic month of Rabi' ath Thani. He was seventy-six years old. His funeral prayer was presided over by the *qadi* of

Damascus, and he was buried in the quarter of Salihiyyah.

The scholars eventually had their revenge. His grave later became the site of a garbage dump. So it remained until the Ottoman Sultan, Selim I, the Resolute, took the city of Damascus.

Sultan Selim believed that Ibn 'Arabi had predicted his conquest of the Near East and Egypt in an essay called *"Shajarat al nu 'maniyyahfi dawlat al-uthmaniyyah,"* which described the Ottoman state long before it existed.

In that essay it was also written, *"Idha dakhalassinufish-shin, yash'aru qabra Muhyiddin"* ("When the letter 'S' enters the letter 'Sh,' Muhyiddin's tomb will be discovered.") The learned men in the Ottoman court interpreted the letter "S" as standing for Selim and the letter "Sh" as the city of Sham, or Damascus. They informed the Sultan that he would discover the saint's tomb when he conquered Damascus.

Indeed, when Selim entered Damascus, the first thing he did was to search. He found the lost grave covered with garbage. The great warrior wept and ordered a tomb and mosque built on the site. Then he commissioned Shaikh Makki, one of the greatest theologians of the time, to write a book on Ibn 'Arabi's life and works.

Shaikh Makki wrote *al-Janib al-gharbifi mushkilat Ibn al 'Arabi,* attempting to clarify some of the misunderstandings about Ibn 'Arabi's thoughts in a language even narrow-minded people would understand. Other scholars of the time were encouraged by the sultan to write forty commentaries on the *Fusus al-Hikam.*

Sultan Selim also visited the mosque where the

attack that may have caused the saint's death had occurred. He found the spot where the Shaikh had said, "The god you worship is under my feet!" and had it excavated. A treasure of gold coins was discovered.

May Allah have mercy on the soul of Muhyiddin Ibn 'Arabi, and may He be pleased with him and bestow peace upon his soul.

May the Creator of All, Master of the universes seen and unseen, known and unknown, Allah—free of all fault, heedlessness, defect and deficiency, pure and most holy, knower and container of all things, the Lord who preserves us from all disasters and calamities—bestow His blessings and grace upon our Master Muhammad, upon his family and companions.

May Allah bestow His peace and blessings upon our Master Muhammad, upon all the prophets and messengers, upon the saints and the righteous servants, upon the angels, upon those who reside by the Throne of Grace, and upon all faithful servants among the peoples of the earth and in the heavens. Amin.

◆

An Ottoman legal edict passed by Kemal Pashazade, Teacher of Sultan Selim the Resolute:

All praise is due to Allah who brought us to the level of knowledge and obedience so that we might pass a just decision, and peace and blessings upon His Prophet whom He has sent with divine instruction to correct the misguided.

We declare to all men:

Know that one of the greatest of all teachers, the

leader of those who believe in divine unity, the Pole of Knowledge, the performer of miracles, Muhammad ibn 'Arabi at-Ta'i, known as Shaikh Muhyiddin of Andalusia, is a perfect man who abided by all that Allah has sent.

He is a virtuous guide, legendary in his incredible miracles. He is responsible for the education of multitudes of men of knowledge, honored by all for their piety and virtue. Whoever denies him and accuses him of blasphemy is himself blasphemous. If someone insists on denying him the praise due him and continues to accuse him, it befalls the sultan to punish him, as well as to insist that the condemned one retract his statements. May the sultan abide with this edict, a reflection of divine justice.

Shaikh Muyhiddin has written many books, the most important of which are *Futuhat al-Makkiyyah* and *Fusus al-Hikam*. These books contain some material the content and expression of which is clear and understandable to all. Other material is veiled and kept secret from the eyes of people who only see the exterior of things. It belongs to those who are able to discover and see the inner reality. All of it is in accordance with divine ordinances as well as the canons brought by our Master, the Messenger of Allah, peace and blessings upon him. The ones who do not understand some things, distort them. Those who cannot understand these refinements should remain silent. They certainly should not accuse the writer of their own misinterpretations. I base my legal opinion upon what Allah, the Ultimate Truth, says in Surah Isra', 36:

> Do not pass judgment upon that of which thou
> hast no knowledge. Otherwise your ears, your
> eyes and your heart will hold you responsible.

IBN 'ARABI

Divine Governance of the Human Kingdom

At-Tadbirat al-ilahiyyah
fi islah al-mamlakat al-insaniyyah

ABOUT *DIVINE GOVERNANCE*

This book is one of the early books of Ibn 'Arabi written in all probability around 1194/590H in Andalusia, certainly before his migration to the eastern realms of the Islamic world in 1201/598H. He explains the cause which induced him to write this guide of how to fare in this life, if one was meant to live it as God's supreme creation: "When I visited the house of Shaikh Abu Muhammad al Mururi (al Mawruri), I found a book called "The Secret of Secrets" (*Sirrul Esrar*) written by Hakim (Aristotle) who was too old to accompany Zulkarneyn (Alexandre the Great) in his campaigns. The book contained instructions of how to rule the world.

"Ebu Muhammad told me, 'This book is about ruling the world. What I want you to do is to write a book about the governance of the human kingdom, of how to govern our own selves where our real salutation rests.'

"Upon this request, I wrote this book in the city of Murur (Mawrur) in less than 4 days. Hakim's is one fourth or one third of my book in length. There is much more circumspection, information, and meaning in the management of one human being and governing of a worldly kingdom, which Hakim (Aristotle) had ignored in his book.

"This book will serve those kings who are the servants of their servants, and lead the ones who realize that this life is but a road leading to the hereafter."

FOREWORD

May God forgive the faults of His humble servant, Muhammad ibn 'Ali ibn al-'Arabi at-Ta'i al-Andalusi. All prayer and praise belong to God, who has raised humanity from their limited existence and knowledge to the realization of Truth.

At first He created man as an atom in the shape of a beautiful jewel, upon which He gazed with love and compassion. When His sight fell upon it the jewel melted into water, and each drop of this water burst with divine knowledge.

Then He poured this water upon the roots of a sapling made out of divine harmony, which gave it the life of knowledge and beauty. He named the tree Human Being.

He gave the human being the faculties of seeing and feeling. He also made the human the wisest of His creation, teaching it all there is to know in His creation. He made it powerful and sovereign over everything. Then He gave the human being the Mind. And God kept man's secrets within His secrets, and hid his origin and nature within His Beautiful Names: the Gentle, and the Mighty One.

Next He presented the human being to the rest of His creation. When they gazed upon him, they felt the presence of divine wisdom, although God had hidden that in the infinite width and depth of His creation. All creation revered the human, and man felt pride in the power that God had placed in him.

Then God manifested His own power upon him.

Man tried to escape from his Creator in fear of His fire, His awe-inspiring grandeur, and His wrath. But God caught him gently, without his even feeling it, and dipped him time after time into the waters of the azure ocean of hope. Thus the divine power revived in man again, and found its right place within him.

God showed man his place in the universe and traced his life upon this earth. He also set him free, not binding him to any place or time, and covered him under the veil of protection of an eternal life.

Thus He placed man above even His angels. He made them prostrate in front of him in allegiance. That is how God taught man His Names.

God made the human being His deputy in the universe and assured his success and predominance over everything. And He gave him Intellect as his prime minister, to help him govern his realm. To him he gave the secret of the word, made him speak even though a red-hot coal should touch his tongue. He gave a staff into his hand, a staff that swallows the snakes of the sorcerers: with that staff He broke the backs of all the tricks of all liars and illusionists.

He gave the human being the measuring stick, as a warning, to differentiate the great and the small. And man learned to fear Him.

Then God took the benefits of His whole creation and divided them among humanity as He saw fit. He put signs on the backs of each of His destined blessings, which come to all. The heart knows these signs, but the mind does not.

Then the human being was sent to his home—in the middle of the desert, without a drop of water—and was taught to seek the secrets under the earth. He taught these to others in turn, and turned the desert into a garden.

God taught man to do, while he could not do. God did for him what he thought he did. God gave all that he has to man only as a bridge to pass over. Blessed is he who passes this bridge in safety.

God knows how to keep His creation clean, or to sully it with what He puts in it, as He wishes. It is all calculated. This world is a testing ground for the believer and the unfaithful one alike.

God has created His kingdom in the human being as a pulpit from which He may be recalled in this universe. He has planted His divine knowledge in the man, and covered it, and forbidden him to divulge His knowledge as his own. He tells man to look out to the skies to see His signs, in so many heavens filled with so many stars, all swimming in the infinite ocean of space in accordance with His ordinances—while all of it is already within man.

All His creation streams between God's two feet, fast-flowing currents of fear and hope. That Eternal Calligrapher, in His infinite wisdom, wrote under His right foot:

> Whoever does an atom's weight of good will see it.
>
> (*Zilzal, 7*)

And under His left foot:

> Whoever does an atom's weight of evil will see it.
> (*Zilzal, 8*)

He who has wisdom and whose eyes of the heart are open knows he can but obey Him, and thank Him for that which he has received—whether little or much—and seek the treasures of Truth that God has hidden in him. He must contemplate his life and his death and be aware and prepared, for he will die the way he lived and be brought back to life the way he died.

Life will be taken away at an unexpected time and in an unexpected way, and it will be given back on the Day of Judgment. On a moonless night darkness hides all that is visible, but when the moon shines again, everything is again seen. This is a reminder of the sleep of heedlessness that hides reality from man's inner eye. Yet if God so wished, He could shed light over the darkness and even upon nothingness, as when the earth faces the moon and the moon faces the sun.

When God gave a staff into the hand of Moses, he struck the rock to test its secret, and water burst out of the rock. See how a frail piece of branch broke the hard rock and brought forth a stream of running water! Who was it, behind the veil of secrets, who hit the stone?

There is a whole treasure of secrets in the pure center of the human being. And what is it but heedlessness that prevents man from being thankful for the God-given treasures in his essence? Who but the godless would kill the human by denying its essence?

Woe to the hypocrite who belittles himself, pretending to be an ascetic! Indeed, his baseness is in his pretense. Why does he have to humiliate his very existence? If he only realized his own existence—even as a hypocrite—instead of denying it, the awareness of his own reality might balance his bad intention, and might save him from the punishment of the Hereafter.

The divine secret placed within you will be a reality only if you know it, find it, become it. Remember always that your Lord has created you only to bow to the Truth all the days and nights of your life.

This little book contains vast knowledge of great benefit to all. It is gathered from the gardens of Eden and from divine providence. It is meant to be a guide to believers. There are neither conjectures nor doubts in it. Even if some may find faults in it, they will concede that they are small, fine, and beautiful. I call this book Divine Governance of the Human Kingdom.

The book is divided into twenty-one chapters. Each section contains instructions for achieving unity, the Lord's gift to humankind. They show how to keep order within the divine order while improving ourselves; how to guide our lives in the right way; how to protect His kingdom, which is the human being, from oblivion; how to rule it in the way that it is meant to be ruled, by the soul that the Lord has placed in it as His deputy. This book is such a fountain that both high and low will be able to quench their thirst by drinking from it. For those who are able to see beneath the evident, there are signs that, if followed, will lead to the Source. For those who see the surface, there are things as plain as could be.

The essence of the mystic path is offered in this book. It is a path for all who wish to reach the doorstep of divine benevolence.

Whoever treads this path will walk in the company of the Owner of this world and His retinue of friends, helpers, and servants. All are intent upon the same goal, they have joy in their hearts, they share their due and are satisfied with their lot. On the way they will realize the reason for their existence, as well as their relations with and superiority to the rest of the creation. They will find that all and everything in the vast universe is within the human being—all this evident multiplicity made pure, concentrated, and unified, and fitted into the human person, with not a single thing left out.

Thus the whole creation in all its perfection is manifested in humankind. We are placed, in the connecting stage of our corporeal existence, between the divine attributes of Might and Grace. We are granted generosity, which we may dispense freely, and power to rule over all and everything. The wise who see the proofs of this phenomenon know it to be true, and say that there is nothing in creation more perfect than the human being whose purity and wisdom are protected by our Creator, the Lord of Beneficence and Compassion.

May God keep you close and obedient to Him: know that the Lord has created the creation in twos in order to have Himself distinguished from all else, so that His name, and His existence, is the only One. Thus it is known who is the Lord and who is the servant.

And the Lord taught man the truth of himself and the trust He leaves in his hand. In God's Holy Book it is written:

> And He it is who spread the earth and made in
> it firm mountains and rivers. And of all fruits
> He has made them in pairs, two of every kind.
> He makes the night to cover the day. Surely
> there are signs in this for a people who reflect.
> *(Ra'd, 3)*

9

Humankind is like the fruits He created in pairs. We are fed as He feeds the fruit tree. He makes us useful to feed others, like the tree. The tree ages and dies and is reborn from its own seed. That is our way, too. And as the tree has to be tended, so must we; as its fruits must be collected, so must ours. Otherwise our existence will have no meaning.

The divine wisdom, placed in abundance in the human being, leads humanity on the path destined for it. In that, we are superior to the rest of the creation, for we are blessed with God's beauty, wisdom, and secrets. The human being is like unto everything that exists. Tiny though we may be, we are the microcosm of the macrocosm. The whole universe is in us, and we find proofs in God's words:

> On the earth are signs for those of assured faith,
> as also in yourselves. Will you not then see?
> *(Zariyat, 20-21)*

> We will show them Our signs in the horizons and
> in themselves until they know that it is the truth.
> *(Sajda, 53)*

> We have not created the heavens and the earth
> and what is between them in vain.
> *(Sad, 270)*

> Did you then think that We had created you for
> no purpose?
> *(Mu'minun, 115)*

Between the two His command descends, [that
you may know that God is Powerful over all
things, and that God comprehends all things in
knowledge.]

(Talaq, 12)

"Between the two" means between the Lord and His faithful servant. He is the one who

teaches man that which he knows not
('Alaq, 95)

and gives him what he needs.

For the heedful there are many things in the greater
universe, yet all are interrelated. One can find the same in
the microcosm of the human being—for instance, in the
relation between the soul, who is the deputy of God, and
others assigned to rule.

For instance the body hair is similar to the forests.
And body fluids—some sweet, like saliva, some bitter, like
tears, some poisonous, like nasal secretions—all are like
the waters of this planet.

As the whole universe is created from the primary
elements of earth, water, fire, and air, so is the body of
man. The Creator says:

He it is that created you from dust.
(Mu'min, 67)

Further He says:

We have created them from clay
(Saffat, 11)

which is a mixture of earth and water.

11

Then He says:

We created the human being . . . of formed
dried mud
(*Hijr, 26*)

which is a mixture of earth and water and air.
Then He says:

He created the human being from sounding
[fired] clay
(*Rahman, 12*)

indicating the fire in man.

Corresponding to the winds blowing from the four
directions, the human body also has four powers: attraction, repulsion, retention, and digestion.

In this world there are both wild and domesticated
animals. In us there is anger, vengeance, the desire to
overwhelm, to war and make mischief. At the same time,
we work to obtain sustenance, to marry, to raise children,
and so forth. God says:

The unfaithful aim to gain their living, to have
fun; like animals they eat, [not knowing where
such heedlessness would lead.] Fire will be
their abode.
(*Muhammad, 12*)

God's angels roam in this world. Man also attempts
to purify himself with sincerity, faithfulness, and worship.
The universe holds things both visible and invisible. So it
is in man, who has an exterior and an interior being. In this

12

world there are the heavens and the earth. The human being also ascends and descends.

If you look at what is around you and seek what corresponds to it in you, you will find the Divine Truth.

You will see only temporal things, some with a shorter life, and some with a much longer one. But if you consider these as symbols, through your religion you will find that which corresponds to them in eternity. In this way you will gather figurative attributes to their corresponding metaphysical meanings.

Examples of this are in the Holy Qur'an, which has a figurative meaning comprehensible to all who speak Arabic. As the Prophet said, "The Lord revealed the Qur'an in the language that I speak." Yet there is also a hidden meaning. For instance, we read *washta'ala ar-ra'su shayba* (Maryam, 3) which literally signifies "my head caught fire," but the meaning is, "I have aged, my hair has turned white." Then there is *ka-ramadin ishtaddat bihi ar-rih* (Ibrahim, 18), which signifies "like ashes hurried by wind," but means that the deeds of the unfaithful are scattered like ashes on a windy day. There are many other examples whose meanings are different from what they seem.

Today, as always, the Sufis aim to understand the real meanings of things, beyond their appearances. Whenever your eye rests upon any existent entity in this world of matter around you, seek its original attribute, its essential meaning, which will explain it or transform it. When you thus find the proof of its existence, you will have found its true reality.

When the eye of the heart recognizes the divine attribute manifested in a thing, it also recognizes the

13

equivalent manifestation existing inside us. Then that thing is no longer outside and separate from us, but is known as a part of the human being. Therefore we assign it its name from among our own names.

A donkey is known to be stubborn; a stubborn man is like that donkey. A lion is powerful, king of the forest; a man with those attributes is said to be "like a lion." When we look at the sun or the full moon, we can associate these qualities with a person and say, "his mind is bright, his spirit is warm." As you see, the qualities contained in human character may be as base as a donkey or as high as the sun.

Ignorance and subjection to the ego abase a person. Intelligence and knowledge raise a person to perfection. But there are eclipses in this ascension, which are caused by the shadow cast upon the moon by the earth. Just so, our love for and attachment to the world and the desires of the flesh cause the interruption of our evolution. But just as the world is brought alive by sunshine, so the human being is made living by the divine light reflected from his soul.

When we compare all existence to what exists in us, and God's attributes manifest in the macrocosm to what is manifest in us as the microcosm, then we see the enormity, almost the infinity, of the 18,000 universes, and the small, limited existence of the human being, who has a very short span of life. Sometimes a difficulty may arise. We may lose hope that this path, this trend of thought, will bring us to salvation, felicity, and perfection.

To eliminate this doubt, it is good to remember two conditions which are our birthright, and which describe our responsibility as a human being.

The first of these is the promise our soul made to its Creator on the day He created all the souls. He asked us,

Am I not your Lord?

And we all responded,

Indeed, You are.
(A'raf, 172)

That is the original promise of the human essence to God, and it exists in every one of us.

The other condition is a threat, a prediction, a menace, with which we are also born: that whether we are able to choose the right over the wrong will make all the difference in our life, first here and then Hereafter.

Both the promise in our souls and our fear of error in telling right from wrong arise from the macrocosm—and even beyond. They come directly from the origin of all and everything, including the right and the wrong and divine justice itself.

If we listen to the soul which has given its promise to its Lord, and follow what it ordains for us throughout our lives, then we will find ourselves obeying what God commands and forbids. All the rest of the created universe follows its destiny without having a choice. It is by following our soul that we are at one with the divine harmony.

In the prophets whom God has sent since the creation of humanity, and especially in the last and seal of them, Muhammad (may God's peace and blessings be upon him), we are given a clear voice that speaks guidance to our souls. And although prophethood has ended

15

now until the end of time, in every age the world will contain a spiritual Pole. His name and place may not be known to all, yet he is the guide of the time, the divine representative in whom God's ordinances are manifest. All outer and inner, material and spiritual decisions in the governance of life come finally from him. Some he blesses with love and compassion and protection. Some he punishes. He is both inside of you and outside of you. When you meet him you will know him. If you do not know him, then he is not there. To indicate the way to find him is the purpose of this book.

Sufism is the path leading to the most beautiful secrets, leading to the conversion and transformation of your state. Only those who have a great need, a great wish, will seek and find this path. From those who have doubt, fear, and denial in their hearts, it will always be hidden.

Denial and fear are a result of not knowing. The terror of the unknown is the greatest weapon in the hand of our personal devil. Therefore this book aims to make the unknown known, answering questions in the minds of all seekers in the simplest and most understandable way.

We hope that the reader will find the desire to submit to the greater will of God, for submission is the key to the secrets he seeks, which then will bring him peace. The foundation of Sufism is submission to, and affirmation of, the will of God.

God's peace and blessings be upon our Master, the Messenger of Allah, who never said a word from himself, nor for his own sake. All that he said and did was said and done by God. That is why the ones who had faith in him and followed him were attached to him with the submission of a slave. They never sought proofs or justifications for what they were asked to do. Few asked him questions, and his Lord stopped them by sending the following verse:

> O faithful, do not ask questions about things which, if made plain to you, would cause you pain.

(Ma'idah, 101)

O seeker, my companion on the path to truth, as you follow this path you may find many obstacles and oppositions. The first of these will try to convince you to question your guide—Why? What is the proof of the truth? How does it compare to what we know? How do you know?

The saint Junayd al-Baghdadi said that if a new thing appearing now is compared to what was in the past, that new thing will disappear without leaving a trace. Do not listen to a teacher if there is an inconsistency between what he says and what he is. If you need a proof of the validity of what you are asked to do, seek it in your own experience and in the result of what you have done. But to find it, you will need a tall ladder to climb, and that ladder also is stored within yourself. When you discover it, the truth will be your own.

Sharif al-Rida, grandson of Hadrat 'Ali, the Gate of Knowledge, (may God be pleased with them both), used to pray plaintively to his Lord, "O Lord, if I do not declare the essence of the knowledge You have given me, but keep it to myself, people say to me, 'We worship these idols. Which idol do you worship?' But were I to declare what I know, then the Muslims would think that shedding my blood is lawful; they would think that their worst sins are better than the pearls of knowledge I would give them!"

So when you are asked about the validity of this path you follow, ask your questioners in turn, "What is the proof of the taste and sweetness of honey?" They will have to concede that the proof of the sweetness of honey is known only by tasting it.

Imagine that someone has built a house away from the eyes of the world. When that house is finished, a person who knows the building trade comes and inspects it. Afterwards he tells people what he has seen. Is it right to ask that expert in building, who has fully explained everything about a house he has seen himself, "What is the proof of the truth of your description?" "What is the proof of the existence of such a house?" Is it not sufficient proof that the one whose profession is to build has inspected the house and described it in detail?

Those who believe the one who has seen the house, and appreciate what he has described, can always go and ask the permission of the owner of the house to enter it themselves.

The ones who know, know by following the prescriptions of the Prophet. Knowledge is only acquired by people who love and fear God. If you see such a person—who is devout, stays within his limits, and behaves as if he is always in the presence of his Lord—listen to him, agree with him, and submit to him, even if the things he says surpass your understanding. God says:

> God chooses for His [special] mercy whomever
> He wills
>> (*Baqarah, 105*)

and:

18

He bestows wisdom upon whomever He wills.
(*Baqarah, 269*)

About Khidr, who was charged to teach divine justice to Moses, (may His blessings be upon them), God says:

We taught him a knowledge from Our own presence.
(*Kahf, 66*)

When God gives His secrets to someone, no one has the right to question that person, for it is like questioning the will and act of the Giver.

One day one of the Companions of the Messenger of God asked why the sunset prayer consists of three cycles while the night prayer is four, and why some prayers are recited silently while others are said aloud. The Prophet did not answer, because these prescriptions of the Lord belong to Him alone, and were not decided by His Prophet. His silence was the proof of the truth of how Muslims are to pray.

When such a question comes to mind, it indicates a doubt as to the authenticity of a truth. Know that it is a sign of lack of faith. Therefore neither ask, nor respond, nor analyze and doubt when you hear the word of God. If you do not fully understand it, ask God, as He indicates in the Holy Book:

And say: O my Lord, increase me in knowledge.
(*Ta Ha, 114*)

This prayer is a proof of your sincerity.

Faith is such a mirror that, if it is sincere, when spots and dirt covering it are cleansed, you will see yourself clearly in it. Will you see yourself as beautiful or not? It does not matter.

If someone comes up behind you and his face is reflected in a mirror, you know he is there, although you have not looked upon him directly—you have only seen his reflection. That is how one sees things, usually. We only look upon the reflection of reality.

We know, logically, that a thing reflected in a mirror must exist. But to see accurately, one's mirror of the heart must be trustworthy, cleansed, spotless, without any dirt that might distort what is reflected in it. What is the process of the cleansing of the mirror of the heart? It is an unending battle with one's ego, whose purpose is to distort reality.

When the mirror is cleansed, the heart tells of all those mysteries which were hitherto hidden. The pure heart does not lie. It cannot talk of things that it has not seen.

It is the mind that listens to the talk of the heart. The truly intelligent person is the one whose mind submits to his heart and is in agreement with it. An action taken in accordance with the decrees submitted by such a mind is a lawful action.

The mind by itself may be lacking. In some circumstances it misses the parts of the whole, thus diminishing the whole. At times it even stops, or it misconstrues. In that case it may try to shake the supporting columns of the religious law, or the foundations of the Unity. But it will be unable even to touch them. What the prophets and saints saw and tell about is what was revealed to their hearts. Thus it lies beyond the realm of mind. The Sufi is the one who knows this, and accepts what they say.

The mind meets with opposition and denial from those who listen to it. Whatever is opposed and denied returns to it and belongs to it. But that criticism which the Sufi suffers at times does not belong to him. He is clear of it.

If a Sufi encounters someone who is lacking in understanding, he protects him before that lack of understanding destroys him. Yet there may not be time to save him; one dies the way one lives and one is brought back to life, on the Day of Judgment, in the way one died.

Beware! Don't be heedless of what is being taught here. Turn the spotlight on yourself, and let the one who is seen, submit. Save yourself from the obscurity of denial. Opt for freedom, and with this new freedom, fight the tyranny of your ego. Sit on the throne of Intellect. Put the crown of service on your head. Judge, not with preconceptions, but by the reality of the Now. The truth is in the present.

When you tell what you know, look at the ones who listen. Observe: they will tell what they heard. You will see yourself, hearing from them whatever you told them.

When you see that happen, it no longer matters whether you were there or not. Then even if you are there, you are not there. Our Master, the Prophet of God, spoke the words of his Lord and said:

> My loving servant comes close to Me by the extra worship of serving My creation for My sake and in My name. Then I love him. And when I love him, I become the eyes with which he sees and the ears with which he hears.

When the Lord becomes your eyes, can anything be hidden from them? When the Lord becomes your ears, can there be an end to what you will hear?

That is the time to stand at the limits of your being and teach what you have heard. Praise your Lord for what He has taught to you. There is no end to knowledge. Don't ever stop learning.

May God keep you among the servants whom He has chosen to know His secrets. And may we say Amen with the might and glory that the All-Mighty and Glorious has bestowed upon us.

CHAPTER 1

THE SOUL: THE DIVINE DEPUTY, THE KING OF THE HUMAN REALM

I t is a fact that the universal soul within man is the ruler of the human being and the deputy of the Creator, for the Lord of Humanity said:

> Behold, Thy Lord said to the angels, "I will create a deputy on earth..."
> *(Baqarah, 30)*

As man is created central to the universe and is the microcosm to the macrocosm, the soul is central to the human being and is the deputy of the Lord. To protect ourselves from the criticism and assault of those who look upon life and the world only from the outside and who are blind to their outer and inner selves, we must explain what we mean.

God, the Ultimate Truth, guides us to Truth and shows us the Truth through the wisdom bestowed upon us by the ones who trod this path before us and who have entered this realm and understood what they saw.

May God shed light upon your inner eye, O follower of this path:

Know that the first being that God invented and thought of and created is a singular basic essence which is not formed into any creed or principle, yet which appears to exist in the next creed or principle. Though some philosophers claim that the first creation is a single being because only one can come out of one, if God had so wished, His will and power could have created many beings at once. To think otherwise would mean that God's will is limited and His power is lacking. God has the ability to create any and all things at once and there is nothing to prevent it. What is perhaps to be inquired into is the location of the source and the place of the divine power. If there is a proof that the first creation is a single being, that also is only His wish and His will.

I, Muhammad the son of 'Ali, Muhyiddin al-'Arabi say:

The rationalists explain their thoughts about the soul as God's deputy in different ways. Some called it the Clear Book of Evidence. Some called it the Divine Throne, others called it the Mirror of Truth. It is a fact that the Creator bestowed upon every human being a different attribute out of His own divine attributes and a different influence from His own esteem and rendered him special.

May God's pleasure be upon Muhammad Abu Hamid al-Ghazali, who said on the subject of the human soul as the deputy of God: The deputy which God sent as the master of all things is the soul, and the soul is not created, it is directly from the realm of God's command. The Sufis have found the proof of al-Ghazali's words in the Holy Qur'an, where it is written:

They will ask you of the soul. Say: 'The spirit
is from the realm of my Lord's command.'
(Bani Isra'il, 85)

Therefore, the soul is under the orders of God. It is within the knowledge of the Lord and is revealed by the Lord.

Thus the man of knowledge, believing that the origin of the soul is divine, believes that it received God's orders directly from His realm of power without any intermediary. And each such command is meant to fulfill certain functions. Thus, the First Cause named by the philosophers is the Absolute Existence of the One and Only. If another existence attached to the causal existence is added to Him, it becomes a second cause, and it becomes the first creation. In the created universe, every existence is the effect of a preceding cause. It is said in the Holy Qur'an:

Is it not His to create and to govern? Blessed be God the Cherisher and Sustainer of the worlds.

(A'raf, 54)

He has created all and everything with His knowledge. Know that He both creates and commands the created. The Lord of the universe is eternal, the nature of His essence is divine. He is One without any other, the Lord, Unique, Mighty, and Glorious. If we believe that the universe is created by Him and governed by Him and that the soul of man is His extension, His command to set and keep order in the universe, the real meaning is learned and understood and no more has to be said. God is the One who tells the truth and leads to the straight path.

Yet I must add, may God's pleasure be upon them, some of the rationalists said that the soul was not the first creation but the most appropriate of all possibilities, the first addition. Yet they named it with the attribute of a created thing. To name a thing with an attribute characteristic to it is not far-fetched. In fact, in the designation of the first created matter, the Lord has created things in twos. One He created without a cause or intermediary which in turn caused the creation of another. God did not create the creation in jest, but created it as necessary causes. The truth is, the first existence was created without a preceding cause and that existence became the cause of the creation of the others. Yet another cause to be considered is the preceding thought, such as the thought of satisfying hunger preceding eating or the thought of quenching one's thirst before drinking, wishing to solve a problem before learning, to wish to do the right thing before taking action, the thought of God's reward instigating a good deed, the fear of His punishment to be considered before sinning, and so forth.

Therefore, when the thinkers realized this and penetrated into the meaning of it, they named the Intellect as the first created matter, and as they didn't see any opposition to it in Islam, they called it the Throne of God. The Intellect that they called it the Throne is because it is conceived as the center of the universe and the source of all that God has commanded and forbidden. It is as if the gravitational center of the whole universe, to which everything is connected. Its place is conceived to be on the ninth heaven.

The soul of man, the deputy of God, is surrounded by the microcosm which is called the human being.

God, most gracious, is firmly established on
the Throne (of authority).
          (*Ta Ha*, 5)

There is a hidden meaning in this verse, to be told

to the ones who follow this path so that they taste the sweet taste of the inner meaning which Sufism seeks. The word "Throne" is balanced by the word "grace," and there is a level of perfect balance of God's attribute and the place of the source of power. The Throne is the place where man's soul resides. The only way in which God's magnificence can be realized is by ascending to that place. The Throne is in the vicinity of the Names "God" and "The All-Gracious." Think of Him in any of His beautiful Names. Call on Him in which ever way you think of Him. All the beautiful names and attributes are about Him and are His, and He is as you conceive Him. And the level upon which the Throne is set is the ultimate level that can be reached by humanity.

Our Master, the Messenger of God, peace and blessings be upon him, said: "God created man in His own image," meaning in the image of His Grace. The divine station, called the Throne, is the station of God's essence, and that which the Throne carries is God's divine attributes. O you who know the right from the wrong, think about this. O you who follow the path and thought you were lost for a moment, be heedful, come to yourself, see the inheritor within you and favor it. God tells the truth and leads to the right path.

Some Sufis who know these secrets call the soul the first teacher. It is so for the ones who are conscious of it and are under its command. They realize that although none of the creation accepted to bear the divine trust, the human being bore it.

The soul's relation to the microcosm is as central as Adam's to the macrocosm: God taught Adam all His Names. As it is said in the Holy Qur'an:

27

And He taught Adam the nature of all things.

(*Baqarah, 31*)

Adam is the being within the two hands of the Creator, whom He taught all His beautiful Names, His own attributes, preferring him to His angels. Then, addressing His angels, He said:

Tell me the nature of these if ye are right.

(*Baqarah, 31*)

To which the angels answered:

Glory to Thee, of knowledge we have none save what Thou has taught us.

(*Baqarah, 32*)

When God asked Adam to be the first teacher and His deputy, teaching His angels the names they did not know, He asked His angels to prostrate in front of Adam as people prostrate toward the Kaaba. In this world, if those who turn toward the Kaaba to prostrate are prostrating to the Kaaba, may God save them. They would then be guilty of the unforgivable sin, setting up partners to God. The prostration round the circumference of a circle whose center is the Kaaba symbolizes submission to that which is central. The prostration of the angels to Adam is the respect and humbleness of the student toward the teacher. When a person prostrates toward the Kaaba it shows that he confirms what he has learned from the All-knowing, and acknowledges his inability to do, his nothingness, his obedience. But it is also an honor bestowed, for prostration is a clear proof of human will. It is a gift of the Creator that

He gives to whom He wishes. Take heed, for here is another beautiful secret to contemplate. Did the Creator examine the attributes of His creation before He named them? If He did not how could He name things which He has not seen and examined?

We know that the Lord taught man as His deputy the names of all and everything and then charged him to teach these to His angels. He could have only taught him the names of things before him. To think that He taught him what He taught him from a distance, unseen, is a false conception. We believe that the Lord knew the things He named, for all the secrets of the universe are from Him and in Him and the Lord knows Himself. And He gave the secrets of the macrocosm which He created to the microcosm which He created so that the latter know and profit from them.

The divine sign of this is given to us by the word *hayula'*, the chaos which preceded the creation, before things were named. Some Sufis named this sign the Mirror of Truth because it is the materialization of the divine thoughts and hidden secrets. There is no way for a false thing to appear on the mirror of named things, for falsity is nothingness, and a thing which has the attribute of nothingness cannot materialize. When a true existence appears, there is no doubt or opposition to it, because the non-existent falsity disappears and is replaced by it. The secret is: the cause creates a necessity and man is this necessity and what the Lord indicates by the term *hayula'* is man and in its origin he is the mirror of the Lord. The Messenger of God, may God's peace and blessings be upon him, said: "The faithful is the mirror of the faithful." Here, the two "faithfuls" indicate similarity. While God says in the Holy Qur'an:

There is nothing whatever like unto Him.
(Shura, 11)

The being of humanity in its clearest and purest form is the appearance of all the attributes of the Lord— not, indeed, of His own Self, for there is nothing whatever like unto Him. The miraculous appearance of His beautiful attributes in man is described by God who says:

We have indeed created man in the best of forms.
(Tin, 4)

O you who are on this path, think how the Lord describes humanity in this verse! If you understand, this verse becomes the gate to knowledge, the source of divine wisdom gushing forth as water gushed from the rock when Moses struck it with his staff. The great man of knowledge, Abul-Hakim, may Allah be pleased with him, used the term *imam mubin*, "the clear book of evidence," to refer to the human soul. By this he means the Hidden Tablet. God refers to it:

And We have ordained laws for him (Moses),
in the (hidden) tablets, in all matters.
(A'raf, 145)

Shaikh Abul-Hakim calls the hidden tablets all and everything, as they contain all things ordained by God to be followed by the faithful. God also says:

And of all things have We taken account in a
Clear Book (of evidence).
(Ya Sin, 12)

which is the hidden tablets. The whole of the universe under and above the hidden tablets is surrounded and strengthened by man, the microcosm. That is why man is the real clear tool of guidance. And his station is close to God; he receives his guidance from Him. That is man's destiny and his joy. So be aware and realize what you have, for in that book which you are, God says:

Nothing have We omitted from the book.
(An'am, 58)

The best of God's creation, containing and realizing all possibilities, the true guide is the perfect man. No one who does not contain all of God's attributes and conditions and commands mentioned in the divine books or whose state does not fully correspond to them can be a true guide. The guidance is in the very being of one whose state corresponds to the conditions and characteristics recorded in the Holy Qur'an, which is the only distinguisher of truth from error. If such a being is available to guide, all others who claim to be guides become invalid.

When we look at man as the guide designated by God and see how this position fell upon him, and question whether this quality is from him, himself, or given to him, we can see that it is because of secret inner qualities and possibilities in man's essence. But the position of guide is given to him as a divine trust. God says:

God commands you to render back your trusts
to whomever they are due.
(Nisa', 58)

This is the divine command! So let us look into the mirror of truth. It is said, "The faithful is the mirror of the faithful": when the faithful looks into the "clear book of evidence," the guide, the mirror, shows the truth. Thus we see the mirror of truth brought forth by the divine command in which the faithful becomes the mirror of the faithful. Although there are two faithfuls, only one is seen.

The guide of the commands of God is verbal while the mirror is visual in which he is dematerialized, refined. The mirror is the keeper of secrets and of the divine trust. It is that guide of guides, our source, our support, the one whom we trust. Abu Madyan called the soul of man the holder of the divine trust. Other saints among the Sufis, as well, gave the soul this name. They considered the material being of man as a place of darkness. As the sun brings light upon the world, they thought of the soul enlightening the realm of the human being. Yet one must understand that although the same sun shines upon them both, the daylight of Baghdad is not necessarily like the daylight of Mecca.

When we think of the divine light which the Creator, the source of all light, kindled in His essence, we think of it as a ball of light and call it the sun, for the sun brings light to all parts of the world facing it. In those places upon which the sun shines there are other lights from the infinite power of the Creator, like other suns. The light that burns within one is called the soul. As the sun in the sky shines in different parts of the world with different intensities, so do the suns within people shine differently, depending upon whether the matter enclosing them is fine or coarse.

Whether fine or coarse, the material being is a close and honored relative of the light of the soul, and at times the soul floods the cup of the body and overflows and runs in different quantities through different organs of the body.

In some parts of the being it appears in abundance, and in others less. As the enlightenment of man and beast differ, so what man contains within may not be acceptable for the angels. Water flows and floods. That is its true character. But we also attribute this to the sun from which the light flows and floods the world. In the case of the sun it is only a metaphor. This the Sufis think: the human soul relative to the total soul is like the governor of a city compared to the king of the realm. If governors are beneficent, the citizens love them and support them. If they are tyrants, the same people condemn them and punish them. God says:

> The earth will shine with the glory of its Lord.
> (*Zumar, 69*)

The Lord is the one who is the owner of the earth.

The light which shines with His glory is His sovereignty and command. God also says, addressing the soul:

> Oh thou soul in complete rest and satisfaction,
> come back to thy Lord, well pleased thyself
> and well pleasing unto Him.
> (*Fajr, 27-28*)

The soul which the Lord addresses and reminds in this verse is the animal soul, which connects the human with the animal. At death, when it goes back to its Lord, it is like the sun setting, taking the daylight with it, and like the shadow of the world falling on the moon, darkening it.

Death is a cloud veiling the light of the soul. Like the sun, the guide sets, leaving in his place his deputy the governor, like a moon shedding light upon the night. In its turn, the moon also sets. But the enlightenment thrown by the governor upon the realm of human beings is not like the light of the king-guide. During the rule of the governor, the light of the guide is a hidden secret soul. When both the king and his governor are gone, what is left are the stars of the divine ordinance. Those are the wise men of canonic law, but they don't have the power to detect and eliminate the beastly attempts of the wild desires of the flesh, which will try to rule the human being.

O follower of the path of truth: if you look deep into the divine secrets, you will find that you yourself are the source of divine wisdom. The Sufis call this source the center of the circle. Someone came and asked the Sufi in which direction to go.

O Sufi, where is the wisdom hidden in the seen?
'Tis within the circle of the unseen.
If I can't find it, is there one like it?
Bits of it are here, you have to connect it.
The beginning is the Truth of which we know little.
For it is hidden in a light which is blinding.
It is spread within the four dimensions, each
overwhelming the other.
All meet at a center called the soul.
The circle ends at the top where it is starting.
Drop by drop it collects but there is always a first
drop.
The art is in it and all the power of other drops.
You ask about the ocean; it is within the drop,
And the life of man flows in it.
Very fast it floats to the eternal union
Of the end and the beginning is
God's gift, the Truth.

My advice to the ones who wish to follow this path: Know that what we call God's deputy, the soul, is the center of the circle of all existence. God entrusted it with this honored state because He knew its potential to rule in justice within the realm of the individual human being.

What moved the Lord to make it His deputy was this attribute of justice: without it, it would have remained a dot upon the circumference. Instead, God took the soul from the circumference and placed it at the center of the sphere. The proof of the characteristic of justice at the center is that all the radii from the center to the points of the circumference are equal. If a circle is to be drawn, the center is an absolute necessity. Thus the center is the cause of the circle. No matter how big a circle or sphere is, its measurement depends upon the center. The Circle exists because of its Center; the center is the guide, the commander.

Without this there is neither circle nor sphere. God existed forever and nothing was with Him. Spreading His arms and legs as radii, He described the circle of existence, a symbol of unending generosity and indivisible unity. The tip of one of His hands reaches to the top of the circle, which is the sacred secret realm of angels; one of His feet reaches the bottom of the circle, which is the realm of material, visible existence. The latter is the realm where God's order of right and wrong resides; the former are the levels of the beginning of creation. God covers all and knows all and addresses His creation, saying:

> I have created you from nothing, even as you were before your creation.

The hand of God does not move, but the circumference rotates. May God shed light upon your inner eye and show you the divine signs, and may the Truth shed light upon your path. If you would see and understand His signs and His attributes and character, you would find such beautiful Names! If you wished to enumerate them, they would not fit into the space within which you exist. Then you would see the honor and the grace bestowed upon you in comparison to the rest of the creation. May this suffice for the time being.

CHAPTER 2

DISCUSSIONS AMONG THE MEN OF KNOWLEDGE ON THE REALITY OF THE SOUL

Muslim scholars have differed over the nature of the soul, the deputy of God. Some have considered it to be the seed of the personality of a human being, thus attributing to it a place. In their minds this seed of individual human character has still a non-material quality quite different from the life-energy of an animal. Others have thought of it as a kind of being that cannot be realized by the senses or the emotions, yet by which the Creator linked the capacity for realization to material human existence. As long as the soul is within man, the living material being can think, understand, and realize. When the soul leaves the flesh, one's senses, and one's ability to perceive and conceive and feel, also leave.

Other scholars have thought of the soul as the deputy of God, acting and doing things in His name, but nonetheless of a fine created matter, versatile as a liquid, which is poured out and spreads and infiltrates into the minutest places in the human body, without a particular place of its own.

One of these scholars, 'Abdul-Malik ibn Habib, says: "The soul is a refined and ethereal existence, not matter but resembling it, with two eyes, two ears, two hands, and two feet, corresponding to every organ in the human body, yet hidden within it. Perhaps the whole of the visible human being is the materialization of the soul within it.

Then the question will arise, can anything prevent the soul from such materialization? The answer will be, no. The soul, the individual self, and their materialized form are united. Yet it is forbidden to them to feel each other, to hear each other. The soul feels the pain of the flesh as well as its joy, but it is eternal."

In both cases the soul is invisible. When we talk about the pain and joy that it feels, these are not physical pain and joy, but their meaning. The soul itself is the meaning of the body. How can a meaning, a concept, feel pain and joy through the concept of pain and joy? Rationally it is impossible. Something that is rationally impossible is not acceptable in Islam, just as the religious law cannot require something that is impossible.

A second question relates to the soul's eternity. If the soul needs a body, a material form to inhabit, and if there are a finite number of souls for created beings, are souls reincarnated in different forms and shapes at different times? Thus the opinions of the scholars which we have exposed are false. Those who do not accept that the soul is the seed-essence of the individual human being must accept that human essence is not of one single kind, but of many kinds. On the other hand, if we do accept the soul as a singular essence, we are obliged to think that the essence of everyone is the same. Rationally this also seems to be impossible. Those who think of the soul as the unique seed of an individual ignore the common role of Intellect. On the other hand if one accepts the soul as other than the individual essence, then one has to accept that it is not material, because the material body is formed of many centers maintaining related sets of essential characteristics.

Other sources say that the soul is a creative force

under the command of someone other than one's self. Abu Hamid Muhammad al-Ghazali, who is one of these, says that the soul is neither inside nor outside of the living being. It has no connection with it, yet it is with it at all times. It has no place, and its influence on every aspect and action of the living being is total. It is both separated from and united with the living being; its special character is that it puts things in order. Some question this opinion and say that even if the soul is the opposite of the flesh, it must be admitted that it is not far away from it.

If the human being becomes dependent on something other than the soul, the soul distances itself from it, returning when this dependence disappears. This means that the soul does not correct the false dependence of the being. Only the disappearance of the thing upon which the being depended solves the problem, and it solves it directly. If this dependence is upon inanimate things, when the being wholly ceases to consider them, they cease to exist for it, and disappear.

The power of the soul as an instrument of equilibrium and order is its ability to detect opposites, including the life in seemingly lifeless matter. So, are all these things illusions? The answer comes from those who claim the soul as the essence of the material being, and that the body is not an appearance resembling the soul.

One should consider the soul as the essence of the being, an ethereal body materialized in the flesh it fills, and see that it really is not an invisible essence inhabiting a visible being—because you are then assigning a place to it. It is not an existence occupying a place.

Al-Ghazali claims that the soul exists without form or place, as God does, yet it is not He.

Which one of these opinions should we accept?

Although they hold differing opinions about the soul, all these scholars believe in the oneness and unity of the Lord. When the Lord created the human soul as His deputy, He made it His mirror within which He saw all that He had created, and all His own Names and attributes. Humanity is the proof of God's existence and a guide to lead the creation to Him. He sent man into the universe as His deputy in order to make the created know the Creator. He gave him His trust and the light to enlighten others. He gave him all that and more, not to support tyranny but so that mankind might rule in justice, and made him responsible for all that might happen in the whole of creation. If we accept this, all that we have said is in concordance with the religious canons and scriptures. All existence is His, and so is all that happens, for He is the Creator. May God make you successful in your search. He is the one who guides one to truth, for He is the Truth.

CHAPTER 3

THE STRUCTURE OF THE CITY OF MAN WHOSE KING IS THE SOUL, THE DEPUTY OF GOD

When the Lord created His deputy, He also built a city for him where he could reside with his retinue and governing officials. He named the city Human Being. When the Lord finished the building of the city, He assigned a special place at its center for His deputy. All the speculations about it—whether the deputy really resides there or just uses it as headquarters, whether it is a throne room or a courtroom or a ministry, or merely a place where his voice is heard—are beside the point. The Lord called that place the heart.

The Lord built this city on a foundation of four walls made of earth, water, air, and fire. Some say that the place of the Lord's deputy is not the heart but the mind. I insist that it is the heart, although no one has evidence or proof. But for establishing stability and for heedfulness and remembrance, the heart is surely the center. Our Master related that his Lord said: "I do not fit into the heavens and the worlds which I created, but I fit into the heart of My faithful servant." Our Master, may God's peace and blessings be upon him, also said: "The Lord looks neither at you nor at your deeds, but at your heart." The Lord always remembers and is heedful, and looks upon His deputy at all times.

The Lord made the soul responsible for the body.

It is not their eyes which are blind, but their
hearts which are in their breasts.
(Hajj, 46)

Men wander upon the face of this world, and within the
space of their lives they see what is being born and dying,
what is being built and destroyed. They have eyes to see
and ears to hear, and should take lessons. If they are not
heedful it is because their hearts are blind. It is not the
vegetal heart that is responsible here, nor what is vulgarly
called mankind—a four-legged animal standing on its
hind legs. God has not given His secret to the animal, but
to His deputy the soul. Yet the vegetal heart is the palace
of that deputy, the king.

Our Master, may God's peace and blessings be upon
him, said: "There is a small piece of meat in the body of
man: If it is clean and righteous, the whole being is clean.
If that piece of meat is rotten, the whole being is rotten.
That piece of meat is the heart." It is the palace of the
deputy of God where the secrets are kept, and it must be
proper and in order. It is the safe where the secret docu-
ments and rules and orders of the deputy are kept.

If the leader is right, the followers are right. If the
leader has gone astray, his companions and followers will
go astray.

When the Lord made the human soul master of the
human city, He taught him the character, the behavior, the
thoughts of the inhabitants of that city. Since he understood his people, his people recognized him and became
his dependents and helpers. If God's deputy, whom He
sent to govern, is disloyal and corrupt and betrays His
trust, his people will be corrupt and disloyal to him as

well. On the other hand, if he fears and respects the One who entrusted him with power, his companions will trust and respect him also.

So look at yourselves: If you are God-fearing, just, and righteous, so is your soul. You are the way you are because of it. First the ruler and the guide must be right; then the signs of righteousness appear in his dependents.

One sees so many things in oneself, without knowing why they are, whether they were there in the beginning or happened afterwards or will be the same tomorrow—for one does not know the procedures of the secret divine government within, or how to protect that little piece of meat, the heart, whose disorder can destroy us all. The Lord created a tower on the higher levels of the city of man. He built it with refined materials and set it to overlook the whole city, and called it Mind. He opened four large windows on the top of it, for the enjoyment of the four corners of the city, and called them Eyes, Ears, Mouth, and Nose.

In the center of the tower He built a vault to protect the treasure of inspiration, and in it He stacked the treasure, all arranged in perfect order. The directors of the senses could consult this Hall of Information, and add new data to it in turn. The dreams dreamt come from this vault. Here too is the wealth gathered by the collector of taxes within the city of man, the monies stacked separately as lawful and unlawful. The Lord built another vault within the tower of the mind which He called the Vault of Intellect. The goods in that vault are brought from the Vault of Inspiration. Here they are weighed and compared; what is right is kept in the second vault, and what is wrong is returned to the first.

In a corner of the mind He built yet another vault,

where memories are kept. The keeper of memories is a high official called Intelligence.

There is another precinct in the city of man where the daughter of the deputy of God, Personality, lives. This place is known as Selfhood. Here there are contradictions, here both God's ordinances and what He has forbidden are kept. On special honored nights the commands of the All-Powerful are distributed here. The place is protected by God Himself, for it is under the Footstool where His holy Feet are set—just as the soul, the deputy of God, is under and protected by His Throne. Abu Hamid Muhammad al-Ghazali says: "The human being is that child whose father is the soul and whose mother is the self." He holds that the Lord of the soul keeps it on a high level under His Throne and our mother, the self, on a lower level under His Feet. As He is the Lord of the parents, so is He the Lord of our material existence, their child. The Sufis know that all states and actions of the self, whether right or wrong, are predestined by the Lord. The only part of man which is not bound by predestination is the soul, which they follow into the future. With precaution and insistence, they hope to rouse the deputy of God.

Even if the soul realizes the danger of the temptations of the commanding self, the human being is left in a difficult position. He is undecided between two powerful entities: the soul calls him unto him, then the evil commanding self calls him unto him. But all this test is by the permission of God, for He says:

All things are from God.
(*Nisa', 78*)

44

He also says.

> Of the bounties of thy Lord, We bestow freely
> on these as well as on those.
> *(Bani Isra'il, 20)*

And He says to the soul

> And the portion and order given to it and for its
> enlightenment as to its wrong and its right.
> *(Shams, 7-8)*

Selfhood is a place of order and enlightenment, but it is also inclined toward the Evil Commanding Self. If it is tempted, then it loses its purity. All things are from God— it is He who made the Commanding Self desirous of evil, and it is He who made human selfhood bent from time to time to evil as well as to good. When the self is rational and heedful, it is pure and in order. Then it is called the Self-Assured Self. That is its lawful state. Although God had created His deputy with the most perfect attributes, He saw that, on his own, he was nonetheless weak, power-less, and in need. God wanted His deputy to realize that he would only find strength in the help and support of his Lord. He created a strong opposition for him to provoke this realization. That is the secret of the two opposing pos-sibilities for human selfhood.

The soul and the self are man and wife. When the man calls upon his wife and she does not respond, people say, "What is the matter that your wife does not come to you?"

The man asks his trusted companion, Intelligence,

the reason for this unresponsiveness. Intellect tells his master, the soul, "O my gracious master, you are calling upon a being who has a station as high as your own. She is a master in her own right, with power, and under the orders of the All-Powerful. She is called Desire for the Worldly, the Commanding Self. It is not so easy to command her!" Then the soul sends his wife a letter by his adviser's hand, explaining his feelings about her. But the self takes the messenger of the soul prisoner. Intelligence submits to the self, under duress.

When Intelligence, now under the influence of the self, is permitted to return to his master the soul, he reports that not only has he lost his wife, but most of his administration and armies have gone over to her as well. Only a very few have remained loyal to him. The mind tells the soul that his enemy has already infiltrated the court-yard of his palace, and is ready to destroy his reign and capture his kingdom and sit upon his throne. He claims that it is his sacred duty to warn him before they are both destroyed. Now, with the warning of the mind, the soul realizes that he is reduced to total helplessness. He is powerless, unable to act. All he can do is to throw himself upon the mercy of the Lord of all and everything. Turning to Him, he begs for help. He knows now that he cannot save himself. Only at his defeat does he know the value of his Lord, the All-Powerful. That indeed was the purpose of all that had happened. If a man lived all his life in complete comfort and safety and had all that he wished for, nothing he had would retain any value for him. It is only pain and trouble that make one realize the value of peace and safety.

When God's deputy, the soul, turns to his Lord for

help, the Lord becomes a mediator between the soul and the self. And so the self abstains from taking total control of the realm of the human being.

The Lord addresses her "O Self-Assured Self, return to Me, pleased with Me; I am pleased with you. Enter My Paradise among My servants whom I love." Responding to this call both the self and the soul bow their heads in submission, satisfied by the divine approval. Now that all differences have disappeared, they come together again at last. The Self-Assured Self, whom the Lord addressed, is this joined existence of the soul and the self, harmonious and at peace, pleased by their Lord and their Lord pleased by them.

The Lord named it the Self-Assured Self because at this point the self has realized its true potential. When she was tempted by evil, it was against her nature, for the Lord Himself said, "all things are from God," and He also said "all His blessings are bestowed freely upon all, on these as well as on those." When He invites the soul and the self to Himself "well pleased themselves and well pleasing unto Him," it is implied that the two are pleased with each other and in harmony. When He invites them to His Paradise, He is inviting them to come to the safety of a secure place away from places unpleasing to the Lord. When they are asked to come into this Paradise together with His servants whom He loves, He includes them among those who have submitted to Him and have connected their hearts to Him in obedience.

The lust of pleasures of this world is the paradise of the unfaithful. It is the true Fire whose exterior resembles the Garden—but beneath the surface is torture. Our Master (peace and blessings of God upon him) warned his

47

Companions, saying, "Paradise is beyond gates that appear displeasing and undesirable while the gates of Hell are, attractive and delicious. They will only reveal what is behind them at the end of the world, when Antichrist comes." He also described Hell thus: "There are two valleys there. In one there is a river of fire and in the other a river of water. Whoever in repentance, accepting his punishment, seeks the valley of fire, will find himself in the cool valley of water. Whoever, unrepentant, seeks the valley of water to save himself from punishment, will fall upon the fire."

The self responds to the one who uses his intelligence. To a certain extent they agree. A grave question: Why is the soul that God has created as His deputy subverted by the Evil-Commanding Self? There are two answers. One has already been explained. God wished to test the soul to make clear to it its total need of its Creator, provoking failure by making it respond to the temptations of the Evil-Commanding Self while deaf to the voice of Intellect. The second opinion is that the soul calls and invites the self to it. When the self responds, it responds in a language the soul does not understand. It is the excitement and ambition of learning something unknown that gets the soul in trouble, just as it was Eve's curiosity about the forbidden fruit that made her believe the devil. Thus, mischief, sedition and war continue within the realm of the human being, caused by the misunderstanding and disagreement between the soul and the Evil-Commanding Self. At times one conquers the other; at times the situation is reversed. Sometimes one reigns in deserts and the other in fertile gardens. This battle will continue until the Day of Judgment.

The faithful who believe in God but who at times fail and are disobedient lose the deserts of their realm in the battle with the Evil-Commanding Self. While it reigns in those deserts, the king of the mind captures its capital. Hypocrites lose their capital city to the Evil-Commanding Self and hold on to the deserts of their being. Nonbelievers are slaves of the Evil-Commanding Self, having lost all the kingdom of the human being.

On the Day of Judgment two groups will form. One will be bound for Paradise, the other bound for hellfire, where they will stay forever. When all are gathered together so that everyone can see, Death will be slain. Then all will live in their assigned places for eternity. Believers who have failed to obey God at all times, after being punished by the fear of Fire will be sent to join those who are bound for Paradise. Hypocrites will be sent to join the unfaithful bound to suffer in Hell.

Division is incidental. Unity is principal. If a hand does something against the principle of the whole being, the whole being responds to prevent it from its error. The sick branch either dries and falls, saving the tree, or the sap of the tree cures it. Such is the state of the faithful who are at times guilty of errors. However if the whole body is sick, a healthy hand cannot cure it. If the whole tree is dead, the few last green leaves will not save it. Such is the case of the hypocrites.

In the kingdom of man, under the rule of the soul, the deputy of God, there are four kinds of citizens. There are pure faithful ones who obey the prescriptions of their Lord and have been able to protect themselves from all evil. Then there are those who are basically faithful, but at times are apt to revolt. There are hypocrites who try to appear faithful while they are not, and there are the unfaithful who take themselves to be God. That is how it is in the kingdom of man, amid the continuous mischief, sedition, and war between the soul, the mind, and the Evil-Commanding Self. This we shall try to relate, investigate and consider.

God the Truth tells the truth, and guides one to the straight path.

CHAPTER 4

THE CAUSES OF CONFLICT BETWEEN INTELLECT AND EGO, THE EVIL-COMMANDING SELF

O reader, may God lead you to recognize that falsehood becomes evident only when the mind and the ego start fighting, for when they attack each other the whole human realm is caught in the crossfire. So every member is rudely awakened and becomes aware of the conflict—that one or the other is striving to get hold, by force, of the whole of the human kingdom.

It is impossible, according to Divine Law and according to Intellect, for a kingdom to be ruled by two rulers. In fact, violent conflict will be the result of the rule of anyone but God. Thus it is necessary that the whole creation join in understanding and equality under Divine Law. Yet no government is ready to rule by it.

The reason for the revelation of the Divine Law is to eliminate disorder and to establish harmony. No one is ready to accept that Divine Law is immutable and applies to everything at all times, and that its purpose is to create a single and unique order. Yet it is known that the Lord wanted to delegate the government of the human kingdom to one single entity. The example of it has been given in the person of our Master, may God's peace and blessings be upon him, who also declared: "If, in a single nation, men swear allegiance to two rulers, eliminate one of them."

When ruling is deputized to someone, as is the case

with everything else, it has an outer and an inner meaning. What has been discussed up until now is the outer aspect of ruling. The inner spiritual, government infiltrating into the human realm—as if through narrow veins and thin nerves, invisibly and secretly—is quite different from the evident, visible outer order. When we understand the secrets of the inner government, we may think that this explanation is conjecture. On the contrary, find some comfort in it.

If you follow the tradition of our Master—who ordered that one contender be killed if there are two who attempt to rule one country—in the country of your being, you are liable, by error, to try to eliminate your Intellect. Thus you may leave the kingdom in the hands of the evil-commanding self. In your present condition you are not equipped to know which is which. In the battle between Intellect and the evil-commanding ego, one may have advanced and the other retreated.

Everything depends on the conditions in which you find yourself. They are like the conditions which decide who is going to lead a congregational prayer: whoever best fulfills these conditions becomes the imam. Thus one of the two contenders who have claims to rule must have the ability to adapt successfully to the existing conditions. The one who is unable to do so must be eliminated by the order of God.

The conditions which an imam must fulfill are ten. Six of these are matters of constitution. They are either existent in one naturally by birth, or else not. Four of the conditions may be acquired from outside. The six natural conditions are:

1. To be an adult, physically and spiritually mature.

2. To be rational, a possessor of Intellect.

3. To be free, not a slave of influences.

4. To be a man.

5. To be related to the tribe of Quraysh.

6. To be sound in the five senses.

The four acquired conditions are:

1. To have a strong feeling for helping and serving other people.

2. To be competent in social and legal matters.

3. To be knowledgeable.

4. To fear God and be determined not to sin.

It is essential that the force which is going to lead you spiritually must meet these conditions. Certainly your soul meets these conditions, and the evil-commanding self does not. Indeed, the soul is not God, but certainly it is from God.

When these conditions are briefly analyzed, perhaps we will be convinced that they are the characteristics of the soul and the antithesis of the evil-commanding ego.

The first condition, of being an adult, is to be dependent directly upon one's Lord and to have a connection with Him. This can only be done through the soul—for when God created the soul He asked it, "Am I not your Lord?" and the soul responded, "Indeed." It is this promise of God, and this allegiance of the soul, which connects them. The meaning of adulthood is the maturity of the soul which becomes worthy of the address of its Lord and the responsibility of being able to answer positively.

Rationality, which is the second condition of being an imam, is an attribute which God has given to the soul, attaching it to the soul as its helper and minister in ruling the human being. Intellect is the character of the soul which is in continuous contemplation of its Lord and connected with Him, for it is Intellect which enables the soul to respond when it is asked if God is its Lord. If the soul did not contain intelligence, no offer, proposal, or choice could have been made in response to the address of its Lord, for lack of intelligence is lack of responsibility.

One of the duties of an imam as spiritual leader is to be in the service of his community. A slave, under the command and obligation to serve only his master, cannot serve others of his own free will. Indeed, although the soul is the master of the human being, it is still under the command of God, and it serves others as His deputy. The soul, as the first creation of Allah, is independent of all and everything except its Creator. It may therefore be totally concerned with the matters of the being which it occupies. Thus it is the symbol of freedom within the whole creation, and:

> Celebrates God's praises night and day, nor
> does it ever flag nor intermit.
> *(Anbiya', 10)*

Therefore, freedom is the third condition for an imam.

The fourth condition of a spiritual leader is that he must be a man. "A woman" represents someone who is a slave to his desires and unable to consider anything or anyone except himself, someone who is imperfect and in need of protection from even himself, someone who is best prevented from exercising authority and influence over others, who is not acceptable as a witness in a conflict. In the realm of the human being this signifies a place of disharmony and fear. The lack of perfection and the need of protection situate this "woman" as the daughter of the imam, the spiritual guide. Disharmony, disorder, and fear are the causes of the conflict between the soul and the evil-commanding self who claims to be master over the human realm.

The fifth condition, to be related to the tribe of Quraysh (to which our Master, Muhammad, may God's peace and blessings be upon him, belonged), means that an imam must have signs of the characteristics of the Seal of the Prophets.

Within our Master, not only the last, but also the first divine revelations were manifested. When he was asked, "When did you become a prophet?", he responded, "I was a prophet when Adam was between earth and water." But the first period of prophethood, beginning with Adam (may God's peace and blessings be upon him), finished with the prophethood of Jesus (may God's peace and blessings be upon him), as Allah says in His holy book:

The similitude of Jesus before Allah is as that of Adam.

(*Ali-'Imran, 59*)

According to divine judgment, the birth of Jesus and his attributes are similar to those of Adam, whom God created of earth and water and to whom He said "Be," and he became. As God starts a thing, so He ends a thing. The period of the prophethood of Adam ended with Jesus.

The words revealed to Muhammad (peace and blessings be upon him) setting order everywhere, from the East to the West, constitute both the second and the last period of prophethood. And as Muhammad was sent not as the prophet of a particular nation but as a mercy upon the whole universe, so is the soul meant to regulate not just a part of our human nature, but the whole of it.

The sixth condition for an imam is to be sound in sight and hearing, for the blind and the deaf are unable to help themselves. The blind cannot lead the blind—but the eye that matters is not the eye that sees only the world. It is the eye that seeks to see reality. The ear that matters is not the ear that hears only the sounds of the world. It is the ear that hears the truth. Our pure Master, may God praise his soul, told us that his Lord told him, "My loving servants come close to Me with extra worship and efforts, and I love them. And when I love them, I become their ears with which they hear and their eyes with which they see ...."

The seventh and eighth conditions which an imam must fulfill are competence and rank, and ability to serve and save others. The realm of the human being, which is a land where a war is waged, needs the intervention of the soul to give victory to the rightful owner of the land. God says:

I will assist you with a thousand angels.
(Anfal, 9)

The "thousand angels" is the soul.

The ninth condition is knowledge. The symbol of divine knowledge is the first man created and the first prophet, Adam (God's peace and blessings be upon him).

56

Allah entrusted to him the names of all and everything and made him a teacher even to His angels.

The tenth condition is to be honorable and to be determined not to sin. This is the source, the center where the spiritual guide is generated. The Divine Law is his robe, the truth is his crown.

Whoever fulfills these conditions is the deputy of God, and may serve in His name.

The conflict between Intellect and the evil-commanding self is caused by their very nature, which induces each of them to try to dominate the whole of the human being and to be the ruler of it. Even when one of them is able to conquer the whole realm, the other still strives to regain what it has lost and to repair what has been destroyed.

What can save the human realm from danger is its obedience to a beneficent influence which comes from outside. That influence from outside of man is the divine law. It is only when man is open and ready to accept the divine law that the soul in him recognizes that its influence has the same nature, the same characteristics, as itself. Only then may it distance itself from the evil-commanding ego. When this happens, Intellect imagines that it has found an ally against the ego, and rises against it—and the war between the two starts.

The two forces fighting to dominate the human being become aware of their differences only in their relation to the divine law. Yet viewed from the outside, it is evident that one of these forces is aimed at bringing the human being to destruction, and the other, to salvation. Both of them fear that the divine wisdom ordains the elimination of their conflict and the destruction of the ones who cause it. If they would stop their hostility towards each other, perhaps both Intellect and the ego could find an argument, a proof to justify their existence—but the Lord has willed it thus. As He says in His holy book:

> He cannot be questioned for His acts, but they
> will be questioned for theirs.
> *(Anbiya', 23)*

Thus the Lord sends whomever He wills to Hell and whomever He wills to His Paradise. The evil-commanding ego and the lusts and desires of the flesh which it commands are the truth of the Fire itself and are bound to it, while the soul is a part of the divine light and is bound to that. Each one feeds itself from its own existence. They only see their own attributes. If the ego knew that burning in hellfire would be its punishment, it would escape from its own fire towards the divine light reflected from the soul—but its intellect does not reach further than itself. Nor is the soul capable of understanding Hell. That is why both the soul and the ego try to pull Intellect to their side.

As a pure wind blows fire into flames, the fire of the ego suffers from the pure divine light. And as the ego feels pain from light, it thinks that the human realm which it governs will also be pained by the divine light generated from the soul. Therefore it tries to protect its realm from pain by covering it with many veils of unconsciousness, imagination, and desires. The soul which generates divine light tries to do the same, to protect the human being from the pain of fire. The two adversaries vie to convince the human realm of their own convictions and impress upon it their beliefs, hoping that it will join them and assume either the attributes of fire or the attributes of light. Thus the realm would adhere to either one or the other, and be subject to it.

This is the sedition, the trouble between the two, the cause of all these inner wars. If only one of them, instead of just looking at itself, would heed the voice always coming from the outside! It would then indeed see who is truly the cause of all this, who is really making each of them do what it does. Then it would have found the truth. Then truth and justice would be established. Then neither the soul nor the ego would be able to say about the other that there is danger in "this" or salvation in "that."

If they were even able to view each other, there would have been a chance of peace within the realm of the human being. Do you think that the opposition to inner peace is only from the evil-commanding ego? If it would just disappear, all that is being discussed here would not have existed. Indeed it is the source of all conflict. If it would have disappeared, all would disappear.

This is a secret which the Lord opens to some and hides from others. The Creator does not have to explain His actions, while the created being is created responsible for its actions. The proof is in the Lord's words:

> If the Lord had so willed, He could have made
> mankind one people, but they will not cease to
> dispute except those on whom thy Lord hath
> bestowed His mercy.
>
> (*Hud, 18-19*)

"Those on whom the Lord has bestowed His mercy" are those whom the Lord has created with characters containing His own beautiful names and attributes, so that the creation will know them.

Allah tells the truth and leads one to the straight path.

CHAPTER 5

ON THE NAME, THE ATTRIBUTES, AND THE STATION OF THE IMAM WHO IS NONE OTHER THAN THE LAW WHERE GOD'S DECREES ARE PRESERVED

There is no doubt that one of the four pillars of Islam is the principle of the *imam*, the source where the Lord's decrees are preserved and from which they generate. According to the divine harmony and order which rules this universe, God's deputy must be known by a unique name, and none other than he could be called by that name. When he distinguishes himself with that name, only the imam identifies Him and understands Him. None, not even His representatives and deputies, can change His name.

In the name of His essence, God is unique. When one says *Allah*, only the cause of everything existing and all that which will exist is meant. When the verse "worship Allah" was revealed to His Messenger, no one asked him who or what was Allah, but when the verse "Prostrate to the Merciful" was revealed, the companions of the Prophet asked him who "the Merciful" was. He then had to explain.

When we look for other names which may identify Him as unique, we cannot find any but the attributes which He gave Himself, such as in the verse in which He says to His angels: "Your Lord will create a deputy to rule the world." His saying that He will send one deputy to rule the world is a proof that two rulers cannot exist. That is why our Master, the Prophet of God (peace and blessings be upon him), said, "If there are two ruling one realm, eliminate one of them." Even if two rulers are in agreement and unified, the continuance of this agreement and unity is impossible. For the Lord said:

> If there were gods other than Allah which
> would mean two rulers governing one realm
> sooner or later they would disagree.

When that happens, the order which one gives will be forbidden by the other, and it is impossible to apply two orders which contradict each other. But those who are governed know that if they do not act upon their orders, they will be punished. So one will follow one order, and another will follow the other. In so doing they will oppose each other and war will start, causing the destruction of the country of the human being. That is why the imam whose duty is to put things in order accepts the rule of one ruler alone.

There is another verse where Allah says:

> It is He who hath made you agents, inheritors
> of the earth.
>
> (An'am, 165)

How is it that the divine law accepts only a single ruler, while God in this verse addresses a plurality as the inheritors of the earth? The secret of this verse is that there will be many deputies inheriting one from the other, but there will be only one at any one time. If another claims to be a ruler while there is already one, he is to be rejected, for he becomes the *Dajjal* of the time, the ultimate liar.

When one ruler leaves, another inherits. That is why the Lord uses the plural in the verse we have quoted. The new ruler must assume the station, the name, the attributes, the character, and the morals of the one whom he is replacing. It is only then that his helpers and his government will rule in his name and in accordance with his attributes. These attributes must correspond to the divine attributes.

If the kingdom of your being is to be ruled well, then protect your religion; be in its service. Don't oppose it. If you do, you will be opposed. Keep in sight the divine commands, whether you know them all or not. His commands are the gift of your Lord to humankind.

Be heedful at all times, for if the whole is aware, its parts are aware. Control your anger, do not seek revenge. Respect the old and love the young. Appreciate the one who spends his own for the well-being of others. Do not look upon the errors of others. Beware of falling into dishonor, for if you fall low, the One who can help you will be out of sight. Don't talk unless your talk means something. Repent for the wrong you have done in the past, for the wrong not regretted is the cause of wrath.

No age is better than another: to be old, famous, or honored are not spiritual levels in themselves. Every age and station has its value, and the young, the humble, may be more worthy of respect. What is important are deeds. To appreciate the good deeds of others may lead one to do the same.

You are charged to rule the kingdom of your being. When you are to pass an edict for something to be done, consider its end. If the end is good, then sign it. If not, do not put it into action.

Show great care in all that you do, especially when you act in obedience to your Lord. There will be a great

63

chance of failure and error, for your ego will continually be commanding you to do evil. So, while you obey your Lord, oppose your evil-commanding self. If you follow it, you may be a lesson to others.

All the members of your being are the followers of the king that you are. They are not aware of the importance and the value of the deputy that God has bestowed upon them. Do not show yourself in their company often, but rarely as a flash, or a passing shadow. For if you show yourself often, they will think of you as one of themselves, and lack in obedience. As God says:

> If He were to enlarge the provision for His servants, they would indeed transgress beyond all bounds through the earth, but He sends it down in due measure as He pleases.
>
> *(Shura, 27)*

The "enlarging of the provision" is the evidence of His presence. If you are present too often, the ones who see you will be spoiled. They will feel familiarity and forget about your uniqueness and the oneness of your position, while they should be anxious, seeking a cause or an occasion for your presence.

If God manifested Himself continuously, it would have weakened the urgency to follow religious requirements. Availability of divine manifestation at all times would certainly not advance but rather cause the decline of the human kingdom, and precipitate its destruction.

If we are heedful in our daily life, we realize that we rarely see the divine manifestation, and then only like lightning in the night sky. This is the divine policy.

Therefore, O master of the human kingdom, lend your ear to this brother of yours in whose heart there is love and compassion for you, and who is indebted to you. When you wish to descend from your proper place of divine wisdom and power down to the realm of matter in the physical body and show yourself, present Reason, a minister in your government, instead of yourself. Let him be your representative with your subjects. Then you will keep your authority. Let him bring your beneficent edicts to them. Let him praise you—then your glory and your power will grow in the public view. Thus your magnanimity, your strength, will be accepted by your subjects, without any doubt or resentment in their hearts. On the contrary, their love for you will increase as your minister tells them of your compassion, care, and generosity towards them. Your people will need you not only in times of trouble and hopelessness, but also in equanimity.

There will be times when they will find cause to revolt against your authority. But they will think twice, for the fear of your power and the respect for your position which your minister, Reason, has inspired in them, will prevent them from attacking you. Then is the time to gather all your people in one place to show yourself to them. Among the beautiful flowers of perfect character, they will view your gentleness and your kindness towards them. They will view you in awe, and they will be inspired both with fear and hope. That will bring health to their sick hearts. They will feel secure in their fear of God. As the poet said:

As the big and beautiful bird soars far above
their heads,
It appears to them as if it is one among them.

They view it with awe, but not with fear,
Yet, as it flies farther, it reminds them of God.

To be that awesome bird is only possible to someone who generates from the angelic realm where the angels closest to the Lord reside. Otherwise, one is a tyrannical ruler sitting on a high throne, watching those who have revolted being punished.

Allah says:

They all revere their Lord high above them.
(*Nahl, 50*)

O master of your human realm, if you must punish the one who revolts against you, do not punish him above his guilt. Only this will bring him back to his proper level.

Have you not heard that the saint Abu Yazid al-Bistami did not quench the thirst of his body for a whole year? That was his punishment to his flesh, because his ego had refused to abide by the divine order.

O master of your flesh, keep your ego cleansed of the love of this world, and free it from dependence on the world. Thus your flesh will practice being useful and serving your kingdom, rather than opposing it. Remember, the Lord assigned you to be His deputy and raised you to a divine station in this world, and taught you your function. These two, you and this world, are interdependent. While He values you above others, He has shown His hatred for the world, not having looked at its face but once since its creation.

The Messenger of God, peace and blessings be upon him, said, "This world is like a stinking, dried up corpse, its bowels rotted, lying on a garbage heap."

He also said, "This world is cursed by God. So are the ones upon it who have forgotten God."

How could this world become beautified by its co-existence with you whom Allah has created as His unique creation, from the essence of His own divine light? To look at this world but once with the corner of your eye suffices for you to attract the horrible hostility of its fiery mood.

Help comes from the Lord who addresses the world saying, "O world, I order you, be a lowly servant to the ones who serve Me, and be a tyrannical master to the ones who serve you."

The Lord makes the world your humble servant and it freely provides your sustenance, as well as the sustenance of the people of your kingdom who obey and serve you. Therefore beautify what you need and you wish from this world, and teach the ones who come after you to do so, so that the world, as your servant, may become beautiful. Yet do not be fooled by it. The way not to be fooled is to limit your needs to what the Lord has rendered lawful. If you resist what is unlawful in the world, if you keep your distance from it and are not fooled by its temptations, you will save yourself from being its servant, and it will become your servant. Then what you expect to receive from it comes to you freely, without your having to reap it.

Kahb al-Ahbar reports that the Lord addressed us in the Torah saying, "O sons of Adam, if you accept what comes to you through your lot, both your flesh and your heart will find comfort and I will be pleased with you. If you are not satisfied with what I have ordained for you, I will make the world your tyrannical master. Then you will be running away from it, like a terrified man running away from a lion in the desert. I vow on My might that you will not receive a morsel more than what is due to you."

So join your body to your heart in comfort while using your will in what you want. Yet that will should not be used unrestrainedly, but under the command of what is right and what is wrong. Your will is your only resource for obtaining your needs. If you use it heedlessly, it will be exhausted. You will not have any power left when you need it to rule the kingdom of your being. You will lose your authority.

Know that there is a Lord above you. Your Lord is God. Use your will to tie yourself to Him. Spend it only for His sake upon the ones who love you and whom you love.

When you direct your will toward the acquisition of knowledge, know that all you may hope to receive is the exterior, practical orders of Allah. The meaning of your will is hidden in your will. Instead of using your will only to know and deal with things, you would better have used it to seek its own meaning, why it was given to you. Then it would not have fallen to the lowly state it inhabits now.

An example: Whether a person is a wise man or a fool, if he needs his sustenance and asks for it, he will receive it. Yet he should know that the wheat does not come from the earth, but from God, who gives it in a certain measure to be distributed to all in accordance with their need. Thus neither should one think that one's sustenance comes from this world, nor should one ask it from the world.

When someone turns his face toward the sun, his shadow falls behind him. If he walks toward the sun, his shadow will follow him but will never reach him. However he wills, whatever he does, he will find his wish only behind his heels. Only when the sun is above his head, in the center of the heavenly dome, will his wish be under his feet. God says:

> Seest thou not how their Lord extends the shade? And if He pleased, He would have made it stand still. Then We have made the sun an indication of it, then We drew it in towards Ourselves, a contraction by easy stages.
>
> *(Furqan, 46)*

If there were no sun, there would be no shadow.

If, instead of turning his face to the sun, he takes the sun on his back and walks towards his shadow, he will not be able to catch up with it either, and he has lost what was due to him when his shadow was under his two feet and the sun at its apex. God will say to him:

> Turn back and seek a light.
>
> *(Hadid, 13)*

He can only reach his shadow when it is between his two feet. That is his lot.

O traveler of this path, you are that person, the sun is a metaphor of your Lord. Your shadow is this earth upon which you live. When the sun is above your head and you are aligned with it, your shadow under your feet is all you could wish from this world, right here and now.

O master of the human realm, has not your Lord created the world for you and you for Himself? Isn't He the one who has given this world and all that is in it into your control?

The Lord says in the Torah, "O sons of Adam, I have created everything for you and you for Myself. For My sake and yours, take care of My creation. Do not mistreat it, for then you will be tearing apart what ties us together."

And Allah says in His Qur'an:

> I have only created Jinn and men so that they serve Me.
>
> *(Zariyat, 56)*

And He says:

> It is out of His mercy that He has made for you night and day, that ye may rest therein and that ye may seek of His grace.
>
> *(Qasas, 73)*

And He says:

> It is God who made cattle for you, that ye may use some for riding and some for food.
>
> *(Mu'min, 79)*

> And He has created horses, mules, and donkeys for you to ride.
>
> *(Nahl, 8)*

And there is much more for you to have and to use and care for which He has created, which He mentions in His Holy Book.

But you, who are the master of them all, you have to care for those left to you in trust. You must love and yearn for the things among them that you wish to have. You must consider, as you consider yourself, the ones under you.

You must know their ranks and their states and their needs, in accordance with which you must bestow upon them what they need. But you must also prevent them from the sin of passing their boundaries.

You must teach them to obey the One who created them as well as their sustenance, and to abide within the limits which are traced for them. You must instill in them both the love and the fear of their Lord. You must teach them to teach those who will come after them. And you must teach them what will come upon them the day after today:

> On the day when their tongues, their hands and their feet will bear witness against them as to their actions.
>
> *(Nur, 24)*

and:

> And follow not that of which thou hast no knowledge. Surely, what you heard and saw and the heart, from of all these it will be inquired [on the day of reckoning].
>
> *(Bani Isra'il, 36)*

These things that God has said should guide you. Don't walk this earth with your chin up in arrogance. Guide yourself and others towards what is right. Forbid the wrong. Yet, do not ever forget the evil-commanding ego which you carry within yourself.

Do not ignore its presence. Instruct your most valuable minister, Reason, to treat it well, to be in continuous contact with it, because it knows best how to govern the barren deserts of your realm. It has power, and it lies in its hands to do good, if it so wills, or to cause disasters, if it so wills.

If it is treated well, there will be peace in the land. Your enemies will be subdued, your treasuries will be secure. Let all your will and efforts be to make order in that which is nearest to you. And that which is closest to you is the result of your efforts and of your work.

If you order that which is good in you to attack that which is bad, in hopes that the bad may turn into good, you may frighten also what is neutral in you. Then you will create hatred against you among them. Even at times when your heart is constricted and hardened, show mercy and tolerance and forgiveness, and ask God's forgiveness upon them. And ask counsel from them in the things you do, because to be loved is only possible by loving. Praise be to the ones who can do it.

O generous lord of the realm of his being, most important in ruling your realm is to give the right work to the right authority, to the one who is best suited to it. And if you wish to show one of your successes, show it at the right time, not before it is achieved and not after it is done and finished with, but just as it is completed. That is the time when its display is most needed. Then your subjects will look forward to your next achievement, and they will forget about other demands while they are waiting for your next accomplishment.

Don't you see? If, instead of the four regular seasons, God sent torrents of rain at unnatural times, and in the place of warmth and sunshine, darkness and frost, then men in their hopelessness would fall into thanklessness.

Even though God still poured His blessings upon them, men would still be apt to lose faith and revolt. And what would happen if He sent upon them total darkness and disaster at all times? Then man would lose all hope of any good or justice coming from Him.

Accept those who have faith in divine commandments and God's Messenger as an example. Then seek divine justice in these. When you have found it, and when you also find it in yourself, you will have achieved salvation in this world and in the hereafter.

When you intend to do something, say *inshallah*— "so please God." As the Lord says:

> Nor say of anything, "I shall be sure to do so and so tomorrow," without adding "So please God."
> *(Kahf, 23)*

and:

> Break not your oaths after ye have confirmed them.
> *(Nahl, 91)*

and:

> Take not your oaths to practice deception between yourselves.
> *(Nahl, 94)*

So beware also of bad friends. They do not only eat your fortune and bring you to bankruptcy, but devour your flesh and drink your blood and bring you to the verge of hellfire. Befriend those who have more faith than you do, and those who know and abide with the divine law. In your communications with your friends, if you find a distortion, even a lack of knowledge of religious precepts, beware of them, they are potential enemies. Watch them and protect your possessions from them. They may be a cause for the collapse of your kingdom and for the destruction of the country of your being. That dangerous friend is not far away from you, but within the borders of your own being. His name is the desires of your flesh, the evil-commanding ego.

Our Master warns us, "Wage war against your greatest enemy, which is your own ego."

And the Lord says:

> O you who believe, fight those of the disbelievers who are nearest to you.
> *(Tauba, 123)*

That faithless one is your ego. Be aware of it. Work against it, for if you do not work against it, it will work against you. The tyrants of this world may destroy your possessions and even you; you will be a martyr and win eternal bliss. But the tyrant in you will not only do the same, but will also burn your faith into ashes and push you into hellfire.

When you give audience to your ministers and your governors, they should not present themselves to you in uniforms which you have gathered from what is customary in the regions around and about you, because these uniforms of the customs outside of you come from nowhere but from your deadly enemy, the ego. They should appear in front of you in the obligatory robes of sincerity, generosity, justice, and nobility.

74

The uniforms fashioned by your ego outwardly may appear ostentatious, even beautiful, but their lining is ugly and treacherous. If you can see through the surface, you will see the truth. When you are able to see what such appearances hide, you will know the antecedents as well as the consequences of what is presented to you.

Then you will have to wash the surfaces of things, first bathing them in the rivers of wisdom, then weighing them in the balance of knowledge. Try to find out if there is any good in them at all. If so, you will find satisfaction. If not, you must accept them, with reserve, as they are. For our Master has said, "Be careful of the green algae which flood waters bring." Meaning: take care of the mischief that presents itself as a beautiful woman.

Everything is created to fulfill a need. A thing returns to its place by retracing its original route. One must consider all that is around one in this light. That need comes from your essence, the noble soul that the Lord blew unto you. Always question yourself about the reason for your existence, the purpose of your creation.

Do not spend the numbered breaths which have been given to you just to wander around the face of this planet, without purpose, with actions of no consequence. Every action, every motion, must be for a divine purpose.

Khidr said: "I did not do this on my own, with my own will." Then he raised his head and looked into the night sky and the far stars and said: "I am a poor sick thing." He was talking about his ego.

I beg you to consider this advice: never act in matters of the welfare of your realm without consulting your ministers, who represent all your faculties. In addition to making you more sure of your decision, this will help to create a feeling of friendship, of confidence, in your ministers. From this feeling of friendship, compassion and concern will be created. And with this wise advice and with justice, your kingdom will be guaranteed its survival. That is why it is said that justice is the basis of the continuance of a realm.

These are the attributes and character of a true leader. Otherwise whoever rules becomes an instrument of destruction and, in the process, also destroys himself.

There are four kinds of leaders. Without forgetting that everything is created from divine beneficence and generosity, the philosophers say that there are four kinds of kings and there is no fifth.

1. A king who is generous, both to himself and to his people.

2. A king who depreciates himself and sees his people as lowly also.

3. A king who is proud of himself and generous to himself but who sees his people as unworthy.

4. A king who is humble, but who is generous and tolerant with his people.

We are not going to point out which of the four would be the best leader, as it is obvious to all in accordance with their own attributes.

Since time immemorial the ones who know the truth have been examining man and what is expected of him. They say that humanity is a station in the creation where everything comes together and where action becomes possible. It is also a station where that which has been gathered is by association and disassociation. Thus it is also a station of separation. This is the location of the Footstool of the Lord. The Footstool is where divine knowledge is preserved:

> To Him belongs whatever is in the heavens and
> whatever is in the earth.
> *(Baqarah, 255)*

Yet, it is separated from:

> What He knows, what is before them and what
> is behind them.
> *(Baqarah, 255)*

It is at this station that man will wish to surrender that which is imperfect in him before the feet of his Lord in return for the intercession of the earth under his own feet, counting on his Lord's mercy expressed on the Night of Power when :

> The angels and the spirit descend by the per-
> mission of their Lord, offering their Lord's
> orders for every affair.
> *(Qadr, 4)*

O deputy of his Lord in the kingdom of the human being: if you have divine knowledge, and have been a channel of good deeds and actions, then you must be generous both to yourself and to your people. If you have none of this, indeed there is no good in you, nor can any good come from your people. If you know but do not act upon your knowledge, then you are full of yourself but your people will be left destitute. If you have the good will but not the knowledge, and spend yourself unselfishly for others, then you will be left humble while your people prosper.

There are secrets in each of these cases, depending on the circumstances. We leave it to the inner wisdom of those who can understand.

Some may protest and say, "We know of two of these cases and we believe them to be right," and say, "the king who has knowledge and acts upon it is the best." We say that if you believe in one, you cannot ignore the others. All the qualities mentioned in the four kings are facts, and what is right depends on what is needed.

If spiritual sustenance is what is needed, its food is knowledge and inspiration. If something is needed for the growth of the physical self, it must be fed through the senses, and the lack of this causes suffering for the physical being.

Is a man of action not a man of knowledge? If that is so, then his spirit is locked up in a cell, hungry for its sustenance. But a man of knowledge who does not put his knowledge into action is drowned in the sea of intellectual lust. Though he may be sustaining his spirit, his inaction may expose it to situations over which he has no control, and which may cause it disaster.

The most important characteristic to consider is the question of generosity and avarice. Generosity is the ability to satisfy a need to its fullest extent. Avarice is not only the failure to satisfy the need, but also the ignoring of it—and in addition, the forbidding of its satisfaction. There are indeed degrees of this. Meanwhile, the one who gives more than the need necessitates is a spendthrift, which is also a sin. To find the appropriate response to a need, and the right dose—and not to go to extremes—is essential.

The outward sign of the deputy of the Lord in the human realm is his actions, which have limitations. His inner quality is knowledge. Knowledge is at all times a departure point. It offers a new response for each need, and it has no borders.

The citizens of the kingdom of the human being are of two kinds: those who have always been there, and those who appear for the first time at every instant. The ones who have always been there are also separated into two classes. There are those who have the nationality of the people of Muhammad in the material realm, and those who do not, but are attached to the world of matter.

The ones who appear every instant, the children of the now, are also divided into two categories: the ones who belong collectively to a group, and the ones who do not have an affiliation with anything or anybody, but are just themselves.

These single individuals are also of two sorts: those who are under the influence of their intellect, and those who are under the influence of their egos.

Those who belong to their egos are also divided into two kinds: the first, who are able to obey in spite of their egos; and the second, the ones who revolt because of their egos. The ones who obey are a part of the realm under the influence of divine power, and the ones who revolt are locked up in the world of torment of their corporeal existence.

The individuals who are guided by reason are also divided into two kinds: the ones whose intelligence is exposed, and the ones who are hidden. The hidden ones are the ones who are safe under the protection of the angelic realm.

[Those ranged in ranks say] not one of us but
has a place appointed.
(Saffat, 164)

The ones whose intelligence is exposed are the
brides of the Lord. Although they are out in the open, they
are like receptacles, holding the treasures of the Lord.
Hidden within His treasures, they are covered by the veils
of the Lord's jealousy, of His love for them. None know
them except their Lord, nor do they know any other except
their Lord. They are a part of real reality. They are the
heart of the city of man. Seek them, so that you will learn.

O generous deputy of the Lord, now that you know
the reality of the people of your realm, give all of them the
different things that they need, while not forgetting your
own needs: to some, knowledge; to some, wisdom; to some,
what they lack in perfection; to some, help with your
actions. To all, show generosity, without surpassing its
boundaries. That is the way of our master, Muhammad,
may God's peace and blessings be upon him.

The perfection of generosity is piety. There is an
asceticism within the one who gives without reserve,
renouncing all except what he has at the moment. The
pride of a nation is the piety and asceticism of their king,
because he has given up everything for the sake of his people. Generosity is the result and sign of care and love for
others. And care and love are signs of one's closeness to
others. And unity is the result of closeness between people
in the realm of a human being.

God says:

And God has created you and your deeds.
(Saffat, 96)

80

Under the veil of the creation of your deeds by God, be selfless. Attribute nothing to yourself—in your actions, in your faith, in your words—so that you can make His realm your home, open the divine light within it, and see that which is real by it.

Leave to others what they have in their hands. Do not want anything from them, and leave what belongs to the Lord to the Lord. Then you will be loved both by the people and by your Lord. Do not claim anything which goes out from you as yours, no action as your doing. Then indeed you will have become a man of conscience and reached true piety and asceticism.

And if one day they bring you a gift from their world which befits the desires of your flesh, thank them for their gift, and beg them to take it from you and give it as a gift to the ones who are in need. But if they insist that you keep it, then take it, and give it to the needy yourself.

Many times before I have warned many in our land, and in other lands, about these same predicaments. They have not valued my advice; they haven't seen the dangers closing in upon them.

When our Master, God's peace and blessings upon him, gathered with his Companions, he used to seat the men of wisdom in the front ranks. They spoke little, for it is best to say the right things in a few words, rather than make long extrapolations. Every excess has poison in it. The one who says little is hidden under his calculated words and is not in need of the approval of others. He is a true ascetic in his silence. This should be the way of a true guide, the imam.

CHAPTER 6

ON JUSTICE AND
THE AUTHORITY OF THE IMAM

The Imam is the leader of a realm where he applies the law, confirmed by divine authority. He dispenses justice, and he is the final authority. As the divinely ordained imam in the realm of your being, you have to rule in justice and dispense justice among your people and the officials of your government. This is necessary for the endurance of peace and order in your realm, and also to keep your enemies subdued. You are the trustee of the divine cause and of justice. A realm governed with justice is bound to be safe and prosperous.

Whether in olden times or now, justice does not age; it is as it ever was, always sought-after and respected, because it is a divine balance with which all is weighed in this material realm. It is the same divine balance which, on the Day of Judgment, will be used to weigh the right and the wrong and to differentiate the righteous person from the wrongdoer. It is the basis of the divine law. What man owns is his physical being, which is judged by his soul is due to law and justice. If there is no justice to equalize and balance the material existence of the human being, that being is bound for destruction. The wise of the olden times have said: "Greater is the benefit of justice than all the gold in the treasuries of a kingdom." The Lord says:

> God commands justice, the doing of good . . .
> (*Nahl, 90*)

And he warns the unjust by saying:

> Woe to those who deal in fraud, those who, when they have to receive by measure from man, exact full measure, but when they have to give by measure or weight to man, give less than due.
>
> *(Tatfif, 1-3)*

and:

> Do they not think that they will be called to account on a mighty day?
>
> *(Tatfif, 4-5)*

When Luqman, God's peace and blessings be upon him, advises his son, he says:

> Do not travel far nor raise your voice.
>
> *(Luqman, 19)*

And Allah says:

> Neither speak thy prayer aloud nor speak it in a low tone, but seek a middle course between.
>
> *(Bani Isra'il, 110)*

And He says:

> Make not the hand tied [like a miser] to thy neck, nor stretch it forth to its utmost reach [like a spendthrift].
>
> *(Bani Isra'il, 29)*

Our Master, the Prophet of Allah, peace and blessings be upon him, said to Abu Bakr, his blessed Companion, "Please raise your voice a little," while he said to his other Companion, the blessed 'Umar, "Speak softly." And one day, when the straps of one of his sandals broke, he took off both of them, to be able to walk in a balanced way.

The wise of olden times said, "Don't be too sweet, you will make people's mouths water. Don't be too sharp, you will turn people's stomachs." The principle of justice is balance, equality, the middle course. It must be applied to all things. Let justice rule in both the exterior expression and the inner meaning of what you say and in what you do. Apply it first to yourself, then to those who are closest to you—your ministers and the officials governing the realm of your being—and then to all those over whom you have authority.

CHAPTER 7

ON THE QUALITIES TO BE SOUGHT IN THE PRIME MINISTER AND THE DEFINITION OF HIS DUTIES

There must be a tie between the owner and what he owns, and that tie is your minister. He is your helper in applying your rules in the realm where you rule. He has to be intelligent and active, so that he is able to put your decisions into action. The name of your chief minister is Intellect. Indeed, when the Lord made you His deputy in the realm of your existence, He also assigned you your prime minister, Intellect. Intellect responds to divine orders. He is the one who rights the wrong. He is the visible ruler of the realm. He is the symbol, the sign of authority.

The Lord says:

> There are indeed signs for men of understanding.
> (*Al-i 'Imran, 190*)

God addresses His ordinances as an obligation to the ones with hearts, but to hear and understand His ordinances, He has created Intellect. That is why He has assigned Intellect as the prime minister to His deputy, the Imam. His duty is to record and analyze and retain the continuous flow of divine messages, ever present and continuously presented in the environment of this universe. You need to be exposed to some of these influences. From some, you must be kept safely hidden, just as a horse must be tied up in the shade, safe from the sun, on a hot day. This precaution, which will keep your realm safe and sound, is the duty of your prime minister, Intellect.

If Intellect is able to carry the responsibilities for which it was created, then indeed he is carrying both the material and the spiritual load of governing your realm. On the other hand, the position of the prime minister, Intellect, is like that of the moon in relation to you, who are like the sun. It is your light which is reflected upon him when you are not visible. He is your mouthpiece, the channel through which the action coming from your power flows. As such, he may appear to be taking initiatives, while he is only following your orders.

When you, as the king of the human realm, appear, like the sun rising, eliminating the veil of darkness where the moon shone like a lamp—then the power of your prime minister disappears. When the order comes from the Imam, the deputy of God, all veils, all doubts, disappear. Nothing but your grandeur and majesty and awe appear.

God Makes the spirit to light by His command
on whom He pleases of His servants that he
may warn of the day of meeting, the day when
they come forth. Nothing concerning them
remains hidden from Him.
(*Mu'min, 15-16*)

Thus the night turns into day, the veils are lifted, doubts are dissipated, barriers are lifted. It is only when the king is in seclusion that his minister is in view. The minister takes the king's place, forbids that which the king forbids, orders that which he orders, does what the king would have done. He is the mouthpiece of the true ruler.

When the moon rises at the same time as the sun, there is no glitter to it, it fades away, as the light of the sun overpowers it. The moon has no rank in the light of the day. But when the sun sets, the moon shines with the light of the sun reflected in it. The ones who see it think that the moon's light is from itself. To understand this is an introduction to the understanding of reality.

Ponder upon what God says:

Say, I seek refuge with the Lord who cherishes mankind.
The ruler of mankind, the god of mankind,
from the imagination, whispered, by the evil one
who withdraws after his whisper.
He who whispers into the heart of mankind
amongst jinn and amongst men.
(*Nas, 1-6*)

My master Abu Madyan, one of the two spiritual guides of this world in his time, said that it was revealed to him that the meaning of the *ruler of mankind* is in the verse:

Blessed is He in whose hand is the kingdom
and He is possessor of power over all things.
(*Mulk, 1*)

He also said that the meaning of the *god of mankind* is the station of the spiritual pole, which God delegates and is present upon the world at all times.

When the Lord Most High first built the form and shape of His deputy, man, and blew his soul unto him from His own soul, He taught him all that is necessary to govern this realm. All that He placed in him was beautiful. Thus God's deputy in the universe has all the faculties to satisfy all the needs of all that is under his rule, down to the smallest detail. Then He poured upon him, every moment, the divine rules and prescriptions to solve all occurrences, and wrote upon his forehead all knowledge, where all could read it. Yet man is unable to judge what solution befits what problem. This is also a secret within the divine wisdom. Perchance the secret is that he too is in need of a helper, a successor who knows himself, who knows what is around him and who knows how to serve.

Then the Lord set His deputy onto the throne of uniqueness and put upon his shoulders the mantle of oneness and bejeweled and crowned him with His own attributes. It is due to all of these that he appears with the majesty and grandeur of his Lord reflected upon him.

If, of all that appears in man, only a speck should be his own, that drop of beauty would cure him of his self. This is the description of the station of God's deputy.

So, look upon yourself. May you be able to see this incredible grandeur and power placed in you. Is it not sufficient proof of God's existence and the existence of a Hereafter, if we can detect this with our own eyes in this life?

God placed His deputy in that high station, and then set Intellect into him. When Intellect entered into him, it sieved his essence and became manifest as its substance. It is only then that all the wisdom and the knowledge written on the face of God's deputy became visible.

But until one sees one's self, one seeks everything outside of oneself, while all there is, is in oneself. The Lord says:

> What you seek is in your own selves. Will you
> not then see?
>
> *(Zariyat, 21)*

If indeed you saw, and stopped looking elsewhere—where you will not find what you seek, and where all that you will get for your efforts will be fatigue— you would find peace. The proverb says: "They take to the road with a hope to find. Wherever they go, their hope to find travels with them. Forever they will hope to find, without finding."

When Intellect encounters a problem to solve, it needs to see the face of the Imam. Upon looking at him, not only the problem's solution, but its purpose, becomes clear to him. He need not be close to the Imam. It suffices to be near enough to make out his voice.

The solution of each problem is as close or as far as the distance necessary for the two to communicate. If the question is academic, the solution is in logic.

Neither the deputy of the Lord, nor his prime minister, Intellect, is material, so the conversation between the two is wordless and soundless. The ear and the tongue in question are not the ear and tongue of the head, but those of the heart. It is left to you to understand their meaning, for the meaning is in the interlocutor. When, in the heart of the mind, the divine spirit overflows, it produces inaudible and invisible signs whose meaning is understood without effort.

That is true communication. That is how the Creator meant communication to be. That is why He placed the mind on a tower at the top of the realm of your being so that it could see, far and wide, the whole of the kingdom. And that is why He placed in the same tower, next door to it, a treasure-house of memory, where all that is worthy in the kingdom is collected and stored. The home of the mind and the treasure-house of remembrance must be close, for the mind must have access to the treasury in order to perform its function.

O one whom God has chosen as His deputy, realize that it is an obligation for you to cooperate with your minister, Intellect, and to support him and to protect him, as you have to coexist. Your peace and order and prosperity in fact, the existence of your kingdom—depends upon his ability to serve you.

If the mind attaches itself to anyone but you, then it can only work against you, which will cause incalculable disasters. Haven't you seen the destruction of men who have lost their minds, and the inability of the spirit to cure this ill? Thus as long as Intellect is safe, you are safe. He is the hand with which you hold and the eye with which you see.

In ruling your domain, before you decide anything, consult with your minister, Intellect. Put your decisions into action only with his agreement. Then, with the security of your solidarity, and with the strength coming from both of you, follow the application of your decision. As long as he is with you and he works for you, do not doubt the righteousness of the advice of Intellect. The Lord Himself has entrusted Intellect to judge what is right, and has protected him from falling under the influence of the mischief of conjecture, doubt, and imagination.

Know that imagination and its effects of doubt and

conjecture do travel among the population of your kingdom, and that they have a trick of disguising themselves in
the appearance of your prime minister, Intellect. They
even appear more subservient, obedient, and agreeable
than he. Many are fooled by them, fall under their influence, and become confused, having lost contact with reality. Hold on to reality, and protect yourself from the distor-
tions in imagination's sight. Otherwise you will be tyrannizing yourself—for there is no good in a realm where
rationality does not rule.

It falls on you to discern in your prime minister,
Intellect, all the attributes of perfection, so that there can
be no chance of confusing him with the imagination which
attempts to imitate him. So here are the attributes which
will enable you to recognize the true prime minister,
charged to serve you.

His personality is justice. The sign of divine inspirations poured upon him is his head. Beauty is upon his
face. The sign of his ability to protect you and your realm
is in the shape of his eyebrows. His eyes show his conscience. His awareness and discrimination are in how his
forehead joins his nose. His trustworthiness is in the shape
of his mouth. Wisdom is in his tongue. His self-assurance
is in the shape of his nose. His forbearance is in his chest.
His valor is in his biceps and his thighs. His confidence is
in his joints. His righteousness is in his wrists. His generosity is in his palms. His freedom is in his posture. His
productivity is on his left side; his ability is on his right
side. His virtue is upon his belly. His chastity is in his pri-
vate parts. His direction is in his legs. His goal is in the
soles of his feet. His heart is heedful, ever awake. His wisdom comes from his soul.

His humility shows in his clothes, his gentleness in his adornment. His humanity is his jewel. His love and fear of God are his crown. His sincerity is his path. His faith is the lamp in his hand to show the way. His advice is in his character; his knowledge is in his foresight. His wealth is in his poverty. His name is Intelligence.

If you ever see such a one, make him your prime minister with certainty, and make him your companion at night, to tell you the tales of other places and times.

Such a helper will make you see reality, distinguish right from wrong and the possible from the impossible, and help you find the truth.

CHAPTER 8

ON INSIGHT, INBORN AND TAUGHT BY THE RELIGION

The Lord says in the Holy Qur'an :

> Behold, in this are signs for those who, by their
> insight, do understand.
>> *(Hijr, 75)*

God's Messenger, peace and blessings be upon his soul, says: "Beware of the insight of the faithful, for he sees with the light of his Lord."

Know that insight is a light shed by the divine light, with which the faithful find their way and reach salvation. That light also makes visible all that there is to see in the material world. If we could see the real realities, they would become signs and proofs of the existence of the Creator, and teach us divine wisdom.

The natural, inborn, human insight enables us to identify and isolate these realities, one by one, while the insight taught by religion sees all as a whole, because religion has come upon us as a divine order and mercy from the one and unique God, who says to us:

> [You] did not do it of [your] own accord. [It is]
> a mercy from your Lord.
>> *(Kahf, 82)*

Only those who have been taught religious insight understand the deficiency of inborn insight, which separates one reality from another and may lead to the wrong conclusion. For the God-given natural insight draws its conclusions from associations, theories, past experiences, and logic—and these are but veils, which can only be lifted by learning the rules of religious insight.

Neither the realization of the existence of an inner eye which is able to detect true reality, nor the wish and possibility of educating this inner eye with the help of religious education, is given to everybody. It is a divine gift bestowed upon a few who are worthy.

What we are about to tell is for all, to enable them to see each other really. Man is a social being. He needs to be with other men to communicate, to understand, to cooperate, to befriend, to love. It is necessary for him to know who is what: who is good, who is bad, who is right or wrong for him. Perchance some signs, which we will indicate, will help to lift the veil and open his insight. Then through the prescriptions of religion, the Lord will open for him a door where His light will show him realms that he has not seen before.

O my brother, may God enable you to see and to understand that you must show all care in choosing your ministers and helpers in governing the kingdom of your being. Choose them from among the most majestic, beautiful ones, with gentle and joyful hearts. Let them be neither too tall nor too short. Their bodies and their flesh should be soft and muscular and cool to the touch. Their skin should be white with a tinge of white and yellow; their hair of medium length, straight and black, without a sheen of red; of smooth face, with dark eyes which do not show any arrogance. Their heads should be round with slight bulges at the sides, upon necks medium in length and thickness. Their whole being should be dignified and calm. Their thighs should be shaped with long and soft muscles, their voices neither sharp and loud nor soft and inaudible.

They should be open-handed, and they should be careful in their speech. They should have a happy disposition, eyes shining with joy and peace. They should not be interested in possessions, nor have a desire to dominate others, and in their actions they should neither move too slowly, nor hurry.

These are the characteristics which have been valued by all of the wise of olden times. Our Master and our guide, Muhammad, may God's peace and blessings be upon him, and my teacher, Abul-Qasim, were born with these traits, and their exterior was the sign of their inner perfection. Therefore befriend those who resemble them.

If the Lord sheds His divine light upon the exterior signs of the inner man, and you appreciate it, then you are among the select who possess both the natural insight and the insight taught by religion. Then there should be no doubt nor fear: the kingdom of your being will be under your rule and control.

The wise men of old assure us—and I know it by my own experience—that those among men who have a uniform and temperate nature are those who have the exterior signs, some of which we have mentioned. There are other signs which have to be considered.

A person who is hairy has an inclination towards depravity, wickedness, and disloyalty. Excessive hair also indicates lack of intelligence. Men with thick hair yet with a natural high forehead, who also have a thin beard, are bad-tempered and obstinate. One should avoid such people, for they are as dangerous as poisonous snakes. Coarse hair indicates bravery and boldness, also strong-mindedness, while soft hair is a sign of cowardice, indecisiveness, and lack of intelligence. Excessive hair on the chest and on the belly is a sign of a harsh and wild nature and behavior, someone who is able to hurt others, and who is lacking in understanding. Blond hair shows lack of intelligence, someone who is critical without justification and who is liable to flare up unexpectedly. Black hair is an indication of intelligence, of heedfulness, and of a just nature. Light brown hair is a sign of someone who is potentially sickly, defective in judgment, yet who makes excuses for wrongdoings.

A smooth and flat forehead is an indication of arrogance and the character which loves to create confusion and hostility amongst people; while a wrinkled forehead, of medium width and height, is a sign of a loyal person who is heedful, loving, prudent, and able.

Large ears indicate a person with an ability to memorize what he hears, though he is unable to understand what he has memorized, and is ignorant of its content and application. People with tiny ears have a tendency to be foolish. They also have a tendency to steal.

Thick eyebrows, extending towards the temples, indicate absentmindedness and confusion and also arrogance. Fine eyebrows, of medium length, are the mark of a heedful, sensitive, and intelligent person.

Blue eyes are a sign of bad character. The worst of eyes are turquoise blue. When eyes are large and protruding, they mark an envious, lazy, and untrustworthy person. If they are also blue, these characteristics are extreme, and that person is also a liar. If someone's eyes are medium in size and dark, inset, with dark outlines on the lids, he is sympathetic, sensitive, attentive, considerate, and trustworthy.

If someone has a hard look in his eyes it is clear that he is not a good person. People with a dull look in their eyes are usually coarse, ignorant, and harsh in nature. A shifty, quick look in the eyes is an indication of deceitfulness, cruelty, and fraud. Eyes with a tinge of red in them indicate someone who is brave, bold, and decent. Reddish eyes with yellow dots in the iris indicate a total lack of conscience, an evil disposition, and malice.

A thin nose indicates a person who is hasty and hypocritical. A big nose which hangs over the mouth is a sign of a brave and valorous man. A short and flat nose is a sign of a lascivious person with heightened sexual appetite. Large nostrils are an indication of a man who is quick in temper. A broad and flat nose, medium in size, shows a person who lacks judgment, who lies, and who talks nonsensically. The best kind of nose is medium in length and thickness and straight, indicating an intelligent, sensitive, and dependable person.

A large mouth is a sign of a brave character. Thick lips are a sign of foolishness. Lips which are of medium thickness and tinged with red indicate mildness, composure, and equilibrium. Crooked teeth with space in between mark a tendency towards intrigue and cheating, and undependability. Straight, even teeth are a sign of a rational and dependable person.

A face with fat cheeks marks the crude and ignorant. A fine, long, and pale face is a sign is an immoral, terse, and insincere person. A person whose face blushes, whose eyes are lowered, and who shows the signs of the slightest smile is indeed someone who is impressed by you and likes you, and is a possible friend.

Someone who speaks with a loud and clear voice is

a valorous person. An audible, gentle voice belongs to a conscientious and laborious person. A soft bass voice is an indication of a logical, organized person who is at the same time serious and calm. A high and measured voice, which produces skillfully chosen words, may belong to someone who is hiding his ignorance, who is a liar and has bad intentions. A coarse bass voice belongs to a person with bad temper and bad character. Someone who mumbles and speaks from his nose is someone, who, in spite of his lack of intelligence, is trying to appear clever. Someone who moves his hands, his head, and his body while he is speaking is over-confident and arrogant. Someone who talks unnecessarily at length, without making sense, is out to deceive. Someone who speaks with measured words, and whose hands move expressively, has a firm understanding of what he says and is logical.

A short neck is an indication of deceitfulness, immorality, and ungratefulness. A thin and long neck is an indication of lack of consideration, cowardice, and an irate nature. If that person also has a small head, there is lack of intelligence. An excessively thick neck shows over-sensuality, gluttony, and ignorance. A neck which is medium in length and thickness is a sign of honesty and sincerity, dependability and a healthy mind.

A large and protruding abdomen is a sign of insensitivity, stupidity, and cowardice. A moderate belly and a narrow chest show superior intelligence, a person who is able to make right decisions.

Wide shoulders and back belong to people who are brave, yet neither too intelligent nor too serious. A curved back and hunched shoulders belong to obstinate and irate people, yet they may also be a sign of weakness and resulting meekness. A flat and straight back is a desirable sign of good character.

Square shoulders belong to people with bad opinions and bad intentions towards others. Long arms are a sign of selflessness, generosity, and courageousness—but short arms belong to cowards, who have a tendency towards wickedness and the causing of mischief among people.

A rectangular hand and long fingers belong to a person with an artistic temperament, whose actions are purposeful and who has the capacity for leadership.

When the soles of the feet are broad and fleshy their owners intend to remain ignorant, are cruel, and have a tendency to tyrannize others. The thin and soft soles of narrow feet belong to intriguers, who have a tendency to instigate trouble. If the heels are fine and pointed it is a sign if cowardice. Heavy and thick heels show bravery.

Thick legs with visible veins mark lack of intelligence and lack of health. Someone who walks with long strides at a medium pace is a person who is capable of calculating the outcome of his actions, and therefore is apt to be successful. Short steps at a slow pace mark someone who is unsure, insecure, and full of doubt.

These are some of the signs which men of insight might use in judging themselves and others. The judgments are based upon the deviation of extremes from a temperate median. Does the spiritual state of someone relate totally to such appearances? All we can say is that the human spirit has a tendency which may turn towards light or towards darkness, and this is reflected upon the physical nature.

The essence of the soul is between light and darkness. The elements of the physical being and the essential nature are created to coexist as a whole creation. It is like the coexistence of Intellect and the atoms of the physical being. The atoms of the physical being are like pure darkness, and Intellect is like pure light, and we are in the middle, in light and darkness, both.

Which of the two conditions will have the power to overcome us? If they were of equal strength—better still, if they were united and one—then all of us would have received what is rightfully ours. Yet, some of us, sometimes, are overcome only by light, and some of us at other times are overcome by darkness. Then we appear either too tall or too short, or white or black.

Each opposite is neither more nor less that its opposite. The white we see pours from that which is white into our eyes. That whiteness has now lost its character; nothing of it is left; it is all in our eyes. Thus its whiteness is harmed and lost—so its state is unacceptable. On the other hand, that darkness whose nature is blind to the light in itself is also unacceptable. So when separate, they are both unacceptable. But from time to time, alternately, they unite in one of us. As our Master the Prophet, God's peace and blessings be upon him, said, "From time to time I have a time when I am filled with my Lord, so that nothing else can fit into me."

Yet he had a time for his blessed Companions, and he had a time for his family. With some he spent more time, and with others, less. What is observed by the senses, and its meaning, are separate, but they are joined together in understanding—like the separation of Heaven and Hell, which are joined together in the expectation of Purgatory.

Hair is hair, but it may be thin or thick. Thus different appearances are reflections of different inner states, which become connected when they are understood.

For instance, a long face with a sympathetic expression is a sign of a positive person who is eloquent.

A pair of eyes which are equal in size and shape is a sign of a conscientious person. If the eyes are inset and dark, that person is capable of understanding hidden meanings and able to solve mysteries.

If the head is symmetrical, it shows superior intelligence. If the shoulders are round, that person is forbearing. A straight neck is a sign of a person who has an inquiring mind, who is not a materialist.

If a person possesses a logical mind, he is able to adjust and direct his words in accordance with the understanding of his interlocutor, and he is bound to be understood and agreed with.

If the hip joints of a person are not bony but fleshy, that person has a tendency to lack principles and shift his opinions according to his self-interest and to win favor. He will need a lot of help to save himself when his alliances are not clear.

A naturally quiet and introverted person is able to keep secrets, but if such a person is clear in his speech when he speaks, it is a sign that he does not know much.

If the tips of a person's fingers are long and finely shaped, that person is a gourmet and very particular in his choice of food. A broad palm belongs to a person who is not attached to the world and the worldly.

A person who speaks little and who laughs rarely is a contemplative who is more interested in spiritual matters. So are people who have a tinge of yellow or of darkness in their skin.

A person in whose eyes there is an expression of

peace and joy is able to attract the interest and love of other people.

If a person is not ambitious, possessive, and desirous of worldly goods, he will avoid most of the problems and dangers of this world.

If someone is not interested in dominating other people, desiring to be the chief, that person is liable to be working for the perfection of his own state.

Someone who is neither hurried nor slow in his actions is not weak; on the contrary, he is a clever person whose actions correspond to his ability and strength.

We have given above a few examples of characteristics which complement the elements of earth, fire, water, and air from which man was created, as indicators of the inborn, natural insight. Now we will explain insight taught by the religion, which is much more important, and which is the foundation of this subject.

May God open the eyes of your heart, shedding His divine light: The angelic realm, which contains the potential of future creation, incorporeal existences, the meaning of all and everything to come, and divine power, is the element from which the visible world is created and, therefore, the material world is under the influence and domination of the angelic realm. The movement, the sound, the voice, the ability to speak, to eat and to drink is not from the existences themselves in this visible, material world. They all pass through the invisible world of the angelic realm.

For example, an animal does not move on its own unless it is motivated for a certain purpose. This motivation comes from inside the animal, from its heart, what we call its instinct, which receives its orders from the invisible world. There the power to move the animal is kept, while the resistance to this motivation is from the elements of this visible world.

We think that we see with our eyes. The information, the influences of perception, are due to our senses— while the real influence, the meaning of things, the power behind what sees and what is seen, can be reached neither by the senses, nor by deduction and analysis, comparisons, contrasts, and associations made through intellectual theories. The invisible world can only be penetrated by the eye and the mind of the heart. Indeed, the reality of this visible world also can only be seen by the eye and the mind of the heart.

What we think we see is but veils which hide the reality of things; things whose truth, whose meaning may not be revealed until these veils are lifted. It is only when the dark veils of imagination and preconception are raised that the divine light will penetrate the heart, enabling the inner eye to see. Then either the sunlight or the light of a candle will become a metaphor for the divine light.

The principal veils which render the inner eye blind are arrogance, egotism, desires of the flesh, lust; as well as the influence of others who are afflicted by these sicknesses. If man truly believed that he had an inner eye, a mirror where only the truth is reflected, and if he made efforts to rid himself of the veils which hide reality from it, then it would be possible for the divine light of the invisible realms to join with the light inside him, and he would see all that is hidden there. As we are now, we are like the blind who feel the warmth of the sunshine, but are unable to see the light. When your eyes are closed, does it matter whether there are objects in front of you, whether they are near or far, whether they are beautiful or not? That is what we are concerned with.

That veil which hinders our vision is very heavy to lift. Only those chosen by God—the prophets, the saints, the ones who love Him and the ones whom He loves—can pierce through it. Then whether the object to be seen is in front of your eyes or not, whether it is near or very far, also does not matter! Our Master the Prophet, may God's peace and blessings be upon him, used to say to his Companions: "I can see you even when my back is turned."

The mystics who devote their lives to come close to their Lord are encouraged by their Lord in their efforts by what we call miracles. They are shown people and places, right in front of them, that are somewhere else, miles away. Though they are in the West, they see Mecca, far off in the East.

Many such visions are experienced by those who seek to know their Lord, especially if their affection for our Master, Muhammad, may God's peace and blessings be upon him, draws them to be like him—for then they inherit his qualities and are blessed with divine favor. All praise be to God that I myself have experienced this.

These people of elevated state are called *abdal*. Sometimes their ability to see the secrets beyond the visible world is taken away from them. That is a sign that they have reached the highest state aspired to by every human being, the state of true servanthood to the Lord. Then they are the heirs of the prophets, and no longer simply people who know what is unknown to others in this world. Their knowledge belongs to the invisible angelic realms; they are between two worlds.

For people in this state, there is no longer a

separation or distance between the visible and the invisible, neither between their exterior and their interior being. The veils which hid things are all lifted. All that is left of them is a ringing in their ears. All their secrets are now raised to the surface and exposed. All the paths leading to the unknown are open to them.

Then when the view of this reality is left behind, it is as if another divine curtain falls upon them. But the loving, generous Lord replaces what He has taken away by a beautiful multicolored light which He sheds upon a part of the material world and a part of the invisible realm both, linking them together, but leaving the greater part hidden in the dark.

I pray and beg my Lord that He cover you with that light when you yourself become pure, clear, and transparent. This is the level of divine inspiration. The proof of it is that the one who has reached it has the joy of hearing and understanding the word of his Lord without sounds or letters. God asks His Prophet to say:

> I am not the first of the messengers and I know
> not what will be done with me or with you. I fol-
> low that which is revealed to me by inspiration.
>> (*Ahqaf, 9*)

And God also says:

> It is not fitting for a man that God should speak
> to him except by inspiration.
>> (*Shura, 51*)

But He also makes His Prophet say:

I say not to you, I have with me the treasures
of God, nor do I know the unseen, nor do I say
to you that I am an angel. I follow only that
which is revealed to me. Are the blind and the
seeing alike?

(*An'am, 50*)

Thus even a perfect man can only see what he is
made to see, and know what is his due to know, from the
hidden realms. But what is seen and known from the invisible will have its effect upon our visible world through the
influence of the words of those who have learned by inspiration. And they will be made to say nothing more than
what they have been taught.

This knowledge, although vast, is finite. This permits us to weigh and measure things and to come to conclusions. God, in his infinite wisdom and mercy, has limited our knowledge, for infinity is inconceivable for the
human being and is only known to the divine wisdom.
Allah says:

Say: If the sea were ink to write the words of
my Lord, the sea would surely be exhausted
before the words of my Lord were exhausted.

(*Kahf, 109*)

And He says:

And if all the trees on the earth were pens and
the sea, with seven more seas added to it, were
ink, the words of God would not be exhausted.

(*Luqman, 27*)

The veil of darkness itself, which hides the unknown, contains infinite knowledge. It is the knowledge of eternal divine logic. Men try to investigate and discover some things in it. The more they know, the more they realize that there is no end to it.

The highest level of knowledge can only be obtained by ecstatic inspired knowing, which opens the eye of the heart and enables man finally to discover that which is permitted to him to know.

The ultimate knowledge which men wish to attain is: Who is it who furnishes this knowledge and teaches the method of learning it? For that answer is the proof of the truth of what we know. Do not seek it elsewhere. He has placed that proof in you, yourself.

God says:

And We record everything in a clear book.
(*Ya Sin, 12*)

That book is the Imam, the soul, the guide of the human realm of which you are the king, the deputy of God. His wisdom and power are infinite, and the sign of that is in the intimate meaning of His words. With what we are able to understand of them, we can see the frontiers that separate us from His infinite realm.

What we see with is insight, the eye of the heart—and the sign of someone who possesses this insight is that a beautiful character and morals are expressed in his actions. Those are the fruits of his understanding and his knowledge. A human being who has reached that state is at the highest level of spiritual union with God. That level is reached only by understanding and living in accordance with the Holy Qur'an. God says:

Behold, in this are signs for those who by
tokens do understand.

(Hijr, 75)

Spiritual communion with God affects the senses
and creates a sharpened sensitivity which enables one to
see the invisible realms. Materialists deny this ability.
Many do not believe in it. But it is a science like any other
science, dependent upon trials, experiments, and continued efforts. It is a knowledge initiated by, and dependent
upon, the faith and pleasure one derives from the glimpses
of truth allowed us by that natural God-given insight which
everyone has.

The one who sees with this insight sees with divine
light. The light of the Lord can make known only truth.
This fact, and the acknowledgment of it, is uncovered only
when natural insight is complemented by the canons of
religion.

The Lord has placed special signs upon all objects
which are visible to everyone in accordance to their
ability.

Someone came to 'Uthman, the third blessed caliph
after the Messenger of God, and said, "Will anyone after
our Master, God's peace and blessings be upon him,
receive revelations from God?"

The caliph 'Uthman, may Allah be pleased with
him, said, "Know that none will receive direct revelations
from Allah in the way that he did—yet I heard him say,
'Beware of the insight of the faithful, for he sees with the
light of Allah.'" And he said to the man, "I see the glimmer of this divine light in your own eyes."

These glimmers of divine light are bestowed by the

Lord upon some fortunate ones whose faith is weak, so that their hearts will be strengthened and warmed towards their Lord. Yet this glimmer will disappear unless it is protected and made permanent by the prescriptions contained in the Holy Qur'an.

So listen to what God says to you in that Book. Seek in it direction for your actions and your love. Your heart should beat with that love when you believe in what you hear, and confirm it with your acts.

When your faith is weak and you forget your Lord, get hold of those signs which God has placed in everything around you to remind you of Himself. Then with the confirmation and proof of their truth, taught to you by your religion, your heart will find strength and your faith will be affirmed.

If you are able to see the signs of your Lord around you, but do not understand their meaning because of your lack of religious training and its result, you may be accused, even by your own self, of seeing only sorcery or illusion.

You may ask yourself, What is the value of seeing someone who is blond, or has blue eyes, or a large nose, and so forth? Those who see these signs with their natural, inborn insight think in opposites—a thing is either good or bad. Signs which indicate acceptable, proper qualities are put on one side and those which indicate bad qualities are put on the other. Then there follows the consideration of very white; whiter than white; more or less; yellow hair or blue eyes; dark eyes or fine nose: they condemn and praise the extremes, but are confused when qualities approach one another, where the bad may become good.

When we see this happening, we question this kind

of categorization of the beautiful and the ugly, and say that in this visible world of ours there is no such thing as beautiful and ugly. We can only attribute such qualities when we consider these signs in the light of religious teaching. Our purpose is not to praise or blame, but by any and every means, to bring the two extremes to the middle, to the median, and to make each thing acceptable and praiseworthy.

Every human being fits one of the following three characteristics:

1. Someone who is aware of himself alone, separating himself from everyone and everything, claiming that his life and his actions are his own. He is thus totally blind and inconsiderate of all that religion teaches, and will indeed go as far as to change the precepts of religion to fit his own purposes. He is an enemy who has set himself to destroy the divine harmony. Thus, he is blameworthy. May God protect us from being one of these, and may He protect us from them.

2. Someone who is open to what is around him and considers himself to be part of it, sees himself as like some people and wishes to be like some others. In his wish to be like others, he may well try to be like the people in the first category as easily as like those in the next, who follow the precepts of religion.

3. Someone who hears and understands the word of the Lord and follows its precepts, walking where it leads him in his life, step by step, moment by moment. He follows in the footsteps of the one whom God has sent as the embodiment of His words. He walks behind his Prophet

and stops when he stops. God loves the one who lives like this.

He made His Prophet say:

Follow me and God will love you and forgive your sins.

(Al-i 'Imran, 31)

The one who follows the Beloved of God certainly loves God, and God will certainly forgive his sins and make him pure. He is the one who has found salvation and eternal joy.

This is how extremes are confronted and two opposites are united: How shall one judge someone who is not participating in prayer while a congregation is worshipping, but sitting and watching them quietly? Is he necessarily a hypocrite or a nonbeliever?

We see a man sitting quietly and not participating in the prayer—that is like what we see of this material, visible world. Whether this person is against worship or faith or God—that is like what we do not normally see in the invisible realms. If we judge what we see with the simple rules of religion, we may come to the conclusion that this man is an infidel unless he confirms his faith by saying "There is no god but God and Muhammad is his servant and Messenger." But according to the canons of faith we are obliged to protect the life and the property of this man, and leave him be. That is how our view, our thoughts, and our actions must be.

CHAPTER 9

ON THE ATTRIBUTES AND DUTIES OF THE SCRIBE

The Lord, to guarantee success to His governor, has bestowed upon him a character more perfect than any other in the creation. He has created for him such a refined, high, miraculous existence that even the souls in the invisible realm are in awe. The Prophet Idris, God's peace be upon him, who was the first among the prophets to write with a pen, glorifies him.

The Imam whom God has charged to govern the realm of the human being is given compassion and generosity. The good which comes from the Lord passes through his hands, and the decision is his, whether to distribute it or not. He is also the one through whom the holy commandments are issued. He is the center of all wealth and kindness and ease; from him, all the blessings are spread to the four corners of the human realm. He is the one who makes the poor, rich and the bad spirit, a good one. He is the place within the universal soul where everything is registered and recorded. That place is an existence in itself, which the Imam, the owner of the universal soul and mind who rules the human realm, has set free.

In that place, where the records of the Imam are kept, the commands of inspirational knowledge are also written. When the commands of inspirational knowledge are acted upon, they materialize, and are given the name of the authority of the Imam.

Now the book, the records, and the one who records

are materialized. Their values and their attributes have to be known.

Know that the Lord has created, in His vast kingdom, a holy element which He swears by: a secret, guarded Tablet and a grand Pen, which writes what no one else can write, nor can anyone change what it has written.

When the first-created Pen moves on the sacred Tablet, it writes the orders of the divine will. The truth thus written reaches all existence and is shared by all existence, and the Lord knows what each being has received. That book is sent so that the creation—which did not exist, nor would have existed, nor could have existed by itself—might face its Creator. Now all we have to do is to find who and where the writer is.

The philosopher says: "The Pen of the Lord and His Tablet are extended to become my pen and paper, and my hand, which holds the pen, moves by what the Lord has sworn in the invisible realms. Thus I am made to walk, and what I see around is just chance, my destiny."

The name "Scribe" and what it represents is such a beautiful, refined, wise quality that the Imam of the human realm swears by it. Its origin is high above. Where it comes from is the source of that divine wine, made of the sacred grapes of truth, sincerity, and purity.

When the Imam wishes to apply a command from the invisible in this visible world, if the message sinks into the human heart, then it will always be known and remembered and the whole being will find peace and comfort. When that happens, the dark veils over the heart lift, and all that the Imam willed will be written in the heart to stay. Thus the heart becomes the mirror of Intellect. The mind sees, in the mirror of the heart's memory, things that it has never seen before.

When that which is seen in the heart is rationalized by the mind, the mind understands that it is an order from above, and asks the Scribe of memory to come. It shows him what it has seen in the heart as the Lord's commands. The Scribe records the Lord's words, felt by the heart, realized by the mind, upon the tablet of the self—and as they are recorded, they are distributed to all the organs of the body, to all the corners of the kingdom of the human realm.

Thus the heart knows the truth by being the truth. The mind learns from the heart by seeing the truth. The rest learn the truth through the Scribe, by hearsay.

Where is this Scribe? Is he stationed under the Throne of the Lord or under His Footstool, or somewhere between the two? Indeed, his position is high. He is stationed where the Holy Qur'an reigns, the place where right and wrong, truth and falsehood, are separated. That place is by the soul. And the Lord says:

> By the soul and the proportion and order given
> to it and its enlightenment as to its right and its
> wrong.
> (Shams, 7-8)

The duty of the Scribe is to record the right as right and the wrong as wrong, according to each different case. He is not given this position simply because he knows how to write. It is because he is from a place like the Throne or the Footstool of the Lord in the invisible realms where there is no right or wrong, where there is no praise or blame.

Below the Footstool is where the self is. That is the place of change, the place of now and later, the place of cleansing and purification. But the place of the Scribe is right above that realm of the self. When an order comes from above for him to write this holy commandment, it is immutable. Thus right and wrong, praise and blame do not apply to it.

The Scribe receives the order to write from a single source—the treasury of the Prophet Muhammad, peace and blessings be upon him. All divine orders to the whole of the human kingdom come through that source. The Scribe receives his orders from that source in letters and numbers and words structured in accordance with the understanding of man. He arranges and organizes them in a beautiful way, records them in the diary of his memory, and distributes them wherever they are meant to go. Thus the whole duty and importance of the Scribe is that he records and distributes what comes from the treasury of Muhammad, peace and blessings be upon him.

What is important is that he is the only one who hears the divine orders. Those who receive them from him have not heard the original commands.

What is written belongs to the realm of things evident. He who writes is hidden in the invisible realm. What holds his hand while it is writing is the hand of the Truth Itself. The hand of Truth which moves the hand of the Scribe is often manifest in what he writes, and results in words and numbers and what they produce. If there is a lack of homogeneity and a lack of harmony in the application of the command, it appears when the hand of the Truth is not holding the hand of the Scribe. For the Scribe, in his essence, is free—but what he does is never for himself, and he is protected by his Lord. Nothing and no one can intrude to prevent him from what he is doing, nor can anyone try to change him.

Some wish to catch and imprison the Scribe under the seven layers of earth, or to send him out to the Seventh Heaven—like the Pharaoh, who declared himself God, and Abu Jahl, who thought of the Messenger of Allah as a poor illiterate, and those who resemble them. These think that they are the masters of their own destiny, that they can achieve whatever they will. They care only about themselves, and revere and sanctify only themselves. They hate the truth, and the one who records and declares the truth, more than they hate hellfire.

But indeed, those who do not look upon what is written and accept it are themselves imprisoned deep down in the darkness of the seven layers of earth, or are burning in Hell. If a person cannot conceive with his intellect what is reflected from his heart, he is already sunk in heedlessness and will sink further.

Often the divine commands which the Scribe writes may appear as if in code, hidden. Perchance the key to decipher them is the cognizance of one's soul.

The Scribe has an honored position. The Ruler of the realm of the human being also employs the Scribe as a teller of tales of past happenings, as lessons for his people as well as for himself. As he is often in the company of the Ruler, the Scribe has to have good behavior, good character, has to know how to keep secrets and how to be patient. He must be eloquent in many languages and able to make declarations that will not be misunderstood and, when he receives orders from above, to record them as received, without interpretation and without feeling the necessity to prove the source of the message. He must be confident of his ability to make a single meaning out of what may appear to have two meanings.

If the Ruler detects some vagueness in the writing of the Scribe which does not correspond to what he has dictated to him, and which may suggest another meaning other than what was meant, the Ruler may discredit his Scribe and may end up disliking him. For if there is a possibility of misunderstanding or if there are doubts about it, then there is no longer any value in an instruction. Precisely to avoid such situations, the Scribe must be a master of understanding and of communicating clearly what he has understood. Thus his words must correspond exactly to the meaning. There can be no heavy words nor complicated sentences which might cause confusion as to who is being addressed: the body, or the heart, or the soul.

When the Scribe starts his registration of daily affairs, he should start with offering his respects and praise of the Imam, the guide charged by the Lord to govern the human realm, because the written word about the importance of the Imam—his honor, his beautiful attributes, his justice, his consideration and care for his people—will increase the respect and loyalty felt towards the Imam in all parts of the kingdom of the human being. It is only after this introduction that he should write the edicts of the Imam's orders.

If these orders are considered by general consensus to be good, then they will be received with favor. If they give an impression of imposition, then they will create opposition. Someone asked the saint Abu Yazid al-Bistami, "How can someone revolt against God's commands when he is a believer and fears and loves Allah?" The saint responded, "If Allah so wills, it happens!"

If the Scribe is as already described, then he is in the right place. He is knocking at the right door, asking to be admitted. Even if he is not let inside, still he knows who the occupant of the house is, for he has come to His door. He must have received blessings and invitation, for God Most High swears by His Scribe. And He offers him all he needs—except the pen and ink and the page to write upon, which the Scribe has to find himself. Then he will make marks on the paper—letters, numbers—which will transmit knowledge, shed light upon truth. But these marks and letters do not have any resemblance to the alphabets of man's invention.

The sacred, secret Tablet of the heavens, where all that is seen and unseen is recorded, is right here with us. Endless words and numbers which guide our existence come from it. As these instructions enter our being and are acted upon, they disappear. Yet they always seem to keep coming. They are always here, and it does not appear that they are ever going to end. This is a secret which enters the heart, and once there, bursts into flames and exhausts itself. It is such a mystery that even those who know best take refuge in it and must seek to learn it.

In truth there are two Tablets, two Books. One is written in the Lord's language and the other is in human tongue. He swears:

> By the mountain (of revelation), by a decree
> inscribed . . .
>
> *(Tur, 2)*

By His oath on His Book, He announces the existence of the Book in our version. His version belongs high up in the Realm of the Souls; our book is down here in the material universe. We can read the one in our tongue, but

121

His Book can reach us only by means of revelations and inspirations.

It is like the two sides of a page. One faces up toward the heavens, and contains words written even before the creation of the heavens. The other side of the page faces downward, toward us, and is written in our language. Why can't we read the other side of the page? Because that message was written for the worlds of unconditioned existence. While we inhabit human existence there are both good and bad, right and wrong, material and spiritual. Only reading the other side of the Tablet will save man from this duality.

The Book written for man in his mother tongue is a sample of a form, a model of what should be, an instruction in how to be gathered together in this world of loose strings. This world is fully related in that Book. All those loyal to this world are mentioned in it. It addresses those who have forgotten all about the spiritual realms, whose hearts are filled with the love of this world, whose minds are closed to secret ordinances, but who are interested in the solution of worldly problems in accordance with divine decree. These people are attached to the instructions in that Book. Such are the Qur'anic lawyers, who themselves are written in the Book, who receive intellectual direction from it, while it does nothing for their hearts, which are all covered with dark veils.

The Scribe, following the way of the rationalists, is able to see both sides of things, is aware that this world is quite close to, and is connected with, the heavens. From some signs in the Book written in our tongue he feels the secrets in the heavenly Book written in God's language— which is not hidden far above in the heavens. He is able to understand it by the combination of his mind and his heart.

On some occasions, when a secret is revealed to him, one hears his screams of awe and fear. When you ask him what his Lord has revealed to him, all he can answer is: the truth. He has asked for an answer to a question, and he has received it in the form of a manifestation of his Lord. When this happens, the Lord covers both His manifestation and the one who has received it under veils. If it were possible to tear the veils aside, the causes would disappear: the effects themselves would be self-existent.

When the Scribe sees how a hidden destiny manifests itself in the creation, he diligently follows its traces, reflecting upon it and analyzing its occurrence. Then he is aware when it is repeated. If he sees fit, he makes his findings known. But mostly he talks to himself and records his findings in his own book, which is in his heart. The book in the Scribe's heart is the sacred, secret Tablet which contains all things to do and all things not to do. In fact, it contains all that has happened and all that is bound to happen.

Those who have this book in their hearts, speak to their hearts, and they speak to each other through the book in their hearts. That book contains all the orders of God, which these chosen ones know in full.

O Soul, deputy of God in the universe of the human being, if you are charged to guide and rule the human realm, know that the Scribe is assigned by your Lord to the rank of your speaker. It is he who has been granted the power of oratory. When he speaks for you and of you, he does not do it on his own. He is created to be your dependent. Anyone who respects him and loves him, enters into his service and obeys him, therefore belongs to you.

Remember that he acts and speaks in your name, assumes your nature and your character. Appreciate that;

then do everything that is necessary to make your Scribe feel your appreciation, so that he loves you and is attached to you. Otherwise he can cause the worst disharmony and mischief in your kingdom.

Your prime minister, Intellect, whose sole objective is that order and peace should reign in your kingdom, is also in need of the Scribe. For your decrees, written by your Scribe, are made known far and wide in your realm by his efforts, not yours. You must surely see to it that your orders are understood in your immediate environment. If there is discord around you, it will spread to all your realm. Only Intellect, your prime minister, is able to prevent the possibility of such intrigue and sedition and the loss of control resulting from it, because the Lord has entrusted to Intellect the knowledge of immorality and evil dispositions and the power to fight them. That power comes from the fear of God. Your Lord and theirs has confirmed the position of both your Prime Minister and your Scribe as your helpers. Therefore take care of them.

If you care for them, you will see the signs of your Lord, who addresses you:

"O My governor, whom I sent to rule the realm of the human being in My name, in whom I have placed the sacred secret of My rules, and whom I have crowned with My own identity and essence—still you are in doubt and hesitant. You wish to see Me to be sure, although I have not willed that to happen. Now I will show Myself!

"I have raised the curtains, and torn them into such pieces that they can never be replaced. I have lifted them up into the invisible realm. Now you are a witness of My existence. You have known the veils, and you have seen what was behind them. So prostrate in front of Me, and know. Read what I have assigned to be written: what will happen to everyone; which deeds will receive My response. There are no words nor sound in this revelation, shown to you in a dream.

"Peace be upon you and upon the ones who are with you, the ones who will never leave you; and all the blessings of all existence; and all love and compassion; and peace be upon those who see."

Your Lord orders His angels, who are in the person of your Scribe, to descend to the heart of His deputy in the human realm. And He indicates to him that He will find you in one of three possible states: either you are with your Lord; or with your ego; or together with your enemy, Satan.

If you are with your Lord, your Scribe is ordered not to even show you the words of your Lord, for the Lord Himself is already your guide. Your heart is in His hand; He will turn it whichever way He wills. Your Scribe has been given the best of character and behavior by the One who sent him, and he was taught not to show off his origins. In fact, if he finds you with your Lord, you will never see him; you will only know of him, by his name and by his rank. Yet you will also know that he is your defense against the desires of your ego and against the temptations of the Devil.

If, instead of being with your Lord, you are under the influence of your ego, your Scribe has been ordered to come to you in secret, without the knowledge of your ego. He will advise you to act upon what you already know, and warn you of what your ego knows: that it will stand against you on the Day of Judgment, when every minute of your life spent under its influence will be a hostile witness.

Beware, avoid not only what is forbidden and what

is disliked by God, but also that which is merely tolerated by Him. Even in lawful acts, such as eating, drinking, and sleeping, you must be more careful than anyone else. Abstain from excess, and begin each act by remembering your Lord. Act only in His name. Do what has been made obligatory for you, so that you will appear in front of Him unblemished and pure. When you show neither enjoyment, nor desire, nor even need of the things which have been made lawful to you, then your Lord will know that your goal is not the sustenance, but the Sustainer. God Most High says:

And He it is that feedeth what is not fed.
(An'am, 14)

When, remembering your Lord, you do that which has been made lawful to you, remember that the purpose of eating is to gain enough strength to worship Him and to fight in defense of His religion and of the laws which He has ordained for the good of the human being. Sleep is for the rest necessary to function in His name. Lawful sexual relationship is for the conception of an obedient and pure child who will walk in the way of the Lord. Seeing is for taking lessons, for distinguishing right from wrong, for following the right path and showing it to others, and for helping those in need. These are divine signs are around you, which correspond to what you have in your heart.

If you are found under the influence of your ego, your Scribe is instructed to remind you that you might very well follow the desires of your flesh, enjoy all and everything that this world offers you, and neglect to ask any favors from your Lord for the hereafter. If you are bound for this world, then it will be your lord. If you are meant to be with your Lord, you will oppose the world.

While attached to this world, you may still be in one of the three states: you may be worshipping your Lord, or you may be with yourself, or you may be in the company of the Devil.

If you are sitting in vain prayer, the Scribe is instructed to prevent you from it, for you are spending your time for nothing. Lifting the veil of the useless pretense of contemplation, he will push you back to your work in the world.

If you are found with yourself, the Scribe is instructed to wait. When the ego goes to sleep in heedlessness and dreams an imaginary life, then the Scribe calls for the help of your Lord. Perchance He will show you the truth.

If you are found in the company of Satan, the Scribe is instructed to come between the two of you. He will seek your sympathy and friendship, so as to help you defend yourself against the Devil. In spite of being your dependent, in his function of defender he will appear to you as your master. He will persist, without showing hesitancy or weakness, because your Lord knows that you will finally return to Him.

If you are under the command of the enemy of humankind, then the Scribe is instructed to test you. He will encourage you to worship others than the Lord, to be engulfed by infidelity, attributing partners to God; to insult that which is sacred; to exalt lust, adultery, envy, violation of the rights of others. If he finds you hesitant to do one evil deed, He will encourage you to another.

In that state, you will find yourself again in one of the three possibilities: either you will still feel a connection with your Lord, or you will be alone with yourself, or you will be under the influence of your evil-commanding ego.

If you still feel a connection, the Scribe is instructed to ask you to identify yourself: who you are; what your name is; in whose service you are, while you are pretending to be with your Lord. He is instructed to throw you out of the kingdom of imagination that your Lord has given to you, so that you will see the difference between your pretense of being with Him and the state of those who are truly with Him, of whom He is jealous, and whom He protects from such conditions as the one in which you find yourself. But if, having been cast out of your imaginary state, you find any of your Lord's own attributes or traces of His divine actions in you, it will mean that you have repented. Then all the faults you have committed will be added to the mischief of the Devil, who will be kept in hellfire for eternity.

If you find yourself alone with yourself, separate from your Lord, setting yourself up as a partner to your Lord, then you are indeed a slave of the Devil, and the wrath of your Lord is upon both of you. Then the Scribe is charged to fight you both. If he wins, what will be left victorious is your Lord. If you win, you will be further strengthened in your blasphemy, and your Lord will brand your forehead and give you to Satan as his property. If your heart wishes for what Satan offers you, you will receive nothing from him. You will be left far from your Lord. And you will suffer, in addition, the pain of avenging yourself upon yourself.

If you find yourself under the influence of your evil-commanding ego, the Scribe is ordered to place in front of you all the desires of your flesh and more; and he is ordered to increase your ambition for, and your designs upon, the pleasures of this world—a hunger that can never be satisfied. But you will be a most devout slave to your ego, and it will tear you to pieces.

One thing you must know: in all of this, whether you succeed or fail, whether, in his function as your Scribe, he is victorious over these states which may plague you or not—he is acting only in the name of your Lord. Both success and failure are from your Lord, for He is the All-Knowing and the All-Powerful.

All these are signs of your Lord, which enter with great force into one's being and settle in the heart. All of this is written. Your Scribe, whose hand is in the hand of Allah, knows it best, for the Lord accedes to what he requests, and he is made to know the state of things in your realm. So value him, and do not underestimate him in any way, because all divine words are in his hand, and what he asks for is granted.

Since the beginning of time, all that might happen, all change that might occur in the realm of the human being, and the very security of the deputy of Allah while ruling his realm, has been in the hand of the Scribe. Therefore hold fast to that hand, and place generous gifts in that hand, for generosity and gifts seal friendship and prevent hostility, jealousy, rancor, and revenge.

CHAPTER 10

ON THE METHOD OF COLLECTING TAXES AND CHOOSING THE ONE TO COLLECT THEM

O generous master charged to rule the human realm! Know that the power entrusted to you is protected by your Lord. The Lord has created beings in different levels. Some are over others, and some under. Some are destined to be leaders and others, followers; some to be masters and others, their servants. But on the Day of Judgment those destined to rule will be asked if they have ruled in justice, and those who have been ruled will be called as witnesses. Those who rule are warned by God:

> Pursue not that of which thou hast no knowledge: for every act of hearing, or of seeing, or of [feeling in] the heart will be inquired into (on the day of reckoning).
> *(Bani Isra'il, 6)*

and:

> On the day when their tongues, their hands, and their feet will bear witness against them as to their actions.
> *(Nur, 24)*

and:

> At length, when they reach the [fire], their

hearing, their sight, and their skins will bear
witness against them as to all their deeds.

(Fusilat, 20)

and:

Ye did not seek to hide yourselves, lest your
hearing, your sight, and your skins should bear
witness against you.

(Fusilat, 22)

The Lord in His Holy Book warns against injustice done to
others on many other occasions.

Your eyes, ears, tongue, hands, belly, feet, and sexual organs are your entrusted workers and helpers,
guardians of your treasures. At the head of these workers
are the senses. It is they that guide and control them. Yet
there is someone over the senses too, who directs and con-
trols them: that director is Conception.

The director who is Conception is not able to differentiate right from wrong. For this purpose he has someone
over him—which is Thinking. Thinking, in turn, is under
the command of Intellect. Intellect is the highest authority in your government, your prime minister. And you,
God's deputy, are above all of them and have the supreme
authority and responsibility. That is why you are called the
Sacred Soul.

O entrusted master, you must understand that you
cannot do all you are expected to do by yourself. It is
impossible. Your Lord often commands you to do many
things at once. To gather together all that He has asked you
to gather, you need the help of totally trustworthy workers
of good will. They will be charged to collect the taxes

which are due on every member of your realm in a proper and just way, and to place this wealth in the treasuries of your kingdom—for a kingdom will not last without rich treasuries. To gather this capital is only possible through collecting taxes. What is expected of you by the members of your country is to be reasonable and just in the collection of taxes, not only for the length of your reign, but also to be an example for the future.

The helper you need to collect capital for the safety and governing of your kingdom has to be knowledgeable in the calculation of what is needed, as well as in what it is possible to collect. He must know this in detail, so that he will not ask any member of your kingdom for dues which he cannot afford and is unable to give.

All you need is one such capable helper. To use many will only result in conflict and disagreement among your workers. For it is possible that each tax collector may wish to do better than the other, in order to please you and to gain your favors. Then they will try to collect, by force, more than people can afford—thus causing poverty among your people and weakness in your kingdom. Any wealth gathered unjustly and by violence will bring no profit. It will be like trying to collect water in a hole in the sand.

The Messenger of God, may God's peace and blessings be upon him, said, "A fertile field is the one which does not hide in it what is going to grow upon it."

He also said, "Whoever makes a tyranny of my religion, and whoever in the future will do the same, will be defeated by that religion."

And God Most High, says:

Make not thy hand tied [like a niggard's] to thy

neck, nor stretch it forth to its utmost reach [like a spendthrift].

Thus, fast and break your fast; worship your Lord, then sleep to rest; be at peace, for your Lord has chosen a helper for you, who will collect your taxes and fill your treasuries and protect you from error. As long as he is with you, none of your good deeds will be lost. They will be safely kept. Your Lord has signified him for you as the best among those who intend to right the wrong, who are heedful of what is present and who preview the future. Make that one your collector of taxes. You will be satisfied with his services.

That collector and keeper of the dues for your Lord (which are your good deeds) is Knowledge. His helpers are persistence, economy, equity, courage, and conscience. When they serve you, the finances of your kingdom will be administered in justice, and you will find prosperity and security in the future. They will know what to expect from the maleficent influences among some of the members of your kingdom, and take precaution. They will know what each member owes and is able to give without causing him hardship, so both the one who pays his obligation and the one who receives will be content.

Now that you know the way of gathering in your treasuries what is due to your Lord and how to choose your helpers, trust in Knowledge as your collector of taxes— and praise your Lord who has given him to you as your helper.

CHAPTER 11

ON SEEKING THE WAY TO OFFER THE LORD THAT WHICH IS DUE FROM HIS DEPUTY

O generous master, deputy of God, know that what is made known to you in this book is not intended for your theoretical education, nor to teach you what to do. It is a warning about your actions.

Your Lord is the lord of all lords, the master of all masters, the king of the universe. All else is nothing, or is in the process of becoming nothing, in comparison to Him. He is the owner of everything; He has no beginning and no end. All that is visible and invisible is in His knowledge. All existences, old and new—their beginning and their end, what is above them and under them, came to be only through Him. Everything is from Him and returns to Him, and whatever is from Him is for Him alone.

All your actions—your deeds both known and unknown to you—are from Him. Only He sees and knows all of them. Every wrong act that comes through you vexes Him and pains Him, and he feels aversion to it. He has created no one better than you to know what is right and what is wrong. You are His best creation, because He acts through you. He does not wish to lose you. He has created you as a sensible and obedient being.

O blessed deputy, take heed that you offer to your Lord what you are collecting for yourself, even though your impressions are collected by your senses and must be evaluated by your heart. Take care how they reach you.

You collect from your environment what you sense

and feel worthy to be collected. Your perception and your conception are the chiefs of your senses, who collect this wealth. They are also the guardians who keep it safe. The experiences collected are classified according to their kind and value and brought to the guardians to be put in the treasury of the mind.

Once it is in the treasury of the mind, the name of this wealth changes from experience to memory. It is kept there in the treasury to be dispensed by a higher authority, Remembrance. But the wealth is kept in two separate places: there is that which is committed to memory to be kept, and that which is to be remembered and dispensed. When the memory which is to be dispensed is called for, it is given to the arbitration of Thought. There it tells what it knows and so directs Thinking, often saving it from dangers, distinguishing truth from lies. It also informs the thought process about the ability and quality of the forces working under it.

Experiences gathered by the senses might also be erroneous, counterfeit. These too might be deposited in memory, remembered, and brought back to thought. If Thought tests a thing anew with the senses and gets the proper response, that means there is no mistake in it. Then it can take that sensation as being true and good, and present it to its master, Intellect. Thought presents the new experience—reinforced with the memory, remembered in all detail and clarity—to its master, Intellect, saying: Here is what the ear heard, here is what the eye saw, here is what the tongue said. The ears, the eyes, the tongue are its helpers. If Intellect accepts this explanation, then that experience enters into the treasury of undeniable truths.

Next Intellect, the prime minister of the kingdom of

the human being, takes this treasury to the Sacred Soul, the master of the realm, and places it in front of him, saying: Here is the wealth, the valuable product of the servants of your realm.

Without wasting a moment, the soul picks up the treasure and flies to the presence of its Lord, then throws itself down in prostration at His door. As the door opens, the soul swoons in awe at the manifestation of the Lord, and drops the treasures of good deeds on the ground.

The Lord asks, "Why have you come to Us?"

The Sacred Soul responds, "O my Lord, I have come to present You with the deeds of the human realm to which you have assigned me as Your deputy. You have asked me to collect what is due to You from them. I have brought You all that has been collected from them and brought to me."

Then the Lord says: "Take this deputy and bring him to what I have written before I created him. Bring him to the Holy Qur'an, and compare his actions with what is written in it. Tie them together until he has read it all, word by word. Release him only when he has reached the height of it."

All this happens under the Lotus Tree in the seventh heaven, above all the other heavens.

If, in that treasure offered to the Lord by the soul, there is a deed which is not in harmony with the Lord's intention in the creation of the human being, a tyranny done to one's self or to others, then the gates of Heaven will not open for the soul to pass. When he reaches the skies of this world he will be rejected. He will be thrown back under the seven levels of earth into Hell, weighed down by the weight of the inhumanity which he offered as his deeds to his Lord.

God says:

Verily, the record of the righteous is [raised with him] in the highest Paradise.
(Tatfif, 18)

and:

Nay, surely the record of the wicked is [thrown with him] in Hell.
(Tatfif, 7)

God Most High addresses the soul in the seventh heaven: "O my servant, as a reward for what you have brought for Me I have made this lofty place lawful to you. Look at the ones who are below you to appreciate your state." And the soul looks below it and realizes the favors of its Lord. Then it is left alone with those favors. When the Lord sees that the soul is content with His favors and is not desiring Him, He hides Himself from it. If it were not so, we would have been able to see Him.

The Lord has created a cause for every secret, and this He keeps for Himself. God says:

[Jesus is] His word, which He bestowed upon Mary, and a Spirit proceeding from Him.
(Nisa', 170)

and:

To Him mount up all words of purity. It is He who exalts each deed of righteousness.
(Fatir, 10)

When deeds are presented to the soul and their identity transformed into something acceptable to it, the soul feels an affinity with them. Now these deeds appear to the soul to be on its level. When the Lord sees this state of affairs, He dresses the deeds in two fine garments, one upon the other. He sets them in their proper niches, but takes their true qualities and identity from under the fancy clothes. He locks them up in the treasury of His secrets, and the soul is left with only the exterior beauty of the good deeds. Their spirit is gone. That is why there is a saying: "Give the due of your deeds," meaning, do not give overdue value to your deeds. That is how the essence of things gets lost while they still appear as intact as before.

What is evident and what is hidden; living in accordance with religious law and living in accordance with truth; the action of hands and the action of hearts—all these may seem to be separate things. Yet their result may be the same, just as true submission and simple obedience may both make us do the same thing.

Practical righteous acts, which are kept in the treasury of the mind, are other than the select acts meant for celestial realms. Therefore, master of the human realm, choose deeds that are greater than this world. Choose deeds that will pierce the heavens above you. When you seek knowledge, seek not only the knowledge which changes, which leaves and is replaced. Seek divine knowledge, which is certain and pure. God's words are like the most perfect and pure pearls. All praise is due to Him.

CHAPTER 12

ON MISSIONS SENT TO APPEASE THE UPHEAVALS IN SOME REGIONS OF THE KINGDOM

Let it be known that divine wisdom is only given to leaders who have rejected the temptations of intellect. If a king decides to send a mission to negotiate with an enemy, his ambassadors must have the following qualities. They must be trustworthy, upright, faithful, religious, far-sighted, valorous, generous, eloquent, convincing, and have other positive qualities related to these. Ambassadors are the representatives of whoever sends them, and it is presumed that the qualities of the one who sends them are similar to their own. If the one who receives them is not convinced of the superior character of the one who sent them, he will be indifferent to their demands. Worse still, if the mission consists of men with a character contrary to these attributes, the enemy will consider the one who sent them as someone who is treacherous, heinous, lying, selfish, and unready to negotiate anything that could be favorable to the opposition.

Therefore, O deputy of God, when you send a mission to subdue your greatest enemy, the evil-commanding ego, who tries to appear in his own state like an obedient vassal to you, let your ambassadors consist of your representatives called honor, sincerity, understanding, perseverance, precaution, good intention, patience, courage, experience, consideration, fear of God, and justice. Every leader who sends a mission consisting of these ambassadors certainly will obtain peace, prosperity, and greatness.

Even the worst enemies, egotism and egoism, will submit to them. Perhaps, though they were your enemies, they may even convert to being your friends. Then the precautions which you have taken to neutralize them will suffice to defeat them without fighting.

And if your enemy—who revolted against you and created mischief in the kingdom that your Lord entrusted to you to defend—sends you a mission, receive them well. Do not treat them harshly. In their negotiations, if they appear to be disloyal to the one who sent them, do not look upon them as traitors. Attribute it to their inexperience and lack of knowledge of politics and diplomacy. If they represent openly the feelings of tyranny, vengeance, treachery, greed, niggardliness, arrogance, ignorance, immorality, cursing, cowardice, and so forth, do not reject them with hatred, nor attack them with words and acts resembling theirs. Test them with diplomatic kindness. It is only when you do not address them in their own style, but in a different mode, that you may attract their attention and start negotiations. In your negotiations, use your prime minister, Intellect, as your translator.

If attached to the mission of the enemy there is an ambassador named Ambition, listen to him. Although he represents your enemy, he is the most trustworthy among them. What he says will be clear and true. He will transmit the message of your enemy thus: "Our lord the ego, whom we are obligated to obey, informs you to surrender and come under our rule, or else we will wage war against you. And his condition for surrender is that you will oppose all the ordinances of your religion and take away from the citizens of your kingdom all that they possess, up to what they need to sustain themselves, and hold everything in your hands."

Your response to him should begin, "O ambassador whose words we value, and whose rank and station are high in our eyes!" The ambassador will be responsive to this introduction, because he has never heard such words from his lord, the ego. Then you will address him and say, "O ambassador, listen to what I say, and reason and be fair. Do you know God? Is He not your Lord and ours?"

He will admit that the One Lord is their Lord also.

Then ask him: "Will you not, as we will, migrate to another world from this world?" And he will also admit that.

Then ask him if this eternal trip is going to be back to our One Lord, or to somewhere else. He will again admit that we will all return to God.

Then ask him, "When we return to God, leaving this life, how will He treat the ones who revolt against Him and who act against His religious laws?" He will have to answer that God will punish those with pain and perdition.

Then ask him, "How will God treat the ones who obey Him?" He will have to answer, "With peace and felicity."

Then ask him, "Is there anyone more powerful and richer than God?" He will have to answer: "Nay."

Then tell him: "O ambassador of ego, greedy Ambition, go and tell your lord the evil-commanding ego: 'I do not care about things which do not please God.' I know that you have a great appetite for owning things, but nothing will come to you except what God has destined for you. What is Ambition for?'" The ambassador will be speechless.

Then tell him: "O Ambition, the truth is true for both you and me. Reality is real for both you and me. So let us spend what is really given to us for God's sake, and in His way, to gain His pleasure. What is given to us in this world is not much good for any of us, and it is temporary. What we hope for from the hereafter is better for us, and greater. O Ambition, I know you are devoted to this world. In spite of all your efforts, don't you feel that something is missing?"

And he will answer you, "Indeed." And he will abandon the path by which he came, and leave you taking the path of knowledge.

Hold on to your religion. Its laws are the laws with which you rule your realm. That is your strength, and that is what keeps the evil-commanding ego in check. You may have similar arguments, worded differently according to their negative convictions, for each of the enemy ambassadors—the treacherous one, the lying one, and the spreader of mischief. But you will be able to make all of them submit to your Lord, and make them Muslims. For Islam—submission to the greater will of the Truth, to the One who created us and created all that His creation needed—is the origin of all and everything. And everything returns to its origin.

Yet your own effort to send your mission to your enemy may not be successful, because all the premises and goals of their argument will be opposed to what the evil-commanding ego demands, and he is apt to reject it. So they will return to you empty-handed. This is the policy and the tactics to be followed in negotiations with enemy ambassadors: it suffices to talk to only one of them, because their demands will all be the same.

CHAPTER 13

ON THE ARMED FORCES IN DEFENSE OF THE KINGDOM OF THE HUMAN BEING, ITS GENERALS, THEIR CHARACTER AND STRATEGY

The army of the kingdom of the human being is the central column which holds the balance of justice. Know that your realm is a home, and a home sits on the four sides of its foundation. That home is you. Its foundation is your attributes and character.

Your foundation is the guarantee of your sovereignty. Its four supports, made of your attributes, are like four generals who command an army to protect your homeland. Watch them very carefully, for your security depends on them.

Each of the four sides of the foundation supports a wall; each of the four generals commands an army. These four armies each have two duties to perform.

Two is the purpose and origin of Four and what generates from Four, and is what connects the numbers generating from Four. It continues ad infinitum. The numbers increase from One to Ten. No other sequence ends in Ten except the number Four, because Four is the reality, the essence, of Ten.

Four is the basis; within it, there is Three. When we add Three to Four, it equals Seven. Within the Four there is also Two. When we add Two to Seven, it equals Nine.

What is left after the Two is One. When we add the One to Nine, it equals Ten. These are the basic numbers. No other numbers add up to Ten except Four plus Three plus Two plus One, which in turn equals Four. So the Ten is within the Four.

We chose the number Four because it contains a divine secret. It is a number of power and weight. That power and weight are under the command of our Lord. The Messenger of God says "The heavens are held by eight supports, but in our time it is four."

And God says:

> And eight [angels] will that day bear the throne
> of thy Lord above them.
> *(Haqqa, 17)*

"That day," in this verse, is the day of the hereafter. But the deputy of God, the human being, has four principal elements in this world of matter, the same four elements from which the whole universe is made—earth and water, air and fire. These four principal elements are the gate to Forty. It is such a wide gate that, if we try to describe it, we will far exceed our intention in this book.

We are also ordered to live within four dimensions. All influences which may cause mischief in our life and being come from those four directions: from our front and our back, our right and our left. In the Holy Qur'an Satan addresses God and says:

> Then will I assault them from before them and
> behind them and from their right and their left.
> *(A'raf, 16)*

No other directions from which evil influences may come are mentioned except these four, yet there are two other dimensions: above us and below us. That which is under us always pulls us to it, and that which is above us belongs to our Lord; it is where He ascends and descends. Do not attempt to reach this, for it is the realm of destiny where we are forbidden to penetrate.

O generous deputy of God in the human realm, watch those four directions from which harm can reach you. Place your four armies, with their four generals, to defend these passages, so that they may protect your realm, your life, and your peace. Your enemies are treacherous and cruel, but they are not brave. They can only enter into your realm when these four paths are undefended.

Your strategy for battle should be this: Put the love and fear of God on your right flank; put your mercy on your left flank; hold knowledge between your two hands in front of you; use intelligence to protect your back.

If the enemy attacks from your right flank, it will be met by the army of your general whose name is Fear of God. You have placed him on your right, for Paradise is in that direction, while your left is the direction of Hell. If your enemy attacks from your right to cut the route to Paradise, his strongest forces will be lust and the love of this world. Often they infiltrate through your ranks as friends. Only the fear of God will be able to repel them; any other force will be fooled by them. Thus, keep the love and fear of God on your right, defending the path to Paradise. Divine wisdom commands that everything must be in its proper place.

If the enemy attacks you from the left, he uses his forces of hopelessness, despair, hatred, spite, and doubt.

Mercy is your strength to repel them. Kindness, forgiveness, compassion will subdue and humiliate them.

If your enemy attacks you from the front, he will deploy his forces of praise, self-aggrandizement, and temptation to arrogance. Arrogance is for the foolish and ignorant; thus the force that will stop it is knowledge, which you hold in between your two hands.

If your enemy attacks you from behind, his forces will be insidious, perverse imaginations to crush you and defeat you, replacing reality with dreams. Only your armies of intelligence and heedfulness will be able to defeat them. Only these will detect this attack, for it will come under the smoke and camouflage of imagination, which imitates reality, enhanced.

That is how you can defend your realm, which is entrusted to you by your Lord. If you wish to increase your security, you may increase your armies up to ten, but never more than ten—for that is the limit, according to the articles of faith, for defending the truth against all defect. When you increase your armies from four to ten, then you will be able to defend your front, your back, your right, your left; what is under, what was before, and what will be after both the whole and the parts of the whole. Thus, all the routes to salvation will be kept open for you, and your realm will be safe from all defect. It will be with your Lord as it is from Him—and you will find security, peace, and happiness.

CHAPTER 14

ON THE PREPARATION AND STRATEGY FOR THE BATTLE AGAINST THE ENEMY

O deputy of God, the first consideration in battle is the defense of the banner of honor which has been bestowed upon you—the honor of ruling in the name of your Lord. This must be set in the safest of places, for it must be defended above everything else. Therefore you must establish for yourself a headquarters which will be secure, yet from which, at the same time, you can control your armies.

This must be under the feet of your Lord, at the Footstool of God. That is the castle where divine laws are generated. That is where the traditions of the Prophet Muhammad, may God's peace and blessings be upon him, are decided upon. That is the place set highest in the creation, having the strongest defenses. Stay there, and do not ever throw yourself into the midst of battle, for if anything happens to you, your armies will be scattered and your realm will fall into the hands of the enemy.

The best strategy is to stay safely in your command post and set your generals and your armies to defend your four flanks. For if any or all of your armies should fall before your enemies in the four directions, you will still be secure. And as long as you exist, your country will exist. Some of your defenses may be able to retreat towards the center, and you may be able to reinforce them and continue the battle. If a branch should fall from a tree, the tree will still be safe, and will be able to grow another branch to replace the fallen one. But if the trunk is cut, the tree dies.

The purpose of the battle is the continuation of life. The sap of the tree, which permits the growing of another branch to replace the severed one, is justice. If, in anything that is alive, justice disappears, it will immediately be replaced by tyranny. And tyranny is the instrument of death.

The country over which you rule is the material existence of the human being, his body. The king of that realm is the soul. If the soul leaves the body, the body is dead—but if a part of the body is hurt, the soul will still remain in it. He is the one who seeks the cure. Therefore, above all, you must protect yourself. Even if you see them close to you, do not let them see you.

If all your armies retreat to the center to wage a final battle, gather them all upon the shores of the sea. Then, with the staff of Faith in your hand, touch the waters of knowledge. The ocean of knowledge will part. Take your armies into the breach opened for you.

Knowledge is the gate of security, the gate of guidance. Satan also seeks this gate. He will follow you into the breach—but when he comes to the middle of it, the ocean of knowledge will close upon him and upon his armies.

Some men of knowledge confess and say, "Although we sought knowledge for others' sake, God has led us only to Himself by it." God says:

And the best of planners is God.
(Al-i 'Imran, 54)

Thus it is in the story of Moses and Pharaoh. When

the armies of Pharaoh followed Moses and his people in their exodus from Egypt, God opened a path in the Red Sea. And after the sons of Israel passed through, the sea closed over the army of Pharaoh.

The agents of your enemy may tempt you to seek knowledge in order to impress others, to place yourself above them, and to make you a master whom others will need and respect. Let that not diminish your appetite for knowledge. Hurry to learn that which you do not know. Haste is what Satan and your evil-commanding ego love— but that is the haste of the seeker who does not know where he is going. They do not know that your haste is to find truth. What the Devil, in his ignorance, hopes, is that you will drown in the ocean of knowledge—as Pharaoh hoped, while he was rushing to destroy.

The proof of the Devil's ignorance given in the Holy Qur'an is in his response to God, for he disobeyed Him when asked to prostrate in front of the newly created Adam:

He said: I am better than he. Thou didst create
me from fire and him from clay.
(A'raf, 11)

He did not know that God had taught Adam all His names.

There will be other good acts which your enemies may tempt you to undertake with bad intentions, hoping that they will thus turn against you. They do not know your intention, which is guided by your knowledge and judgment. So do not refuse everything your enemy demands.

The one who works hard even without conviction is always better than a trusted friend who is lazy and does nothing.

The one who works, even if he does not have his heart in it, will have a glimpse of divine light that will enlighten his heart. That light will blind those deeds that he did without considering their results, without judging whether they were wrong or right. It will guide him on the path of salvation. Thus the enemy will himself fall into the trap which he has set for you.

So in your battle against the Devil and your evil-commanding ego, stay safely in that high place, close to God, at the center of your realm. That castle is the heart. It casts fear upon your enemies to know that you are there, because they also know they cannot reach you there. Their only hope is to get you out of it, into the open, where they can trap you; and their principal tactic is to push you to haste. If you are careful, you will not fall into that error. For you can see where the enemy is, from that high tower; you can observe his defenses.

CHAPTER 15

ON SECRET CODES AND WARNINGS OF DANGERS IN THE OFFENSIVE AGAINST THE ENEMY

Know that, among the numbers known to man, the numbers mentioned in the Holy Qur'an and in Islamic teaching hold a divinely-kept secret. If it is sought, it will enlighten the path to follow.

All creation is created from Two to Twelve. Twelve is the final degree of all numbers.

There are four stages in counting: Ones, Tens, Hundreds, and Thousands. Four is the perfect number. Twelve is the last number. Whatever aspect of the human realm is considered, you will find that it is composed of Twelve. Twelve is the unification of the four creative numbers and the three original numbers.

The four creative numbers represent being, reason, man, and his station. These four creative elements are the preoccupation of life. From this Four, many a knowledge generates. From these many knowledges, many seek—and some find—unity.

If we unite the number One, through the intermediary of the word "and," with another One similar to it—"One 'and' One"—the number Two will appear. The number One is not counted as a number, yet all numbers generate from it. When One disappears, all else disappears.

When One is added to Two, it becomes Three. When One is added to Three, it becomes Four. If we keep counting, adding One to the resulting numbers, we will reach a Thousand, and when we subtract a Thousand from a Thousand, the Thousand disappears.

Thus, the beginning of preemptive numbers is Two. The first of the individual numbers is Three. Two is the origin of, and is similar to, all preemptive numbers. Three is the origin of all individual numbers, both for that which is less than it and for that which is more than it.

Even numbers are higher than and ahead of odd numbers. This is natural and impossible to be otherwise.

It is impossible that Four be before Three or that Five be before Four. Thus, if you detect a number which is within and under the control of an even or an odd number, the one which contains the odd number will defeat the one which contains the even number. But the one which comes before and after that number, if it contains an even number, will defeat the one which contains the odd number.

It is lawful for man to fight against his personal evil, the ego, and against evil influences outside of him which aim to destroy him. This fight becomes necessary when there is rebellion against the decrees of the Creator within or without one's self. It must be done, not with violence, but in ways that have been made permissible by God. If one fights against rebellion within one's self, then the even will have to defeat the odd. If one is fighting against the evil forces around one's self, the odd will have to defeat the even. If there is a rebellion within the enemy of the outside after it has been defeated, then the even must defeat the odd.

There are two kinds of unity. One is the absolute oneness of all and everything. The other is personal unity and oneness. Absolute oneness applies to everyone, even those who are against Islam, who think of it as a numerical oneness, based upon material numbers with no spiritual bearing, despite its truth. Personal oneness is the unity and oneness of the messengers of God, of the prophets Muhammad and Moses, may God's peace and blessings be upon both of them. It is also the goal of all men of wisdom and knowledge and of their people: an attempt at unity and oneness to be created from the apparent multiplicity in man.

Absolute oneness has the power to defeat everything false, everywhere, at all times. Beware that your enemy not use this power against you before you can use it against him.

Personal oneness does not guarantee victory at all times. In some circumstances it may save you; in some circumstances it may not be able to defend you. Therefore, you must find the right circumstances, where it will help you to be victorious—and then, depend upon it. And if it fails you, then you must seek your salvation in the absolute oneness.

All this is secrets from among the divine secrets. Each thing that is said depends upon and relates to the other. Each has many ramifications and can only be understood if one knows it in detail. A sign suffices for those who know.

CHAPTER 16

ON THE REGULATION AND PREPARATION OF THE SPIRITUAL DIET, ACCORDING TO THE DIFFERENT SEASONS, FOR THE GROWTH OF THE DEPUTY OF GOD

Know that one's diet is to be regulated in accordance with the causes and conditions created by God. A created being needs food for its existence and survival, and there are clear rules set by the Creator for its sustenance. The difference between the human being and the rest of creation is that the human is the ultimate consumer. The rest of creation is made to be used by it.

That which we consume is regulated according to different times of the year and different seasons. The warmth and humidity in the body, which regulates the natural conditions for life, is influenced by the intake of food. The Lord permits man to eat as long as He permits him to live, and people see and feel and behave in accordance with, and are conditioned by the food they eat and that they grow around them.

This is such a clear situation that it does not even need to be discussed.

People who seek to find themselves in order to better themselves do not follow a path in which opposites clash. They are centered in their hearts. Now I ask them: "You wish to better yourself, but do you know what you want, and how you wish to be?"

Then know that the months of Spring are warm and

humid. They correspond to the natural state of the living organism. The body has a tendency to motion—to move, to travel, leaving pain and trouble behind. You see it all around you, in plants and in animals—all living things are in motion. So too, the vegetable and animal souls which exist in every human being are agitated. They tremble, they gyrate. The seeker who ignores his natural instincts is gravely mistaken.

O deputy of God, to rule the kingdom of the human being, know that God is the Lord. He bestows a state upon the time and the place and that which dwells in them, giving it as their nature, which they obey and with which abide. So when you see the people of your realm in the same state, accept it. Order your prime minister, Intellect, and his servants of Intellect, and your forces of Memory, to gather all that they can from that nature which corresponds to the precepts of your faith. For God says:

> In this is a warning for such as have eyes to see.
> *(Al-i 'Imran, 213)*

and:

> But when we pour down rain on the earth, it is stirred to life, it swells, and it puts forth every kind.
> *(Hajj, 5)*

and:

> It grows till the earth is clad with its golden ornament and is decked out in beauty.
> *(Yunus, 24)*

The Lord has made the season of Spring to bring the earth to life and to make each thing in it move, to seek and find and to become what is its due among that which the Lord of all has kept in store. So gather from this plenty all except that which poisons and constricts your heart.

There is no struggle or difficulty in this divine transaction between man and the Sustainer. Let your people do the same. You may worry that they may not be able to differentiate the real from the false, but let them go out to nature and wander around the green fields and along the clear rivers, smelling the flowers in the mountains and in the forest, and enjoy themselves. Thus, with your care and beneficence to them, you will profit from their joy and experience. And you will be loved and esteemed by them as if you yourself were wandering in Spring on the mountains and in the valleys where clear rivers flow, gathering flowers.

All this will remind you of Paradise and of what your Lord keeps in store for the ones whom He loves. The Spring is the season of Paradise, and Paradise is the home of the living. As it is wet and warm here, so is it in the climate of Paradise. When your people feel the same, it will encourage them and give them energy. Use that energy to lead them to work, but eliminate the difficulties in their work, so that their wish and hope for the eternal bliss and comfort of Paradise will increase. They will find signs of it in this world in the Spring.

Spring is analogous to youth in the life of man, but its end is not like its beginning.

The Summer season is warm and dry. It has the nature and character of fire. It is a season of contemplation, a time which overpowers and defeats man. It makes one think that life is advancing and one will be old, for action is difficult for the old. The heat reminds one of the fire of Hell, and you will remember God who says:

When the blazing fire is kindled to fierce heat.
(*Takwir, 12*)

You will remember the Day of Reckoning, when the sun will descend low, brains will boil, men will drown in their sweat in utter thirst, and the sinners will be chased from the fountain by angels of wrath.

But all this may be the fiery food, a lesson and punishment for your evil-commanding ego, thus relieving you of his tyranny.

The Autumn is the season of cold and dryness, which is the nature of death, and it should remind you of death—the cause of death, the awe of death, the pain of death. And along with all that, think of this: will you be able, at the last moment, to remember and be with your Lord, or will you die heedless, separate from Him, caring for yourself alone, as you did all your life? Reflect upon how your enemies will rejoice when the angel of death tears your life away. Will the gates of Heaven open for you, or will you be rejected and sink to the lowest of the low?

While you are among the living, it is as if this world is pregnant with you. Your physical being in this life is as thin as the placenta which will be discarded as nothing and left behind when you are born to death. God says:

It is He who brought you forth from the wombs
of your mothers when ye know nothing.
(*Nahl, 78*)

At death, all that you know about this life will be left behind. So feed your heart with the divine knowledge of the Hereafter. Know that the promise of your Lord will certainly come true.

The fourth and last season of the year is Winter. It is cold and humid. It is the nature of Purgatory. The food your soul needs in this season is the contemplation of two states, one or the other of which is waiting for you. You will feel either the fear of being chained and dipped into fire among the tyrants of this world, or the yearning to be free, looking upon your place among the gardens of Paradise. You must measure the little time left to you, and decide whether to spend it in obedience to, or in revolt against, your Lord. You will not ever be able to relive your life. The case is like the plight of those who will reach Purgatory empty-handed and beg the Lord to return them to the world to do good deeds; they will be rejected. The regret of your past, and the desire to redo the things you have done wrong, is of no use. That is only fooling yourself. Yet you may still have time to balance your wrong by doing right, for God promises:

> Unless he repents, believes, and works right-
> eous deeds, for God will change the evil of
> such persons into good.
>
> *(Furqan, 70)*

He also warns:

> Of no effect is the repentance of those who
> continue to do evil, until death faces one of
> them, and he says, now I have repented
> indeed.
>
> *(Nisa', 18)*

161

Purgatory is like a continuation of this life, but in it you have no will of your own. Whatever may be done with you there will give you no benefit; what will count then is what you have brought with you. This should feed your thoughts in the Winter of your life.

Thought and action are two foods for the maintenance of this life. They should be consumed together. Thought will evaluate the results of an action. If an undertaking is favorable and in accordance with the wish of your Lord, act upon it with His permission and in His name. Then it will bring health and strength to your being.

O master of the human realm, save yourself and your kingdom. If you govern with justice and treat your subjects with gentleness, leading them on the straight path that your Lord has set out for you, then on the Day of Judgment they will bear witness in your favor, and the Divine Judge will accept their testimony. But if you lead yourself and those who depend on you to harm, corrupting their good intentions with your injustice and perversity, then on the Day of Reckoning every member of your kingdom will be a witness against you and you will not be able to defend yourself. God says:

> That day shall We set a seal on their mouths,
> but their hands will speak to Us and their feet
> bear witness to all that they did.
> (*Ya Sin, 365*)

You have been informed of the different foods offered to you by the different seasons. You must also be warned that each of the four seasons of the year has particular ailments and difficulties which you should try to

162

ward off. These ills will attack the body at different ages and stages of your life. Worse still, there are also spiritual ailments.

Actually, the foods offered to you at different seasons are preventatives and medications to protect you and cure you. They are effective only if you are able to see the symptoms and take your medication in time. If you learn the symptoms and causes of these ailments, and the times when they are apt to be epidemic, then you can eliminate the suffering and keep yourself in good health during your life in this world.

Knowledge is your principal food. That is what sustains your spiritual life, but not without putting into action what you have learned. You must acquire the knowledge corresponding to the specific seasons of your life. You must also act upon what you have learned at the proper times, exactly as you take medication when the doctor prescribes it to be taken. The diet and the medication suggested to you are meant to balance either that which is in excess, or that which is lacking in you. This is what has to be discovered.

Your Lord is the great doctor who knows the constitution of all His creations. If your doctor told you to take some tender meat and add almonds, saffron vinegar, and pepper, cook it on a slow fire and eat it at specific times and in good measure—if you did it, you would grow strong. And you would have carried out, yourself, an instruction given to you by someone you trusted. You would have mixed it yourself and cooked it yourself and eaten it yourself—and your own body, after taking what it needs, would have excreted the dregs of it.

What turns into curative life-force in you is the spirit that your Lord has entrusted to you; it will cause you to live and be strong. Your actions are its instrument, although they are also the result of the strength thus received. And none other than your own being will reject the dregs of unfaithfulness—of imagining partners for your Lord, of arrogantly installing yourself as master—and throw them into the sewer of Hell.

The most bitter of medicines, perhaps, is what your Lord orders you to do: to wake up in the middle of the night to say your prayers; to take your ablution and wash yourself many times a day; to walk to mosques far away to participate in the congregational prayers; to fast; to pay alms. Honey tastes bitter to the one who is sick—but if you have faith in your Lord, if you trust in His promises and His rewards in the Hereafter, if you fear Him and love Him and wish to be with Him, the bitter will turn into sweet. For He says:

> And those who strive in Our cause, We will certainly guide them to Our paths, for verily God is with those who do right.
> (*'Ankabut, 69*)

and:

> So fear God, for it is God who teaches you.
> (*Baqarah 282*)

It is certain that your sustenance is gained through your own actions. According to the Law, the best food is that which is obtained by your own efforts. Even eating it and digesting it is your own work—therefore, it is service. Thus if you gain your food heedfully and lawfully, prepare it, chew it, taste it, swallow it, digest it—you will serve the

One who created you and keeps you alive, and who placed your soul into you from His own soul. Thus you will help Him by receiving that which He has given you.

If somebody else chewed and ate your food, what possible good could ever come to you from it? Therefore you have to do it yourself.

Many heedless ones are unable to receive what is given to them, nor can they taste what nourishes them. For nourishment must be absorbed through one's own efforts and thankfulness. When the likes of these appear in front of their Lord on the Day of Reckoning, their actions and good deeds will not accompany them to witness in their favor. For you need at least two witnesses— good deeds, and thankfulness to the One who enabled you to do the deed.

Every living creature needs sustenance to exist. Your Lord has charged the Archangel Michael with the sustenance of all living beings. He guides them through their senses to the food which is destined for them, and even spreads life-sustaining strength in their being through their veins.

Your Lord has charged the Archangel Israfil to sustain the material bodies with their souls.

He has charged the Archangel Gabriel to feed the souls with intellect and knowledge.

The existence of every living being depends on a command of its Creator. That command of the Lord comes in the form of sustenance. It all comes from one source, and that source is the essence. Without it there is no life, neither for the body, nor for the mind, which feeds on the knowledge of it. The body and the mind care only for things which have shapes and forms, while the eternal soul, which has no form and shape, wishes to stay only within itself. Its sustenance is divine knowledge. That is why the pure soul who was the Messenger of God, may God's peace and blessings be upon him, needed knowledge to sustain himself, and in the Holy Qur'an begged his Lord, saying:

O my Lord, increase me in knowledge.
(*Ta Ha, 114*)

The Prophet, may God's peace and blessings be upon him, said that he saw in a dream that his sustenance was brought to him as a cup of milk. When he drank from it, his satiation came out from the tips of his fingers, and he gave that milk to 'Umar to drink. His blessed Companions asked him how he interpreted that dream, and he said that the sustenance was knowledge. When he spoke with his Lord after his ascension through the heavens, his Lord told him that just as milk was sent to him in the dream, knowledge was going to be the sustenance of his people, too.

O deputy of God, to rule the realm of human beings, be with your Lord in His command. Do not count on the soul alone to obtain its own sustenance. You are responsible for it. Besides, the appetite of the soul for knowledge is insatiable. The Prophet of God, may His peace and blessings be upon him, said: "Two kinds of people are never satiated: the first are those who love this world, and the second are those who seek knowledge."

Know that the knowledge under your feet is not worth picking up. Seek the knowledge that God has bestowed upon the chosen few. That knowledge contains the mysteries of divine nature. Practical knowledge is satisfying, beautiful—but its value is no more than logic over philosophy. The knowledge which you wish to seek is beyond the mind. Its light is all-encompassing, like a perfect mirror reflecting all that is. Practical knowledge is discoveries of already existing things. It enlarges your scope and brings you satisfaction and joy. But real joy is not in the knowledge of things, but in the truth of things.

It is hard work and a lot of pain to attain truth, and none who attain it imagine that they did it themselves. They do not stand upon it, sullying it by stepping on it. It is an unsoiled mirror, pure, the mirror of the soul—the place where the Lord manifests Himself. It is not like what one discovers through one's evil-commanding ego. That is more like a blinding fog which prevents one from seeing the reality of things.

But the knowledge of truth, when it penetrates into the visible, material elements constituting the reality of things, quickens the evolution of the one who attains it. Although now he walks and sits and eats and sleeps with his Lord, remembering Him, totally conscious—this only shows his weakness, and that he cannot keep it. But if he devotes all his care and attention to living in peace and moderation, he may be able to hold on to the truth. Then he will be the master of the high state which he has attained because of it.

The knowledge of the truth of things, which is among the mysteries of divine nature, does not require the memory with which a human being is provided for the recording of his other experiences.

CHAPTER 17

ON THE SECRETS WHICH GOD HAS ENTRUSTED TO MAN

How should one proceed on the path to Truth, which is divided into five? O you whose hearts are yearning for secrets hidden from the eye: know that what has been said here does not contain anything that the writer has added from himself; nor does he seek any honor or benefit from what he says; nor claim that he has earned, merited, or deserved that which was given to him. He does not display anything from his own thoughts as proof of the knowledge contained in these writings, nor claim to have heard anything which he has not heard.

You must be told how these secrets, hidden deep inside you, sometimes surge into your consciousness, sometimes sink deep into your unconscious. This is manifested within you as things which become evident and things which are hidden.

Those who live in and for the exterior world of visual reality know about what is evident. But the inner realities cannot be seen by the eye, nor understood by a worldly mind. One can only do it through divine inspiration. The Lord has kept that knowledge as a secret to separate the men of this world from those who seek and come close to Him. Among these are His prophets and His saints.

Our guide and master, the Prophet Muhammad, may God's peace and blessings be upon him, is totally dependent upon and obedient to his Lord. A mystic saint is someone who is guided by the Prophet and totally obedient to him, who has lighted the lamp of his heart from the flame in the heart of the Prophet. Such saints are the living proof of the articles of faith which came from the Lord as divine revelation to His Messenger, and from the Messenger to the world.

He is the knot which ties the Lord to His creation. They are the ones who say the Lord exists because we exist: if we did not know that we exist, then we could not know the meaning of existence. The Lord exists: He created us and created knowledge—and knowledge is from Him, for Him and to Him, the All-Knowing One.

So the life of man, also, is from Him and for Him, and the return is to Him. To hear, to see, to speak; power, will, generosity, compassion, the ability to forgive—these are not just words, but are attributes given to man from His attributes. In identifying with these names, man can know himself and know his Lord, for they are attributes common to both.

But all these attributes are hidden inside of us. It is hard—indeed, it is impossible—to raise them into our consciousness and live according to them. If we knew them, then they would not be a secret.

What we know by hearsay about our Lord is that since He is ever-hidden, He is ever-timeless and therefore, placeless, and has no attributes or proofs. But we know that His existence is the beginning of the creation, that He is with the beginning, and that the beginning of knowledge is with Him. The very existence of knowledge is the proof that everything contains its beginning, its origin. Therefore every human being created contains his origin, his creation, and his Creator.

As things transform from one thing to another, they appear in different shapes and pass from one place to another, and finally disappear.

If we consider eternity as an extension of continuity which has a beginning and an end, like life, and if we attribute that to the Lord, so that an idea of living suggests an idea of ever-living, we will construe it falsely.

A concept is always understood either in comparison to something that is similar to it or by contrast to something that is opposite to it.

The oneness and uniqueness of the Lord are thought to be the same as the single beginning that exists for all and everything, but that is an understanding governed by a state which is passive and under the influence of exterior forces. However our master the Prophet Muhammad, may God's peace and blessings be upon him, said, "He who knows himself knows his Lord." In this saying he suggests an active state, one that depends on man's knowledge of the qualities of his Lord. A person's understanding can exist only to the extent of the minute traces of qualities common to both him and his Lord. This is the connection—the only means of knowing the Lord, and of union with Him.

As we see, there are two parallel paths to truth: one passive and one active. The active way necessitates the total annihilation of self for eternal union with God. The passive way is easier, because that which brings us from nothingness to the realization of our existence, the proof of our creation and the purpose of our creation, is the beautiful names of God which He taught to the prophet Adam: His own attributes which He has placed in man.

If these attributes, which connect man to his Creator, were excluded from him, there would be nothing left—no means to know Him, no proof of His existence, no path leading to Him, and no possibility of union with Him.

Without their traces in ourselves, the teaching of God's attributes would have caused terrible disasters for us, because we could have fooled ourselves into thinking that opposite negative characteristics in us were similar to His. Meanwhile the divine names that belong to Him alone render Him perfect and devoid of all imperfection.

There is an inner preparation for all this, which you must do by yourself. To reach the level of detecting the connection between the Lord's attributes and their traces in you, you have to first establish your relation to the universe around you, to see the similarities between the whole of material existence and yourself, to see that man is the microcosm of the macrocosm. You have to trace the order of the heavens within yourself in order to seek the nature and character of each heavenly realm in man.

Know that the whole universe revolves around four heavenly realms: the highest realm, the evolving realm, the self-renewing realm, and the realm of the interrelated worlds. Each of these realms has a purpose and a function.

The highest realm contains twenty truths, realities of the greater universe. The evolving realm holds twenty-five realities of the greater universe, the self-renewing realm has four, and the realm of the interrelated worlds contains ten. All these realities exist also in man. The principal realities particular to the greater universe are thirty-nine. All these are also included in man. Thus, the whole universe has a total of ninety-eight attributes—while man holds one additional special attribute which connects him personally to his Lord, and is a secret between them. It is this which makes the human being fit to be God's deputy on earth. That is why the Lord says, "I have created everything for you, and you for Myself." That is why all and everything depends on him.

The truths, the attributes, the commands, the beautiful names given to man, are ninety-nine. Whoever realizes these in himself, enters Paradise. But one truth over and above the ninety-nine belongs to the Lord of Power alone, and is His Greatest Name. This one name is the master of all names. Thus, the whole of existence is contained within these hundred names.

Paradise has one hundred levels, and at the hundredth level is the Paradise of sand dunes. There are no rivers of honey and milk, nor fruits which grow as soon as they are picked: it is a Paradise of dreams. No created being can enter this Paradise except the select, called by their Lord to see Him. It is a place of awe and unimaginable amazement. It is man's duty to foresee to which of the hundred levels of Paradise he belongs.

Hell also has a hundred levels. The man who attains these hundred levels during his life reaches the level of total veiling and is rendered blind. Yet the Lord sees him, and will cast him from the hundredth level of Hell until he falls to the level he deserves.

The Creator has created man as the best of His creations and placed him in His highest esteem, but man can reduce himself to worse than the worst, which is the lowest level of Hell. Indeed it is not a place that the Lord wants man, his supreme creation, to inhabit—He has prepared his place at the highest level of Paradise. Why, then, does man aim to reduce himself to the lowest, and deserve the Hell that is not meant for him?

The highest place that God has prepared for man is a place of resolution and moderation. That is where the truths of Muhammad are gathered, that is the place where man is meant to live, resolved to obey his Lord and to be moderate in everything. Corresponding to that high place meant for humanity there is a place in man which is called the divine soul. It is eternal, because God blew it into the human being from His own soul. It is this divine soul that aspires to live in that place where God meant man to live.

Corresponding to the realm of the Lord's Throne is man's physical body; it aspires to that Throne. Corresponding to the Footstool of the Lord in Heaven is man's ego. The Lord's feet are upon what He praises, what He condemns, and what He forbids, and that is where the ego wants to be. Corresponding to the original Kaaba in the seventh heaven is man's heart. That is what it yearns to be. Corresponding to the angelic realms is man's spirit, and toward these it aspires to evolve.

Corresponding to the heaven of Saturn is the strength of human knowledge; there it aims to rise. Corresponding to the heaven of Jupiter is human memory, at the back of the mind. Corresponding to the heaven of Mars is man's mind and lungs. Corresponding to the Sun is human reason, in the middle of the mind. Corresponding to the heaven of Venus is human imagination and the animal soul. Corresponding to the heaven of Mercury is human creativity, at the front of the mind. Corresponding to the Moon are the five human senses. These are the principles of the higher realm which relate to what is in man.

The evolving realms contain the heaven of fire, where there is no atmosphere. Its nature is hot and dry. It corresponds to the bile in man, the function of which is digestion. The character of the heaven of air is warmth and humidity. It corresponds in man to the living blood, the source of strength. The world of water corresponds in man to phlegm. It is the force of rejection. Earth, whose nature is cold and dry, corresponds to man's liver, which has the force to hold.

Our own earth is in seven levels. Their colors are white, black, red, yellow, blue, green, and violet, corresponding to the skin, the fat, the flesh, the veins, the nerves, the muscles, and the bones.

Within the self-renewing realms live the creatures with souls. They correspond to the energy in the living man. Within this realm is the world of minerals—existences without life, which correspond in man to whatever in him does not feel or sense. The realm of vegetation corresponds to that which grows out of man. The animal kingdom corresponds to human feelings and emotions.

The interrelated worlds hold the contrasts of light and shade, black and white—the pairs of opposites. Within these is the world of qualities, which corresponds to the right and wrong in man. The world of parts corresponds to youth in man, when he is growing. The world of the moment, the world of things done, corresponds to man's palm. The world of time corresponds to man's face, and the expressions on his face. The world of compound things resembles what is above and below man's waist. The world of situations corresponds to man's faith and words. The world of action resembles man's eating. The world of wrath corresponds to man's satiation and to his violence. The world of differences corresponds to the existence of characteristics in man which do not belong to him, but resemble that which is other than he: it is often said, "he has the memory of an elephant," "he is as obstinate as a donkey," " he is as strong as a lion," "he is as scared as a rabbit."

Now you know how you relate to your environment, and what the interaction is between the human being and the world. You know that when you save yourself from the tyranny of your evil-commanding ego, you will reach the level that honors you. So why is it that you are still a slave to your ego and your imagination?

Your Lord has entrusted to men many of His secrets, and each person takes from this fund in accordance with his nature and character. Few people are able to return to their destined state and attributes. Examples include the prophets and the saints, who are under the guidance and control of divine secrets. That is what happens when the soul of your Lord guides the human soul. People who are directly under the influence of divine secrets do not appear different from the rest of us who worship our Lord and remember Him in our actions.

The Messenger of God, may God's peace and blessings be upon him, described the revelation of these secrets to him. He reported that they came upon him in waves, sounding like waterfalls or things dropped in water, and that the strongest of them sounded like bells. That is the sound of the angelic light in flames, setting on fire the human soul and eliminating that darkness within the human being which is part of his natural constitution. When the divine command thus reaches the soul and sets it afire, the body shakes and trembles, one's natural disposition crumbles. The person changes, for the physical body is affected by the change in the soul. Strange constrictions and contractions appear in it. When the angelic light leaves a human being, the body is drenched in sweat, the face is flushed, but the person is relieved. He returns to his normal state and is happy, as if released from something which ties him tight. The Lord explains the coming of revelation to those who have been chosen to guide others:

> With it came down the spirit of faith and truth
> to their heart and mind, that thou mayest
> admonish.
>
> *(Shu'ara, 193-194)*

That is how and why the Holy Qur'an was revealed to the Messenger of God. His secrets entered directly into his heart and mind. They were not told to him by an angel in the shape of a man.

To the saints, those who come close to their Lord, the state of ecstasy, when inspiration comes upon them, starts with a feeling of extreme thirst. They lose themselves in it and pass out. At that moment their thirst is quenched and their constriction is turned into expansion. Then when they return to their normal condition, if they remember anything of what was revealed to them and find themselves in a state of total peace and joy, that is termed divine inspiration. This result depends on the preparation, effort, and previous state of those who are blessed with such inspirations. Some who are not ready to receive this experience think that they are ill—but even in this case, what they have tasted is still truth.

For those whose disposition is such that these inspirations are given to them and they are unable to recall or find anything in them, it simply means that they are not conscious of what they have received. In some cases it is due to a heart too preoccupied with the devotion and remembrance of God, which is set afire by the wish to imagine Him. A mist is raised from the chest up to the brain, covering it and rendering it unable to see and causing them to faint. That is what happens to some who are in ecstasy, which therefore has no value for them. In fact, if asked, all that they could say would be, "I felt a cloud covering me like a black blanket."

A more dangerous state is one which not only affects you negatively, but also may harm those around you. This usually happens in the circle of mystics during the ceremony of the remembrance of God, when someone thinks that he is in ecstasy, although he still has all his senses. He then imagines that he is receiving some extraordinary knowledge, which brings him to a state of excitement and agitation. This is an evil state created under the influence of demonic imagination. It is also contagious.

Know and beware that the Devil does not have the power to lift the ordinary function of your senses and enable you to see secrets with your inner eye. In the states of false ecstasy, all he can do is to make you imagine strange phenomena. These may be able to induce a state like an epileptic fit, which can only harm you. This process starts with a feeling of heat and a false hope that you will see things hitherto hidden from you. You will discover a voice—which is his voice—which appears to be coming from inside of you. In reality, you will be talking to yourself. This is the voice of your own ambitions for higher spiritual states. You imagine your aspirations realized, and so you take a lie to be the truth.

At other times, the Devil addresses you pretending to be your Lord. You will hear him say, "O my servants, I am your Lord! Do not look at anything but me, or else I will cover you with veils. Always see things with my eyes. If you attempt to look with your own eyes, you will be attributing partners to your Lord. I am the one who sees, I am the one to be seen." And so you believe that you hear the truth, while falsehood has taken hold in you, and you run the risk of becoming its servant for the rest of your life. If you had only known that the Lord does not speak to His creation either with letters or with sound; cannot be heard with ears; cannot be imagined, whether from the outside or from the inside! Then you would not have been fooled by the words of Satan.

This happens often to many seekers in their worship, contemplation, and meditation. Those who fall victim to their imagination are apt to be condemned to oblivion. It is better to receive nothing than that. Any inspiration which does not bring you or those around you any real knowledge or benefit, is false. When you are aware of that, you are safe from evil influences.

O follower of the mystic path, you have to be heedful and knowledgeable! Your greatest enemy is unconsciousness and ignorance. Learn from your own experiences, rather than from the experiences of others, for others cannot solve your problems. You must do it yourself.

Know that inspirations that come during ecstatic states have no power to command or to forbid. They can only inform—and what is informed should not be from the inspiration itself. If you fall under such an influence, you must observe whether or not it is in accordance with doctrine. If the inspiration leads you to anything that opposes or is outside of the prescriptions of your Lord, you must reject it. Take refuge in the Holy Qur'an and that which it prescribes, for it is the touchstone of truth.

If the ecstatic inspiration is simply a new experience which does not induce you to act against the doctrine but is only news, then you have to judge for yourself whether it is an evil influence or not. If this news came to you in bits and pieces, in different images, disconnected and not coherent, you must suspect that it is evil. If it becomes coherent in spite of this, then beware that you may be going along with a mischief.

If the inspiration is neither symbolic nor allegorical, but directly affects your heart without affecting your senses or imagination, then it is apt to be true. For instance, if you feel in a state of awe and grace, without having seen anything; or you find clarified some teaching which you have hitherto not been able to understand; or if you meet with a reinforcement of good morals, or answers to pressing questions or needs; or if you discover a sense of unity within yourself, and other such secrets—you can be sure that these experiences are beneficial and therefore true.

There are jewels in man which have influences on him. The jewel of awe and marvel, the finest of these jewels, is in the center of the human heart. It is where the essence of the being is hidden, a store of energy and power. In that dark hidden place many an unknown secret is kept. Although others cannot see it, it sees that which is beyond the eye, for it is the eye of the heart. It is said that the Lord has hidden a moment in the middle of Friday, among the days and hours of the week, when all prayers are accepted. That spot in the center of the human being, in his heart, is like that moment: a black spot.

The Messenger of God, may God's peace and blessings be upon him, said that to him, this dot in the heart, like the moment in the middle of Friday, resembles a mirror.

Every element of consciousness within the human being—the senses, the feelings, the mind—is constantly watching that spot in the heart in order to see, to hear, to touch reality.

When the heart shines with the remembrance of God as a result of sincere contemplation, meditation, and worship, divine truth is reflected in it on the surface of that spot, for that spot belongs to the kingdom of your Lord. Then an intense light is generated from it, a light which reaches to the deepest corners of the whole being, and the whole being is conscious and in awe. Then not a single member of the human being will move on its own, for none has its own will any longer. That is why that dot at the center of the heart is called the essence, the jewel of awe and marvel. Its effect is overwhelming and paralyzing.

If your Lord wills to keep you in a state of intense wish to reach Him, then he sends a mist and places it between your heart and that light which generates from the essence of the heart and spreads into the being. That mist reflects the light in the opposite direction. It covers the heart, thus permitting all the souls within the being to wonder in their places, seeking the light behind the mist, hoping that it will not disappear. This state is the state of repose, the normal state of people who believe that God is invisible, is unlike anything that He has created, and is hidden from His creation. In that state, attributes common to both Lord and creature are different from each other. Yet the yearning persists.

You will hear some people say, "I was not with my Lord, until I saw the traces of His beautiful face," or, "Who else but the Lord puts faith in His servant's heart?" It is the voice of that spot in the heart. It is only there that the face of the Beloved will be seen. The Lord says:

When the awe is removed from their hearts
will they say: what is it that your Lord commanded? They will say: that which is the truth.
(Saba, 23)

The character of those who are in that state endures
as long as that mystery, and the yearning for it, is in their
hearts. They cannot be tempted, nor are they deeply interested in anything that the world presents them, for they are
above these influences. Nor would they expose themselves
to the world and its influences.

Some jewels in the material world have particular
characteristics, symbols of that jewel of the heart.

The emerald is the symbol of the power of remembrance in man. God says in the Holy Qur'an:

Those who fear God, when a thought of evil
from Satan assaults them, bring God to remembrance when, lo, they see!
(A'raf, 200)

The power of the remembrance of God renders
Satan blind. He can no longer see the trap which he was
about to set for you—and it frightens him, when he cannot
see his victim. If the believer falls back into heedlessness
after remembering His Lord, which saved him from the
Devil, the Devil will try him again. But if he is in continuous remembrance, he is with the One whom he remembers, and the Devil cannot come into the presence of the
Lord, for he will burn to ashes.

The red ruby is the symbol of what God says in the
Holy Qur'an:

There is nothing whatever like unto Him.
(Shura, 11)

If one's sacred secret soul could view what this jewel represents, it is said that it could obtain knowledge about the reality of certain things without even seeing them. The viewing of this stone leads to something different if one looks at it under the influence of one's ego: then one might be moved to submit to a tyrant who comes one's way.

The value of the sapphire is that it represents that which is meant in God's words:

There is none to put back His command.
(Ra'd, 41)

That power of God's command, which cannot be undone by any other power, is entrusted to some men who will rule others. That power is innate and from birth.

The topaz is the symbol of God's declaration:

But God has created you and your handiwork.
(Saffat, 96)

It is the symbol of those who come close to their Lord, humbly and in need, realizing that neither they themselves, nor what they have done, belongs to them.

The clear diamond represents water, about which God says:

We made from water every living thing.
(Anbiya', 30)

Water is the essential element in everything. It has the power to change things which are similar. It is that which is common to everything. It is the truth in everything, around everything—yet when it flows from one thing to the other, it separates one from the other. It is the essential element in alchemy, and can change iron into silver, or copper and lead into gold. In living things it has the same effect. It is able to transform someone who is in revolt against his Lord into an obedient servant, and an unbeliever into a believer.

Red sulfur is an element that God has created from those who are closest and most loyal to Him. It is an element of great powers and great value. Whoever can attain it will not find it in himself. The one who obtains even a trace of it becomes terribly possessive and jealous of it.

There are dark shadows cast upon man which hide him, and noises which prevent him from being heard. God says:

> Then we draw it towards Ourselves—a contraction by easy stages.
> *(Furqan, 46)*

Meaning, then He lifts the shadows from around man, one by one, by shedding His light shed upon him, just as the sunlight gradually replaces the darkness of the night.

These shadows have a function. They hide the ugliness and that which is shameful in man. If you do not have the beautiful jewels within you, then it is a sin to uncover and expose yourself. That is the time when a guide is necessary, to help. If you cannot find a guide, seclude yourself in a place away from men, remember God and call unto

184

Him by His name. Fast, and avoid the tastes of this world, and count upon the meaning in the verse in the Holy Qur'an:

> There is nothing whatever like unto Him.
> *(Shura, 11)*

Stay in that state seven days and nights at least, forty days at most. Then perchance you will uncover the jewels in you, and then the veils of darkness will leave you.

To rid yourself of the noise which renders one deaf, God says:

> For, without doubt, in the remembrance of God
> do hearts find peace and satisfaction.
> *(Ra'd, 28)*

This noise is the noise of the wind and storm that your ego causes to be raised between the angelic influences and the world in which you live. The storm can only be quieted, and your heart find peace, through the remembrance of God.

CHAPTER 18

ABOUT THE MIND
AND THE LIGHT OF CERTAINTY
THAT ENLIGHTENS THE HEART

The Earth does not have its own light, yet when the Sun is reflected upon it, it shines and is lighted, and the Sun cannot cast a shadow upon it to darken it. And the Sun shines upon the Moon, making it visible to the earth. The eye yearns for the source of light, but you cannot look upon it, for it will blind you. When you see light reflected upon the Earth, it is as if you have seen the Sun. Here are three points of a triangle: the Sun, the source of light; the Earth, upon which its light falls; and the Moon, which becomes visible with the light of the Sun.

Know that the physical body, which is the domain of the animal self, is made of coarse matter, like the Earth. Yet the light from the heart, which is the domain of the human soul, reaches to the farthest corner of the body, and from there is reflected upon the mind, where the inner eye starts to see.

Just as daylight enables the eye of the head to see, so heart-light shining upon the inner eye makes man worthy to be addressed by his Lord. He says:

> Verily in this is a message for any that has a heart.
>
> *(Qaf, 37)*

In this state the senses have no more use, for the

light by which the inner eye sees is far brighter than that by which the eyes of the head see.

What is now seen is the awesome sight of the angelic realm. Then—light upon light—a second eye of the heart opens. This is the eye of certainty, the eye that sees true reality. With this eye you can look upon the source of light itself, which is called the light of certainty.

There are two divine lights that come from your Lord: one shines upon the path of knowledge and wisdom, and the other shines upon the path that leads to Him. He has created two inner eyes in your heart: one is the eye of understanding, and the other is the eye that guides you to salvation. He says:

> God doth guide whom He wills to His light.
> *(Nur, 35)*

That light by which He guides you is the light of certainty. This will guide you to the path to Paradise, for He says:

> He will provide for you a light by which ye shall walk [straight to Paradise].
> *(Hadid, 28)*

If the source of light is added to the light shed upon the path of guidance, it will make visible all the hitherto unseen angelic beings in the heavens and on earth. These are the angels who are the agents of your Lord, who carry His secret commands of your destiny. God explains this divine light as:

> Light upon light . . .
> *(Nur, 35)*

CHAPTER 19

ON THE VEILS WHICH HIDE THE ANGELIC REALM FROM THE SIGHT OF THE EYE OF THE HEART

There are three lights within man: besides the light of the mind and the light of certainty, there is also the light of life.

The light of life is the light which energizes the animal self in man. Three influences weaken it and render it impotent. These influences manifest themselves as a terrible ringing noise, which deafens; a veil that blinds the eye; and a veil that blinds the mind. All three are mentioned in the Holy Qur'an. They are caused by the influence of the material world upon man's ego. Then the ego, in turn, renders the heart sick.

When the heart is sick, the mind radiates a beam of light upon it to immunize the heart against the tyranny of the ego. But while burning the maleficence of the ego, it also burns the heart—and the heart, on fire, is covered by the dark smoke which it generates. This smoke separates the heart from the mind, breaking all communication between them. Thus the heart is darkened. It is this dark cloud fallen upon the heart which becomes a blinding veil. Let your conscience be the judge of the devastation caused by a blind heart.

That which puts out the light of certainty and obscures the sight of the eye of the heart is lack of sincerity, lack of trust, faithlessness, and an inability to distinguish right from wrong. The resistance to these ills is within the range of human possibility. With intention and effort and God's permission, they can be cured. That will restore health to the heart, and produce peace of heart. Then light upon light enters—and with it, miraculous signs are seen. For the heart becomes a mirror where God's light is reflected. He says:

> God is the light of the Heavens and the Earth.
> *(Nur, 35)*

and:

> For any to whom God giveth not light, there is no light.
> *(Nur, 40)*

and He promises to the ones to whom He has given light:

> An evident sign for any people who understand.
> *('Ankabut, 35)*

CHAPTER 20

ON THE HIDDEN TABLET WHERE THE ESSENCE OF THE HOLY QUR'AN IS KEPT

The Hidden Tablet is a level where proof of all that is true and denial of all that is false is written. It is a place where the prophets, the messengers, and the saints meet, and where they are separated and distinguished from one another.

The Creator has made the Pen the interpreter of the ink-well. With it He drew the forms and shapes of all that was to be kown, and wrote out their names. He is the one who composed the mother of all books, and set right what is in it. He is the one who knows whatever will be known by man and whatever will be kept from him. He, the All-Powerful, is the one who acts upon what is written in the Book. He wrote it Himself, yet He looks into it each time He acts.

The front, the back, the edges of the Hidden Tablet are made out of green emerald. They look like the ever-changing days within the created universe, its ever-changing reality. All around it are angels of unimaginable beauty, worshipping, facing it.

You have your own pen given into your hand from the Pen in the hand of your Lord. That pen is your faith, which writes different things day by day, while that which is on the Hidden Tablet changes. And day by day, different things happen. Whatever is written and happened today erases what happened yesterday and will happen tomorrow. This is the proof of the reality and truth of the moment of Now. It is the denial of the memory of yesterday and the expectation of tomorrow. If that which is erased is to be reconstituted, it will happen in heavens far above, reentering the Divine Pen in the hand of the Lord. The prophets may inherit that Pen, but it is not for your hand. The pen in the hand of the prophets has two dimensions, while the pen given into the hands of those close to their Lord has only one.

The knowers of God and the sincere believers are themselves written in this Tablet. Some are privileged to have their names on the top of the page, and are above the ones whose names are written under them. Further than that, God the All-Knowing knows best.

CHAPTER 21

ON WHIRLING DERVISHES AND ON WHIRLING AS A MEANS TO COME CLOSE TO GOD

Whirling is a secret among the divine secrets of the Lord, who is highest, without limit, and who is unique and other than everything that He has created. It is an exercise performed by mystics in order to feel and hear their Beloved.

Those who wish to penetrate this secret and participate in the ceremony of whirling do what they do in one of two ways. Some whirl in an ecstatic state, and some others whirl under the influence of their minds. There is no third way. If someone says, "I whirl to reach the consciousness of my Lord," the highest stage he can reach is with his mind. That, in itself, may be accomplished in two ways: first, in accordance with the natural character of the mind; and second, through the mind's dependence on the acquired personality.

The example of the first is when somebody says, "I whirl to hear my Lord." Then he may indeed hear, for as the Messenger of God says: "When the servant of God comes close to Him, God becomes his ears with which he hears."

Sometimes, under the influence of one's mind, one whirls with every part of one's being, excluding nothing, while intending to be conscious that all and everything is whirling. Then one is not attached to any one place or to any one thing. When one is able to do that, the sign of it is that the whole body is frozen like a statue while whirling with the awe and marvel of the things it observes.

Those who whirl in an ecstatic state are under the influence of the beautiful music and rhythm which accompany this exercise. From the outside, they look like beautiful dancers. They are well coordinated with the accompanying music, and their faces show a serene expression, as if they have taken leave of all their senses. Even if this looks very beautiful, the performer has become a clown in the hands of the Devil. The best of it is if that person becomes unconscious in his whirling, without purpose, without decision, and without feeling it happening. Then there is some benefit, some truth in his state—indicating only that he is a person with a self, and is under the influence of it.

Those who wish to lose themselves in God through the exercise of whirling should know that if one truly reaches that state, what happens afterwards does not occur through one's own efforts, nor is it the result of some knowledge attained through the exercise. If someone claims that the high result is produced by knowledge attained during whirling, he is not telling the truth—for if that is what happened to him, he did not really lose himself.

The ones who claim to whirl in an ecstatic state are aware of their own motion—therefore they are whirling under the command of their egos, for themselves. That is not an exercise controlled by the mind. In whirling influenced by the mind, there is no motion, nor any coordination of previous knowledge with motion. Whoever whirls and claims that he has brought knowledge and motion together ignores the truth and is lying to himself.

Know that if God, the All-Knowing, is going to bestow knowledge and wisdom upon the heart of one of His servants, He will choose someone who has attached himself to his Lord sincerely, selflessly, and with infinite love of Him—and with a totally cool rationality. It is this rationality that cools the heaven of the heart, causing it to descend, while the natural warmth of the mind rises to meet it. Then there is a meeting of the heart and the mind. Then they ascend together in spite of the pull of the self—and like thunder, caused by the clash of the cold and the warm, screams issue from the inner being.

When the fire overwhelms the cold and keeps him rising, the one who whirls feels a burning in his chest, and may even smell the fire of yearning. Then the heart floats in the void. There is a moaning sound and a scream, unheard by any but those who have the reflection of divine power in their hearts. They are affected by it and feel a stillness and stiffness in their bodies. That is the sound of the heart set afire, spreading to the hearts of others.

Some deny the existence of such state. They say that they have never seen it, nor ever heard that such a thing existed. Yet our Master the Prophet of God, may God's peace and blessings be upon him, used to receive such states continuously, while he neither screamed, nor moaned, nor showed any physical signs. Therefore, O follower of this path, do not listen to the words of these deniers, because their hearts have been sealed.

Thus we have explained the ways of sacred whirling as a means to come close to one's Lord:

When the fire rises from within and meets the cool clouds, which are too cold to allow it to continue its ascent, it becomes confined within the heart and lungs, and burns them. This may cause death. Or it may be led to the mind from the heart, and heat the mind. Then the one who is whirling moves far too fast, starts jumping, and produces a movement disharmonious and unbalanced.

The right motion is to turn in good measure around the axis of the body. Man is created round, not like a cube, and the natural movement of a sphere is around its axis. When the mist rising inside the whirler is a fine mist that spreads to all parts of the body, it becomes the air that the fire needs in order to breathe. Then no storm or thunder is created within the one who performs this mystical exercise. No sound comes from him, not even the beating of his heart. The only expression of this state is a beatitude and a slight smile on the face, an expression of peace due to the comfort of the purity and expansiveness of his inner atmosphere.

O follower of the mystic path, now you know the way. Whether you whirl for yourself or whirl with your mind, do not fool yourself. May God lead us all to the straight path and render us pure and sincere.

IBN 'ARABI

What the Seeker Needs

Kitab Kunh ma la budda
minhu lil-murid

BISMILLAH IR-RAHMAN IR-RAHIM

NOTE

What the Seeker Needs is also known as *Kitab Kunh ma la budda minhu lil-murid*. This short work was written in Mosul in 1204 in answer to the question of what the seeker "should believe in and what he should do in the beginning, before anything else."

Translations of this work have been printed on several occasions: in Turkish (by Mahmud Mukhtar Bey, 1898); in Spanish (excerpts by M. Asín Palacios, 1931); and in English (by A. Jeffrey, 1962).

All praise and thanks are due to Allah Most High, and
may His benedictions
and salutations be upon His Messenger,
and the progeny and Companions of His Messenger.

This short guide is a response to one who wishes to take the path of faith, hope, and love so that he might become complete and perfect as he was created. It was written to answer his questions about what he should believe in and what he should do in the beginning, before anything else.

O you who yearn for eternal beauty, traveler on the path of the true wish, may Allah make you successful in knowing the true way, finding it, and being upon it. May He use you and us in actions that please Him and are done for His sake. For the beginning and the end and what is in between, and success in them all, belong only to Him.

The way and means to eternal salvation and bliss is in coming close to the Truth. Allah Himself teaches us the meaning of His closeness to us. He teaches us by sending us His prophets. We say "We believe." It is the truth. We accept and confirm it. The only thing then left for us to do is to follow the teachings and the example of His prophet.

First, you must believe in the oneness and uniqueness of the One who is before the before and after the after, who created us and everything else, and you must not associate with Him anything unbefitting the purity of His Essence. He Himself says in His Divine Book:

If there were in them gods besides Allah,

199

[the heavens and the earth] would both have
been in disorder [mixing and clashing and
being destroyed].

(*Anbiya', 22*)

The wills of many creators would clash and cancel
each other, not permitting anything to be or to happen.
Therefore, if we and all existence exist, He—the One and
Unique Creator—exists, and He has no associates.

O you with beautiful nature and pure heart, do not
debate, discuss, even talk with people who attribute partners to Allah. There is no use in trying to convince them.
Even the deniers will finally concede:

And if you ask them who created the
heavens and the earth, they will say, Allah.

(*Luqman, 25*)

They as well will finally admit an unknown force as
the initial Creator of the creation—but they will add to
Him further creators. The difference between them and the
believers is that they suppose that others, among the created, are also able to create. You do not have to prove to
them the existence of Allah. Let them prove, if they can,
the existence of His associates.

This is sufficient advice for you on the subject of
professing the oneness of Allah. Time is valuable: you cannot be careless with it. If the mind has reached a state in
which it is free from doubt and the heart is safe and
secure, it makes no sense to disturb this peace with super-
fluous proofs.

The second matter of importance for one who wishes

to learn is the belief that Allah Most High is free from all resemblance to anything visible or invisible in the creation. He is free from all defect.

There are some who, wanting to see the image of their Creator, err, and liken Him to a human being. Let His own words be your guide in this. He says:

> Nothing is like Him ....
> (*Shura, 11*)

Any thought, any word, any quality or attribute not corresponding to this principle is a falsehood, unworthy of the Divine. Therefore seek no further than the fact that none resemble or are like Him. That is His reality. This is also confirmed by the declaration of His Messenger, who said, "At the beginning was Allah, and none with Him." The ones who followed him added to this statement, "It is now as it was."

As it was before the creation, it is after the creation. From the time when matter was hidden under the veil of nonexistence and there was no form, nothing has been added or subtracted. Though He has created the creation, still there are none like Him. Nothing is like Him. Nothing is Him, but everything is from Him. The divine word that He is without likeness cancels all other thoughts, claims, and interpretations.

You must also accept and believe, even if you do not understand, the allegorical verses of the Holy Qur'an and the ambiguous statements of the Messenger of Allah concerning the unity and the ultimate cause, as well as all the declarations of the prophets which have come to us unaltered. You must consider that the significance of these words is a part of divine knowledge and that as such, you accept them. The monumental meanings of these holy expressions are for the understanding of people who are close enough to Allah to be able to see His beautiful attributes.

There is no better proof of the perfection of the Divine, who is self-existent and whose existence is a necessity for the existence of all else, than the holy verse:

Nothing is like Him....

Allah declares with this verse His being, His essence, His divine nature, His limitless greatness, His glory. So write in your heart and mind this principle, this foundation of faith, and believe in Allah's prophet and the message that he brought from the Divine Truth, and in Allah's orders and justice. Furthermore, have faith in the true declarations of all the prophets known and unknown. Love their companions; accept the truth of their mission. Do not speak against them. Do not value one over another. Think of them with terms of praise, as they are described in the Holy Qur'an and in the words of other prophets, which can only be the truth. Show respect, as did the prophets, for the character that distinguishes the perfect man, and for holy places. Accept and believe in the deeds and the words of the saints, even though you may not understand their state and the miracles attributed to them.

Look upon the whole creation, and above all, mankind, with good will—accepting, approving, forgiving, serving, loving. Make that your nature in your dealings with the world. Listen to your conscience. Cleanse your heart. In that clean heart, keep up prayer for your faithful brothers. Help and serve, as much as you can, the people who hide their misery, who are content with their poverty, the travelers on the path to truth. Do not attribute to yourself virtue, goodness, and graciousness because of your service to the creation. Consider that you owe other people thanks for having humbly accepted your help. It is incumbent upon you to lighten the load of those who are burdened. If people whose pain you have helped to alleviate cause you pain in return—if their responses, their ways, their habits are dark and cast shadows upon you—show patience and forbearance. Do not forget that Allah says:

> ...surely Allah is with the patient.
> (*Baqara, 153*)

Do not spend your life in empty endeavors and your time in idle talk. Instead, reflect and remember Allah, read the Qur'an, guide the misguided to the enlightened path. Help others leave evil and turn to doing good. Mend broken friendships. Help others to help others.

Find the right friend, who will be a support for you, a good traveling companion on the path of truth. Faith is a seed. It grows into a tree with the beneficent watering and sunshine of faithful friends. Beware of being close to those who do not discriminate between the faithful and the unfaithful—not knowing either faith or the faithful, they do not care about them. They are either strangers to or enemies of the truth in which you believe.

Look for a perfect teacher who will lead you on the straight path. In your search for a guide, be sincere, because sincerity distinguishes the true seeker. It is certain that if you cling to sincerity and truthfulness, the Lord will manifest His attribute of the Ultimate Guide upon you and will guide you to a perfect teacher. Sincerity in the seeker is such a blessing that when it is present, Allah will even turn the accursed devil himself and the seeker's personal devil, his ego, into angels of inspiration serving him. Sincerity is such a catalyst that it turns lead into gold and purifies everything it touches.

A matter of the greatest importance, one of your greatest needs, is to be sure that the morsel of bread you put in your mouth is lawful. Lawful sustenance, the lawfulness of all you enjoy in this world, is the foundation of your faith. It is upon this foundation that your religion can be built.

To advance in this path, in the footsteps of the Prophets (peace and blessings be upon them), you have to be light—light in worldly goods, light in your concerns about this world. An unmistakable sign of the heaviness that will prevent you from advancing is to be a burden on people. Neither be a freeloader nor let others carry your load. Particularly, don't accept goods and favors, either for yourself or for others, from people whose hearts are dead, submerged in the sleep of heedlessness.

In what Allah permits you to gain as your sustenance—in all your actions, behavior, and words—fear Allah. Do not seek comfort and luxury, especially when you have not worked hard for it. Lawful sustenance is obtained by working harder than is demanded of you. A clear sign of the lawfulness of one's gain is that it will not permit you to be either stingy or a spendthrift.

Take care, since if the love of this world takes root firmly in your heart, it constricts your heart, and it becomes exceedingly hard to pull it out and throw it away. This world is a trial ground; don't seek comfort and riches in it.

Eat less. That will leave more space in your heart

and will increase your desire to pray and be obedient. It will make you more active and less lazy.

Cleanse and beautify your days and nights with worship. The generous Lord asks you to His presence five times a day. Do your prayers at the times He calls you, five times daily, and at each prayer make an accounting of your actions since the last prayer. It is to be hoped that only good deeds and actions befitting a Muslim are done between the times of prayer.

Most people complain that this world, their work to secure their sustenance, and their work as householders for their families, take time away from their worship. Know that work done heedfully, with consideration for others, in accordance with proper behavior, for the pleasure of Allah, is also worship.

Allah has blessed you with intellect, knowledge, profession, strength, and health. All grace and power are due to Him. Use these to gather as much of your suste-nance as possible in the minimum of time. If possible, secure in one day your week's sustenance. Take the exam-ple of Ahmad al-Sabti, a prince, the son of the 'Abbasid caliph Harun al-Rashid. He used the maximum of his tal-ents and strength and effort and worked exceedingly hard as a manual laborer on Saturday. With what he earned in one day he was able to live a whole week. He dedicated the remaining six days of the week to working for Allah and worshipping Him.

After you perform your morning prayer, stay with your Lord until sunrise, and after your afternoon prayer stay in His presence until sunset. These are two periods of time when spiritual powers and enlightenment flow in abundance. Keep your heart tied to Allah in humility and in peace.

There is great virtue and merit in performing extra worship of twenty cycles of prayer between the afternoon and evening prayers, and between the evening and night prayers. Perform extra prayers of four cycles just before the noon prayer, after and just before the afternoon prayer, and after the evening prayer. Perform another ten cycles of prayers in sets of two after the obligatory night prayer, and the three cycles of closing prayer, *witr*, as the last worship of the day.

Do not sleep until you are unable to stay awake. Do not eat until you are hungry. Dress only to cover your body and to protect it from cold and from heat.

Make it a habit to read from the Holy Qur'an every day. When you read, hold the Holy Book with respect. Keep it in your left hand at the level of your chest, and move your right hand along the words you read. Read aloud, but just loud enough that you can hear your own voice.

Read without haste, slowly thinking of the meaning of each word. Wish for divine mercy and beneficence when you come to the verses that inspire His mercy. Take warning from the verses of admonition, and when reading them, promise your Lord your determination to act upon His command, repenting, taking refuge in His mercy, seeking salvation. When you read verses describing the praiseworthy qualities of the truly faithful, think of your own qualities. Be thankful and praise Him for your good qualities, and feel shame for the qualities missing in you, so that you may hope to find the character of the faithful in yourself. And when you read about the faults of the nonbelievers and of the hypocrites who hide and distort the truth, think about whether you are also afflicted with such faults. If you are, try to stop them, to chase them away, to eliminate them. If you do not have them, take refuge in Him, be thankful and praise Him.

What is essential for you is to be heedful at all times, to be attentive to what comes into your mind and your heart. Think about and analyze these thoughts and feelings. Try to control them. Beware of the wishes of your ego, settle your accounts with it.

Have conscience, shame, in front of Allah. That will be a motivation to make you heedful. You will then care about what you are doing or saying or thinking, and the thoughts and feelings that are ugly in the eyes of Allah will be unable to settle in your heart. Your heart will then be safe from wishing acts not in accordance with Allah's pleasure.

Give value to your time, live in the present moment. Do not live in imagination and throw your time away. Allah has prescribed a duty, an act, a worship for your every moment. Know what it is and hasten to do it. First perform the actions He has given to you as obligations. Then do what he has given to you to do through the example of His Prophet. Then take on what He has left you as voluntary, acceptable good deeds. Work to serve the ones who are in need.

Do everything you do in order to come close to your Lord in your worship and prayers. Think that each deed may be your last act, each prayer your last prostration, that you may not have another chance. If you do this, it will be another motivation for becoming heedful and also for becoming sincere and truthful. Allah does not accept good deeds done unconsciously and insincerely as readily as deeds done in consciousness and sincerity.

Cleanliness is an order of Allah. Keep your body and your inner self clean at all times. Whenever you make an ablution make two cycles of prayer following it, except when you have to make an ablution at times when praying is not permitted: at sunrise, at high noon, and at sunset. Friday is an exception to that rule; it is permissible then to pray at high noon.

Above all, what you need is high morals, good character, proper behavior; you must identify your bad features and rid yourself of them. Your relationship to whomever you come into contact with must be based on the best of conduct—but what this means may vary with conditions and circumstances.

Whoever neglects a single item of good behavior is considered to have bad character. Men are created different from each other. Their levels are different. Good behavior and character are also in different levels. Behavior is not a form. It is not to act in the same way on every occasion towards everyone. You have to consider each case, each person, in accordance with the circumstance and the need of the person. A good rule to remember is that if a thing is done to bring salvation, truth, comfort, and peace to others, to oneself, and to as many people as possible, protecting them, eliminating pain and hardship, it is good behavior—on condition that it is not done for personal benefit, but for Allah's sake.

Is not man the servant of Allah? Are not his life and his deeds dependent on divine predestination? He is in a frame whose limits he cannot leave. His will, his freedom of choice, his destiny written on his forehead, are in the hand of the All-Powerful upon whom all acts, all moves depend.

Proper behavior is the means by which an intention becomes a good deed. Therefore it is the greatest capital in the hand of the seeker. The proof is the word of the one who was brought with the most beautiful character, the last

prophet, Muhammad (peace and blessings be upon him),
who said, "I have been sent to perfect good behavior."

Allah says in the Holy Qur'an:

And the recompense of evil is punishment like it,
but whoever forgives and amends, his reward is with
Allah....

(Shura, 40)

The religious law says that you may choose to
demand your right or you may choose to leave it. Choose
to leave that which is due to you and forgive, instead of
punishing, so that you will be counted among the compassionate, the peaceful, the righteous, whose rewards are
promised by Allah.

It is also within good behavior to be angry and to
seek to punish when this is justified by the religious code.
Anger and its manifestation are one of the great sins if
aroused by wrongs done to you personally. But it is permissible and right and a part of correct behavior and good
character to become angry because of something done
against Allah and His divine precepts, to manifest it, and
to fight for Allah's sake.

It is best to separate yourself from people who do
not believe in what you believe, who do not do what you
do, and who are against your faith. Yet at the same time
you should not think badly of them or condemn them for
what they are. Your intention in ignoring them should be
that you prefer the company of believers. Spend your time
in remembering, glorifying, and worshipping Allah
instead of being with them. Treat well those who are
dependent upon you: the people who work for you, your

children, your wives and husbands, your mothers, sisters, and friends, the animals in your care, the plants in your garden. Allah has given them into your hands to test you. You are in His care. Treat the ones in your care as you want the One in whose care you are to treat you. The Messenger of Allah says, "All of creation are Allah's dependents." He has left a few of His dependents, such as your family, in your hands. That is why His Messenger (peace and blessings be upon him) says that the one who is best loved by Him is the one who is best towards his dependents. Show love, compassion, delicacy, generosity, and protection towards those who depend on you—and in fact, to everyone. If you wish His compassion and protection, remember that you yourself depend on the One, the lord and owner of all and everything.

Teach Allah's words in His Divine Book and the good behavior of Islam to your children. Secure for them conditions in which they can exercise what you have taught them. Do this without expecting any return from them. From the very beginning, teach them to bear difficulty, to have patience, to think. Do not place in their hearts the love of the world. Teach them to dislike the things of this world that will render them proud—luxuries, beautiful clothes, delicacies, excess of ambition—because all these, if obtained, will be subtracted from the good due them in the hereafter. Let them not get accustomed to good things; break their habits. Beware that this, which may seem austere, should not bring forth in you the ugly character of miserliness towards your children. Do it in respect and attachment to your religion.

Do not seek to be close to the heedless, to the ones who are slaves to the desires of their flesh. They take hearts away from the light of truth and throw them into the dark hole of heedlessness, as they did with their own hearts. If you are placed with them in the same time and space, then face them and advise them. If they turn their backs on you, it is because they do not know their fronts from their backs. Do not stab them in the back. Be the same way to them whether they turn their faces to you or their backs. Then they may like and respect you and perchance they may be attached to you and follow you.

Do not be satisfied with your spiritual state; advance. Advance ceaselessly, without interruption. With firm intention pray to Allah, the Ultimate Truth, to bring you from the state in which you are to a state beyond it. In every state, in every move, while doing a thing or while being inactive, be sincere and truthful. Be with the Ultimate Truth. Do not ever forget Him. Feel His presence always.

Learn to give, whether you have plenty or little, whether you are happy or in pain. This is a proof of your faith in Allah. Try to satisfy the needs of the needy. This is an affirmation that Allah has assigned everyone's sustenance and nothing will change it. This is a proof of your trusting in Allah.

A miser is a coward. The accursed Devil whispers in his ear that there is no death, that he will live a long time; that the world is hostile; that if he gives he will be left destitute, dishonored, and alone; that he should not be fooled by the plenty that he now has, for no one knows what will happen tomorrow. Worse still, if the miser has little, the devil tells him that soon he will have even less. No one will help him; he will be a load on others and will be detested. He has to look after himself. If these evil imaginations capture the heart, one may be led to the edge of hellfire. On the other hand, the ones who give their ears to Allah hear His blessed words. Allah says in the Holy Qur'an:

> ...and whoever is saved from the miserliness of his ego, these it is that find salvation.
> *(Hashr, 9)*

> ...whoever is miserly is miserly to himself.
> *(Muhammad, 38)*

The final warning is:

> If you turn back [on the path] He will bring another people in your place.
> *(Muhammad, 38)*

That is to say, after having been taught and after having been brought to the path of faith, if you begin or continue to be a miser, you may lose your place, your level, and Allah's favor. Someone else, who is generous and believes in Allah's generosity, will be brought in your place.

The one who is niggardly has not realized the terrifying meaning of Allah's words:

> Destroy their riches and harden their hearts.
> *(Yunus, 88)*

This is the curse of the Prophet Moses (peace be upon him) upon the Pharaoh. When Allah willed the destruction of Pharaoh and his chiefs, the Prophet Moses (peace be upon him) prayed to Allah, the Absolute Judge, for them to be cursed with miserliness. With the effect of this curse the Egyptians were afflicted with miserliness and envy. The poor and the weak died of hunger and Allah judged the Pharaoh and his followers and punished them because of their miserliness.

The ones who are cursed with stinginess do not listen to the words of Allah's Messenger (peace and blessings be upon him), who says, "Allah has two angels next to Him who pray every morning, 'O Lord, increase Your bounties upon the ones who give, and take away what they have from the ones who keep it!'"

When Hadrat Abu Bakr (may Allah be pleased with him) wished to donate all that he possessed and brought it to the blessed presence of our master, the Prophet of Allah asked, "What have you put aside for the care of your family?" He responded, "I leave them in the care of Allah and His Messenger." When Hadrat 'Umar (may Allah be pleased with him) brought half his fortune to donate and was asked the same question, he answered, "I have left half of my goods for the sustenance of my family." The Prophet of Allah told them, "The difference between you two is in accordance with your response to my question."

The one who gives from his sustenance attracts more than he has given from the Ultimate Sustainer. The miser, in addition to his sin of miserliness, accuses Allah Most High of stinginess and prefers and trusts his miserable goods over the generosity of his Lord. This is the unforgivable sin of attributing partners to Allah and may cause one to be rejected from Allah's mercy and lose his faith, may Allah protect us.

Therefore, spend from what Allah has given you. Do not fear poverty. Allah will give you what He has promised, whether you or everyone asks for it or does not ask for it. No one who has been generous has ever perished in destitution.

If you wish to find the truth and have Allah's pleasure and support in it, then avoid being negative and control your temper and anger. If you cannot stop anger, at least do not show it. When you do this, you will please Allah and disappoint the devil. You will begin to educate your ego and straighten and shorten your path. Anger is a result and a sign of the ego not being under control, like a mean wild animal untied and uncaged. As you hold your temper, it is as if you put a bridle on its head and barriers around it. You begin then to tame it, teach it how to behave, to obey, so that it cannot hurt others or itself (because it is a part of you).

When this discipline reflects from you, revealing someone who can control his temper and hold his anger, your adversary will be calmed. You will not be reacting to his provocations. You will not be punishing him or responding to his negativity, but ignoring it. This is more effective than punishing him. He may be led to see the reality of his acts, to realize what is fair, and to confess his faults.

Give heed to this advice and make it a habit. If you do, you certainly will see the positive result and the rewards here and in the hereafter. You will be the winner on the day when your deeds will be weighed. That is the greatest reward and the greatest grace that you will receive. For if you hold your temper, the All-Just will also hold back His punishment for your sins, which are punishable by His divine wrath. Your forgiving will be rewarded by His forgiving you. What better benefit may one expect for effort in bearing hardship caused by your brothers and sisters in faith?

Allah will treat you the way He has ordered you to treat others. So try to assume the good qualities of being just, peaceful, helpful, gentle, and loving. Persist in these qualities; act with them. You will see that this character will spread from you to others around you, creating harmony, mutual love, and respect. The Beloved of Allah, our master the Prophet (peace and blessings be upon him), orders us to love each other, to be in a continuous loving state. He repeats this in so many ways, in so many statements. To leave anger, to replace it with bearing hardship, with forgiving, with caring for the one who causes the hardship, is one of the cornerstones of the foundation of love.

* * *

Open your heart in order to receive divine benevolence. A benevolent heart becomes the mirror in which Allah's favors are manifest. When the divine favors manifest and come through you, when you feel His presence, you will feel shame at your improper actions. This will cause both you and others to have conscience. Thus your benevolence will protect you and others from sin.

When the archangel Gabriel asked our master the Prophet (peace and blessings be upon him), "What is divine benevolence?" The Last of the Prophets answered, "To pray and glorify Allah as if you are in His presence, as if you see Him." Reverence reflects in the heart of a believer who has reached the level of praying as if he sees Allah.

Then our master the Prophet continued, "For if you are unable to see Him, He certainly sees you." The one who has reached that level of realization of divine benevolence will have conscience. He will feel that gaze of Allah upon him and will be ashamed to sin. The Prophet (peace and blessings be upon him) said, "Conscience is total good." If a believer has conscience, he is aware of what he is doing and he cannot do wrong; when a heart is filled with conscience, the possessor of that heart encounters no harm either in this world or in the Hereafter.

The sign of a man with conscience is his lack of arrogance and self-importance. He never oppresses or tries to dominate others. May you also reach the level of benevolence and have conscience, and may you have the strength and foresight to try to attain it.

* * *

Wake before sunrise, remember Allah, and repent. When repentance follows sin, it erases it. The sin disappears as if it never happened. When repentance follows a benevolent action or prayer, it is like light upon light, grace upon grace. To remember Allah and to praise Him unifies the heart when it is scattered all around—like a mirror broken into a thousand pieces—and mends it, makes it into one, and turns it towards the One. Then all trouble leaves the heart, and it is filled with the joy of the One whom it remembers.

When your heart is filled to the brim with remembrance, then read the Holy Qur'an. When you read, reflect upon the meaning of what you have read. When verses remind you of His oneness and of His being without likeness and free from all defect, praise Him. When you read verses describing His blessings, bounties, generosity, and love or His wrath and punishment, take refuge from Him in Him and beg for His mercy. When you hear the parables about past prophets and their people, take heed and draw lessons from what happened to them. There are infinite

216

meanings within the verses of the Holy Qur'an, within every word—changing with your states and levels, knowledge and understanding. Therefore you cannot possibly be tired, weary, or bored in reading them.

* * *

Try to undo the knots of your persistence in sinning. Knot over knot ties you up. How are you going to save yourself? You will need the help of the one who tied those knots, your own self. Talk to it, reason with it. Tell it: "O temporal flesh, you resent listening to reason, but listen. Are you sure, as you inhale, that this is not your last breath? Allah knows best, but the next breath may be your last in this world to which you are so attached. Death will seize you by the throat; yet you persist in piling wrong upon wrong, sin upon sin. The Ultimate Judge warns the ones who persist in sinning with such punishment that mountains of rock cannot bear it. How then can you, flimsy as a straw, imagine that you could bear such horrible torments? Do not turn your back on the One who created you. Face Him and repent. Do it now, without delay, for you do not know when death will break you in two."

> And repentance is not for those who go on doing evil deeds,
> until when death comes to one of them he says,
> "Now I repent...."
> *(Nisa', 17)*

Say to the self: "Indeed, after the aura of death has rendered you prostrate and life is fading away, if you can remember at all and repent, that repentance will not be

217

accepted by Allah. The Prophet whom He sent as a mercy upon the universe said that though Allah accepts your repentance until the time when your breath is being choked out of you, at the moment of your death throes it is too late. Death comes without warning—to some while eating, to some while drinking, to others while sleeping with their wives, to others in deep sleep from which they do not awake. Whoever, before that, has not turned from falsehood to truth, has not repented but persists in sinning, will fall into the abyss of death."

Talk this way to your self. Try to discipline and educate the desires of your flesh. As they are persistent in sinning, be persistent in convincing them to stop sinning. If you keep warning your lower self, with the help of Allah the knots binding your heart will be untied. That is the only way to be saved.

* * *

Fear Allah both in your actions and deep in your heart and thoughts. Fear of Allah is the fear of Allah's punishment. Whoever truly fears the warnings of torment of the Absolute Judge cannot but act in accordance with the pleasure of the Creator and seek the right over the wrong. The Owner of the Final Word Himself said:

... and Allah cautions you against His retribution
(Al 'Imran, 27)

... and know that Allah knows what is in your minds, so beware of Him....
(Baqarah, 235)

The fear of Allah is a protection, the thing that

guards you from harm. Allah's protection is the strongest of all armor, of all fortifications; no harm can penetrate it. That is what divine fear secures for you. The Prophet of Allah, whom He sent as His mercy upon the universe, himself took refuge in his lord. Praying to Him, he said, "I take refuge in Your pleasure, in Your beauty, in Your gentleness, from Your wrath and Your strength. I take refuge in Your divine mercy and compassion, from Your punishment. I take refuge in You from You."

Seek, learn about, and imitate the beneficent acts of your Creator that manifest all around you. Protect yourself against divine wrath with acts and deeds in accordance with Allah's pleasure. Whatever act, whatever thing, whatever path is under the shadow of doubt and fear, do not come close to it. Leave it.

Know that knowing your Creator and obeying Him is the only path that will lead you to peace and felicity. Revolt and selfishness are a dead end. Only by gaining the divine consent can you save yourself from your Lord's wrath. Only be entering the straight path can you get out of the abyss of that dead end; only by actions proper to paradise can you keep away from the fire. Allah says:

Fear Allah . . . and fear the Fire.
(Al 'Imran, 130-31)

With the fear of Allah, rise away from fire and towards felicity.

* * *

While you persist in sinning and stubbornly refuse to see your errors, why are you so proud that Allah treats you with patience, kindness, and generosity in spite of your sins? Is it that you are fooled by what the devil

219

whispers in your ear, saying, "If it weren't for your sins and your revolt, how would Allah manifest His infinite mercy, compassion, and generosity?" Don't you see how irrational that evil teaching is? Would it be less merciful and beneficent for the Owner of Infinite Wisdom to prevent His servant from opposing His will and pleasure?

Then the devil may whisper in your ear again: "You have no hope of attaining the level of benevolence of those who are born with good character and obedience. They have come to this world and shown their obedience to the will of Allah, gathered their Lord's mercy and beneficence in this world, and left it. The real mercy, generosity, and kindness of Allah will be manifest in the Hereafter on the Day of Judgment, when He judges His disobedient servants who are in need of His mercy."

Only someone who has lost his senses could believe in and be deceived by such thoughts. Protect yourself against such temptations and tell your devil: "What you say about Allah's infinite patience and generosity towards His servants is true. Indeed, if there were no revolt, disobedience, and sin, we would not see the manifestation of His divine attributes. So many examples are related to us in the holy books and statements. But you, evil one, are using the truth for your own purposes—so that Allah's mercy be manifest, you encourage me to sin! You are trying to make me revolt because Allah is patient and kind.

"You ask me to test Allah' s mercy and beneficence. How do you know, O accursed one, that I am of those who will be forgiven? Indeed Allah forgives whom He wills and punishes in justice whom He wills. How do I know to which party I belong? All I know is that I am full of sin. And just as I was left in this world without the ability to

220

repent and ask His forgiveness, He may well refuse me His mercy before I enter hell and punish me with the fire. Although one dies as one lives, and sin is the messenger of disbelief, if I am fortunate and give my last breath as a believer, then He will purify me in hellfire and take me out and give me peace in His mercy.

"If I knew for sure that there were no day of reckoning with my sins, that there were no punishment, and if I were certain that I would receive divine absolution, I might have considered your twisted reasoning. Even then, it would be no better than admitting foolishness, for it is certainly an unforgivable behavior for a servant to test the patience of his Lord.

"On the other hand, even if I were certain that I would receive divine punishment, the proper thing for me would be shame and thankfulness for His delaying His punishment and spending of all effort of which I am capable in trying to obey the commands of my Lord.

"I have not heard of any good word that all sins will be forgiven. On the contrary, one is left free to choose between the right and the wrong, and the Ultimate Judge is free to forgive or to punish. In your case, though, O evil-commanding ego, there is no choice. You are constant in your wish for the wrong and the forbidden!"

* * *

Be chaste; chastity is to be cautious, to try to abstain from all that is unclean and sinful. It is protecting yourself from all that is doubtful and suspicious in and around you. When the Messenger of Allah said, "Leave that which is doubtful and reach for that which is sure," he was speaking of the necessity of abandoning things that render you doubtful and hesitant, that create uncertainty, suspense, and fear in your heart—and of turning towards things that render you secure and peaceful.

It falls upon you to examine each act, each word, each act of worship, each relation with others such as friendship or marriage. You must find whether each thing is good or bad, clean or unclean, right or wrong—in other words, lawful or unlawful. In some cases it is clear; then you must choose the right over the wrong. In some cases it is doubtful; then you must leave it as if it were wrong and seek that which is sure.

Follow the advice of the Prophet (peace and blessings be upon him): Even if you feel in need of that which is doubtful, even if you are unable to get anything else, do not take it; leave it for the sake of Allah. This is chastity. Be sure that Allah will reward the chaste with abundant goods much better than the doubtful thing that was abandoned. But do not expect your reward immediately.

Chastity is the foundation of religion and the path to truth. If you are chaste, all your deeds will be pure and sincere; all you do will end well; you will be in harmony with the divine order. You will be the recipient of divine generosity; all will turn to you. You will be under divine protection. If you are chaste and pious, avoiding the wrong and the doubtful, there is no doubt that you will receive all these blessings. But if you turn your back to chastity and piety, the Absolute Judge will place you in a shameful state—helpless, terrified. He will leave you by yourself in the hands of your ego. Then you will be a toy for the devil, who will find no resistance, no opposition to his tempting you, to his taking you away from truth.

Spend all your effort to stay on the path of piety, and may Allah help you.

* * *

This world is a place of preparation where one is given many lessons and passes many tests. Choose less over more in it. Be satisfied with what you have, even if it is less than what others have. In fact, prefer to have less.

This world is not bad—on the contrary, it is the field of the hereafter. What you plant here, you will reap there. This world is the way to eternal bliss and so is good—worthy to be cherished and to be praised. What is bad is what you do with the world when you become blind to truth and totally consumed by your desires, lust, and ambition for it. Our master the Prophet (peace and blessings be upon him), in whom wisdom was as clear as crystal, was asked, "What is worldliness?" He answered, "Everything that makes you heedless and causes you to forget your Lord." Therefore the goods of this world are not harmful in themselves, but only when you let them render you forgetful, disobedient, and unaware of the Lord who has generously offered them to you. It is your sense of the world, your relationship to it, your preference of it over the One who gave it to you, that makes you insensitive and causes you to break your connection with divine truth.

The Messenger of Allah (peace and blessings be upon him) said, "Whoever prefers the world over the Hereafter is made to suffer three things: an unbearable load that is never lightened; a poverty that never becomes richer; and an ambition, a hunger, that is never satisfied."

Therefore the one who lives for this world alone is

223

bound to bear its pains and difficulties—trying to resolve its problems by himself, being totally dependent on it like a beggar, trying to obtain the needs of his flesh and his ego from it. That flesh, that ego whose appetite never knows satiation, whose ambitions are endless, is always wanting, always hungry, always dissatisfied. These are the rewards of the world to those who make the world their lord, forgetting the Lord of all the Universes.

This does not mean that you should abandon the world, not do your duties in it or participate in its affairs—retiring to a corner, making no effort, doing no work. The Messenger of Allah (peace and blessings be upon him) says, "Allah likes to see the believer working at his profession," "Indeed Allah likes the one who has a craft," "The one who earns his sustenance lawfully through his efforts is beloved of Allah." These sayings mean that Allah's beneficence encompasses all who work hard in a craft or business in this world. It is for this reason that all the prophets worked for their sustenance.

It is related that one day Hadrat 'Umar (may Allah be pleased with him) met a group of people who were sitting around lazily doing nothing. He asked them who they were. "We are of those who put their affairs in the hands of Allah, and we trust in Him," they replied.

"Indeed you do not!" he angrily responded. "You are nothing but freeloaders, parasites upon other people's efforts! For someone who truly trusts in Allah first plants the seed in the belly of this earth, then hopes and expects and puts his affairs in the hand of the Sustainer!"

Some true theologians come close to claiming work—in the professions, crafts, and businesses that are lawful according to divine law—as a condition of faith. They have claimed that certainty of faith is defined by the carrying out of religious obligations, and that work is one of these. They based this on the verse:

But when the prayer is ended, disperse abroad in the land and seek of Allah's grace, and remember Allah much that you may be successful.
(Jum'ah, 10)

Thus to leave the worldly and the world does not mean not to do your duties in it.

Perhaps what is meant by being worldly is giving yourself up solely to gathering the world's benefits. The worldly person identifies with what he has gathered and is proud of it. Full of ambition, he devotes himself to amassing the goods of this world without any consideration of whether they are lawful or unlawful, his rightful portion or the portion of others. Worse still is not to see any wrong in all this, to think that it is the right way, the only way.

When the love of the world fills your heart totally, it leaves no space for the remembrance of Allah. Forgetting the hereafter, you prefer this temporal world.

All that you need from the world is something lawful to satisfy your hunger, something with which to cover yourself, and a roof over your head. Let these be the only things you ask from this world, nothing more. Don't be envious of the apparent temporal abundance the world-bound seem to enjoy, nor wish for the riches they have gathered without any consideration of right or wrong, of lawful or unlawful. How long does one stay in this world?

Someone who chooses this temporal world over the true good of the eternal Hereafter will never reach his goal, either here or there. For the ambition of one who is ambitious for this world will never be satisfied. Don't you see that the Maker of Destiny decides your lot in this world, and that you receive neither more nor less than what you are destined to receive? Whether you care or not, what Allah has set forth does not change. Whether we want more or not, we can only attain that which is reflected in the mirror of our destiny. Allah says:

> We portion out among them their livelihood in the life of this world.
>
> (*Zukhruf, 32*)

But people who take this world as their god have endless wants, and those wants of theirs that are not appointed to them, they will never receive. Thus they will be dissatisfied and unhappy all of their lives—and in the Hereafter they will have to face the wrath of Allah.

The desires of this world are like sea water. The more you drink of them, the more you thirst. The Messenger of Allah likened this world to a garbage heap in order to tell you to keep your distance from it. Be satisfied with the portion of it that Allah has included in your fate. Whether you like it or not, that will be your lot.

Allah advised and warned the Prophet Moses (peace be upon him), "O son of Adam, if you are satisfied with what I have apportioned to you, I will set your heart at rest and you are worthy of praise. But if you are not satisfied with what I have apportioned to you, I will grant the world power over you. You will race in it as a wild beast races in the desert. And by My power and majesty, you will not receive from it anything but what I have apportioned to you, and you will be worthy of blame!"

This means that man will attain peace of heart and the level of Allah's praise and grace if he accepts and is content with his lot in accordance with Allah's divine apportionment. On the other hand, if you do not accept the lot that is your fate, Allah will render the world, which you so desire, your enemy. The world will become like a desert to a hungry animal. You will run and run and tire yourself without being able to find anything in it. Allah vows for the world-bound that no matter how they run after the world, they will receive nothing more than their lot. The only things they will receive beyond that are fatigue, dissatisfaction, and disgrace.

Let us suppose that Allah has bestowed upon you all the goods of this world, all the material properties of which you may conceive—how much can you use besides the food and drink your stomach can take, the clothing that will cover your body, and a place to live? The humble of this world have no less, yet they are much better off. For they are at peace, without worry, in this world; and certainly in the hereafter they have less to account for.

Do not exchange your spiritual peace and the possibility of eternal bliss for the temporal, decaying goods of this world. No matter how grand and secure they look, they will die when you die. Death may come in your next step upon this earth, and all your dreams of this world will evaporate.

As the world-bound are sons of this world, there are also people bound for the hereafter, sons of the hereafter. As the Messenger of Allah advised, "be sons of the hereafter, bound for eternity, not temporal sons of the earth who will return to the earth." Read these words of your Lord and abide by them:

> Whoever desires this world's life and its finery,
> We repay them their deeds therein and they
> are not made to suffer loss in it. These are they

for whom there is nothing but fire in the hereafter. And what they work therein is fruitless,
and their deeds are vain.
(Hud, 15-16)

Whoso desires the harvest of the hereafter We
give him increase in his harvest, and whoso
desires the harvest of this world, We give him
thereof, and he has no portion in the hereafter.
(Shura, 20)

* * *

AFTERWORD

May the Eternal Truth wake you from the slumber
of heedlessness. May He make you aware of the
Origin, to which we will all return and in which
we will all remain for the rest of eternity.

May the Divine Seer of all and everything open your
inner eye, so that you can see and remember what you
have done and said all through your life in this temporal
realm of experiments. Then you will know and always
remember that you must account for it all and that you will
be judged on the day of final judgment.

Do not leave your accounting to the Day of
Reckoning. This is the place and the time to do it. See
yourself; close your accounts. The only way to salvation is
to go into the Beyond clean and clear of debts. Give heed
to the advice of the Prophet (peace and blessings be upon
him) who said, "Make your accounting before it is made

for you, weigh your sins before they are weighed for you."
Examine your life; weigh your transgressions against your
good deeds. Do it while you still have time in this world of
numbered breaths, while you can, before you are left alone
in that dark hole in the ground.

While you are alive, your worldly self is like a collector of benefits from Allah's bounties, which come to you
from myriads of hands. What you receive is not really
yours; you are like a cashier who distributes what he has
received, and you are responsible for the accounting of it.

If you do not do this today, be sure that tomorrow on
the burning Day of Reckoning you will scream and ask for
help. No one will come to your aid. You will hear the
divine voice coming from the center of all divine orders,
the voice of the Absolute Punisher who punishes the
guilty, reducing them to nothing. It will be saying:

> Read your book. Your own soul is sufficient as
> a reckoner against you this day.
> (*Bani Isra'il, 14*)

Hasn't the Lord sent you messengers; hasn't He
shown you the right way; hasn't He ordered you to remember Him and praise Him day and night? Hasn't He given
you time within the day and within the night to follow His
orders?

If you wait until the last minute, you will receive no
good from your regret. If you insist on waiting and delay
the accounting of yourself, know that all doors and windows will be closed to you and you will be left outside. If
this is the case, know that there is no other door, no other
place in which to seek refuge. There is no place to go—for
you or for anyone or anything in the creation—except

Allah's door of mercy. Go and kneel at its sill. Shed tears of repentance and beg for entrance. Try and see what is behind the curtains.

There are three dangers which may keep you from examining yourself, making the accounting of your acts, and being thankful to your generous Lord. The first of these dangers is unconsciousness, heedlessness. The second is the flood of tastes and desires that gush from your ego, your lower self. The third is bad habits, in fact all habits, which make one like a machine. The one who can protect himself against these three dangers, with Allah's help, will find salvation in both worlds. Blessings be upon our master Muhammad and his progeny and his Companions—in all tongues, in all places, and at all levels.

◆

Whoever theorizes his religion
offends against the Way of God, and
peace. Heretic!
Deviate *toward* the Law! Don't complicate.
All that's forbidden. All this learned talk
is ignorance. Station and state discard it.
It's not discussion: Religion's what my Lord said
or what he said—the master guide, the envoy
(and peace be his)—for he said not a word!

IBN 'ARABI

A treatise on
The One Alone

Kitab al-ahadiyyah

In the Name of Allah the Merciful,
the One Who is visible
with all His beautiful names and attributes
in the realm of images.

"He who knows himself, knows his Lord."

All praise and thanks to Allah, Almighty, the First with no other before Him. He is the only First, and there is no last but His oneness. The end is with Him alone, and He is the end. He is All-Existing: with Him there is no end. Neither is there nearness or farness; nor is there a will or wish, or time, or above, or below, or place; neither is there a universe. Allah is now as He was before. He is eternal. He is One without oneness and Alone without loneliness. He is not named with a name, for it is He whose name is "He," the self-named one. There is no name other than "He," and none other than He is named.

He is the First without anything before Him. He is the Last without anything after Him. He is Visible in all that is seen. He is Known, clearly, in all that is hidden. He is in all forms and images without any relation to any appearance. He is the secret and the appearance of the first letter announcing the beginning of existence. He is the presence of all the letters that belong to the First and all the letters that belong to the Last and is the presence in all the letters that are visible and all the letters that are hidden. Therefore He is "the First" and "the Last" and "the Visible" and "the Hidden." He is the First and the Last and the Visible and the Hidden. All the letters that form the words, from the first to the last of realms seen or unseen, are without any relation to His Being and are without any effect on His Being.

* * *

Do not fall into the blasphemous error of the sect called *Hululiyyah*, who believe that another soul, even another being, can be infused into them and that they may have God materially existing in them. Know that He is never in anything, nor is anything in Him. He is neither inside nor outside of anything. None can see Him, whether with the eyes of the head or with an inner eye; nor can any conceive Him through the senses, the mind, intelligence, knowledge, or imagination. Only He can see Himself; only He can conceive Himself. None can know Him; only He can know Himself. He sees Himself by Himself; He conceives Himself by Himself; He knows Himself by Himself. None other than He can see Him. None other than He can know Him. That which hides Him is His oneness. None but Himself can hide Him. The veil that hides Him is His own being. He hides His being with nothing other than His being the Only One; therefore, none other than He can see Him.

Neither a prophet whom He has sent to humanity, nor a saint, a perfect man, nor an angel close to Him can see Him, for they are not apart from Him. His prophets, His messengers, His perfect men, are none other than He, for He has sent Himself, from Himself, for Himself, without any other cause or means besides Himself. He sent His essence, from His essence, by His essence, to His essence. There is no difference between the One who sent and His messengers who were sent. The letters of His being are the being of His messengers. There is no other being than He. Neither does He become another; nor does His name become another's name; nor is there any other named by His name.

That is why our Master, the Light of the Universe, the Prophet Muhammad (may Allah's peace and blessing be upon him), said:

I know my Lord by my Lord.

He also said:

He who knows himself knows his Lord.

By this it is meant that surely you are not you, and you—without being you—are He. He is not within you; nor are you in Him. He does not exclude you; nor are you excluded from Him. When you are addressed as you, do not think that you exist, with an essence and qualities and attributes—for you never existed, nor do exist, nor will ever exist. You have not entered into Him, nor He into you. Without being, your essence is with Him and in Him. You were not; nor are you temporal. Without having any identity, you are Him and He is you. If you know yourself as nothing, then you truly know your Lord. Otherwise, you know Him not.

You cannot know your Lord by making yourself nothing. Many a wise man claims that in order to know one's Lord one must denude oneself of the signs of one's existence, efface one's identity, finally rid oneself of one's self. This is a mistake. How could a thing that does not exist try to get rid of its existence? For none of matter exists. How could a thing that is not, become nothing? A thing can only become nothing after it has been something.

Therefore, if you know yourself without being, not trying to become nothing, you will know your Lord. If you think that to know Allah depends on your ridding yourself of yourself, then you are guilty of attributing partners to Him—the only unforgivable sin—because you are claiming that there is another existence besides Him, the All-Existent: that there is a you *and* a He.

Our Master, the Prophet (peace and blessings be upon him), said:

He who knows himself knows His Lord.

He did not say:

He who eliminates himself knows his Lord!

The proof of the existence of something is that when it is presumed nonexistent, its opposite appears. As there is none other than Allah, proving His existence does not depend on the disappearance of some existence other than His. And as you do not exist, you cannot cease to exist, nor be transformed into anything else. Your being is neither temporal nor eternal, for you have no being.

Our Master, the Messenger of Allah, said, "Actually you do not exist, as you did not exist before you were created."

Allah has no partners and there is none like unto Him.

Allah Most High is the meaning of before the before and after the after; without Him, before and after have no meaning. Were this not so,

He is alone. He has no partners.

would have no meaning. It must be so; otherwise something other than He would have to exist on its own and not depend on Him for its existence. Such a partner would not need Allah for its existence and so would be a second god—and that is an impossibility. Allah Most High cannot have partners, and there *cannot* be any like unto Him.

If one believes that things exist in Allah—from Him or with Him—and that these things depend upon Allah for their existence, even so, such things are appearing to one as lords. Though their lordship may depend on Allah, still one who believes in them is guilty of recognizing some other lord as a partner of our Lord. It would be a grave error to consider any other existence as valid alongside of Allah the Self-Existent, even if the thing is seen as dependent on Allah for its existence. A being that has given up its existence and has become naught after having given up its existence, is still far from a breath of knowledge.

If one contemplates oneself as such a being, one is far from knowing oneself. If someone thinks of himself as existing among other beings and things that disappear as he does, whose nothingness becomes naught in nothing—if such a person believes that there are others who exist beside Allah, he is nothing indeed, and his nothingness will go on as long as he thinks he exists. He will be guilty of the unforgivable sin of attributing partners to Allah, while he may think that he knows his Lord, since he knows himself.

The way of knowing oneself and knowing one's Lord.

Then how is one to know oneself in order to know one's Lord?

The answer to this question is: Allah Most High exists and none other exists with Him. He is now as He has always been.

If one sees oneself as other than the only existence, which is Him, or if one does not see oneself as a part of Him, then the answer came from the Messenger of Allah when he said, "He who knows himself, knows his Lord." He did not mean by "self" one's ego—that self which favors the pleasures of the flesh and its lowly desires and which tries to command all of one; nor did he mean the self that first deceives—making one believe that the dirt and the ugliness is proper, then flagellates itself for the wrong it has done and forgets and does it again; nor did he mean the self-satisfied self. He meant one's truth, one's reality. When the Prophet (peace and blessings be upon him) prayed and said:

O my Lord, show me the reality of things

what he meant by "things" was those things that appear to be other than Allah. He meant, "Teach me those things other than You. What is all this around me? Let me know. These things—are they You, or are they other than You? Did they exist before or did they come to be? Are they here forever or are they going to pass away?"

And Allah showed him that the "things" had no being and He showed "them" to be Him, and it was seen that all that appeared as other than Allah was His being. He was shown things without a name, without time, without quality, as the essence of Allah.

The name of a thing is suggested by the thing to the one who names it, and by him is given to others. Thus, in a thing, the existence of the thing and the existence of its self are equivalent. Therefore, when the thing is known, the self is known and when the self is known the Lord is known.

You presume others to be other than Allah. There is nothing other than He, but you do not know this. While you are looking at Him you do not recognize Him. When the secret opens to you, you will know that you are none other than He. Then you will also know that you are the one whom He wished (but you need not disappear), and that you are forever and will not disappear with time, for there is no passing of time. Your attributes are His. Without doubt, your appearance is His appearance. What is in you is in Him. Your before is His Before; your after is His After; your essence is His essence—without Him entering into you or you entering in Him, for

Everything is perishing but His Face.
(al-Qasas, 88)

That which exists and is visible is He. There is nothing but He, so how could nothing cease to be? There is only Him, His essence, which always will be. Therefore, if one knows that a thing exists that cannot cease to be, then the doubt and the ignorance about that thing will cease to be. That being is eternal, without changing into another being. When one who is sure of an existence joins with one who denies that existence, they do not unite. At best, the doubt about that existence disappears.

Therefore, do not think anymore that you need to become nothing, that you need to annihilate yourself in Him. If you thought so, then you would be His veil, while a veil over Allah is other than He. How could you be a veil that hides Him? What hides Him is His being the One Alone.

That is why the utterance became permissible for Mansur al-Hallaj, when the words

I am the Truth.

came from his lips, and for Abu Yazid al-Bistami when he cried:

Praise be to Me, the essence, absolved of all defect!

for they were both united with Truth.

These are not people who have annihilated themselves in Allah; nor have they come to be in Allah; nor did they exist before, becoming naught afterwards. They are those who see their attributes as Allah's attributes, their essence as Allah's essence, without their attributes and essence being either in Allah or out of Him. Their selves are only Allah's being. These are the ones who have reached Allah. They are eternal. They never ceased to be, for they never were, since there is only Allah's self, Allah's essence. Neither is there any existence. There is only the existence of Allah.

Our Master, the Messenger of Allah, said:

Do not curse Time, for Allah is Time.

pointing out that Allah's being is free from likeness or equals or partners, but is manifest in eternal time.

The only existence is the existence of Allah. Allah Most High speaking through His Messenger said to Moses:

O my servant, I was ill and you didn't come to visit me; I was hungry and you didn't feed me....

Allah Most High clearly declares that the being of the one who is sick is His being, and that the one who is hungry and in need is also He. If the sick and the needy are He, then your being also is His being. In the same way, everything made out of elements and events is also He.

When the secret of a single atom out of all the atoms from which the elements are made becomes known, the secrets of the whole universe visible and invisible will be revealed. Then you will not see anything but Allah either in this world or in the Hereafter. You will see all the existences in this world and in the Hereafter, all the names and the things named with those names and their being, as His Being alone. You will see Allah creating nothing forever.

You may see His revealing, His being, and His attributes in another kind of image, without qualities and references, as He reveals Himself:

> Every moment He manifests Himself in anoth-
> er glorious state.
>
> (ar-Rahman, 29)

Then you will see that all the things you thought He made, He did not make. Their appearance is a reflection of Allah's revealing His essence and His attributes, every moment, in a different form and shape.

He is the Before, for He is self-existence. He is the After, for He is endless. He is the Visible because He is the Only One. He is the Invisible, for He is the One Alone. He is the First because only He exists. He is the Last, for there is no end after Him.

He is the first letter and all of the letters until the last letter. He is the letters seen and the letters unseen. He is the name, and He is the named. His being is the only necessity; therefore it is also a necessity that there be no existence but His.

On Dying Before Dying

He who thinks of himself as other than Allah is certainly not other than He, because Allah Most High is free of all existence except His Divine Essence. All, visible and invisible, that exists in Him, with Him, apart from Him, is not other than He, for the other itself is He. Whoever sees himself thus and is endowed with these qualities has neither bounds nor end.

One dies when, by Allah's will, one's borrowed time ends. One's material being—which is called life—ending at an appointed hour, loses all its character and qualities both good and bad. One who dies a spiritual death while his material life continues also loses his characteristics whether good or bad, and nothing of him remains. In their place Allah comes to be. His self becomes Allah's self; his attributes become Allah's attributes.

That is what our Master, the Prophet of Allah (peace and blessings be upon him) meant when he said:

Die before dying.

meaning, "Know yourself before you die." Allah, speaking through His Prophet, said:

My servant comes close to Me with the worship of good works until I love him; and when I love him, I become the hearing in his ears;

I become the sight in his eyes; I become the words on his tongue; I become the hands with which he holds; I become the strength of every part of his being.

With these divine words the Messenger of Allah indicates that the one who dies before dying realizes his whole being as Allah's being and sees no difference between himself and Allah, between his attributes and Allah's, nor does he see any necessity for nor possibility of any change in his state. For if his being were not already Allah, he could not even know himself.

Thus when you know yourself, your self and selfishness will leave you, and you will know that there is nothing in existence but Allah.

The condition for self-knowledge is to know that if you had a being of your own, independent of other being, then you would neither have needed to annihilate yourself in Allah nor to know yourself. You would have been, yourself, a god—self-existent and without any other existence but you—while it is Allah Most High who is free from the existence of any other god but Himself. And when you come to know yourself, you will be sure that you neither exist nor do not exist, whether now, or before, or in the future. Then the meaning of *la ilaha illa 'Llah*—There is no god but Allah—there is no being but His, nor any other except Him, and He is the Only One—will become clear to you.

Do you think it possible to interfere with the sovereignty of the Lord? How could the Absolute Sovereign over all and everything be constrained? He has ruled forever. He is God. He is the Ruler, not the ruled. He is the Eternal Creator, not the created, and is now as He ever was. He does not need His creation to be Creator; nor does He need the ones He rules to be Lord. He possessed all the attributes before He manifested them in the universe He created, and as He was, He is.

The manifestation of His essence does not differ in any way from His being as it was before. The manifestation of His oneness requires His having been the First. He is hidden in being Visible; His secret is manifested in what is seen. His Before is His After, and His After is His Before. His multiplicity is in His Oneness, and His Oneness is in the multiplicity. He is One, and all is One.

His quality is His appearance at every moment in a different form and a different state. In His Blessed Qur'an, in the chapter Ar-Rahman, The Beneficent, He says:

> All those who are in heaven and on earth ask
> of Him. He manifests Himself at every moment
> in another glorious state.
> *(ar-Rahman, 29)*

Nothing existed nor does anything exist; yet at every moment He manifests Himself in another glorious state. There was no first; nor was there a before; there is no more manifestation now. In truth, there is no being other than Him: for what only appears to exist, existence and nonexistence are the same. If one conceives it otherwise, one must conceive that a thing may appear from nothing, which negates the oneness of Allah, and that is a defect— while His oneness is free of and above all defects.

The only existence is Allah's existence. If you know this and do not consider yourself to be the same as, or other than, or together with, Him—then truly you know yourself. That is why our Master the Messenger of Allah (peace and blessings be upon him) said, "He who knows himself, knows His Lord" and not, "He who annihilates himself knows his Lord"—for he saw and he knew that there is nothing but Allah. And that is how he knew himself.

Know yourself; know your being. Certainly you are not you; yet you do not know. Know that this existence is neither you nor other than you. You do not exist; yet you are also not a nonexistence. Your existence is not someone else; nor does your nonexistence make you someone else. Without being and without not-being, your existence and your nonexistence is Allah's being, because it is certain that the being of the truth is the same as your being and your not-being, and at the same time the truth is you and not-you.

Then when you see what is around you as not other than you, and all and everything as the existence of the One—when you do not see anything else with Him or in Him, but see Him in everything as yourself and at the same time as the nonexistence of yourself—then what you see is the truth. Then indeed, truly, you see yourself and you know yourself. When you know yourself with these qualities, you know your Lord without being in Him, with Him, or united to Him. The knower and the known and the one who joins with the one joined are one. Someone might ask, "How then is one to be with Allah, when there is none other than He? One cannot be united with oneself!"

The answer is that there is no union or being with Him, because to be with someone or to be united with him is only possible when there are two entities. As there are not two, as there is only one, there is neither being with Him nor uniting with Him. Unification may occur between two things which are either the same as or different from each other. If the two are not the same, then they are the opposite of each other. Allah Most High is exempt from having another the same as, different from, or opposite to Him.

In the oneness with Allah which we describe, coming close has no nearness and being far has no distance, for there is no space or time.

Someone might ask, "What is being close without nearness and being far without distance?"

The answer is: in one's state of closeness or farness one must realize that there is nothing but Allah. Yet you do not know yourself, because you do not know that you are naught but Him. You are He without yourself.

It is only when you are He without the letters and the words of knowledge that you know yourself, that you know that you are the Truth.

You were not aware that you were the Truth, that there was nothing else but the Truth, and that the Truth was you. When the knowledge comes, through the understanding of the One and Only, then you will know Allah by Allah, not by yourself.

To give an example: suppose that your name is Mahmud; yet you do not know that, and you think that you are called Mehmed. One day you learn that you are Mahmud. You continue being what you were; yet when you learn that you are Mahmud, the name Mehmed is taken away from you. Your realization that you are not Mehmed has not made you cease to be Mehmed [because you never were Mehmed]; the disappearance of a thing requires its pre-existence.

The one who knows and the thing known, the one who joins and the thing joined, the one who sees and the thing seen—are all one. The Knower is His attribute; the

Known is His essence. The Joiner is His attribute; the Joined is His essence. The Seer is His attribute; the Seen is His essence. The one who assumes the attribute is the same as the attribute. This is what is meant by the words of our Master the Messenger of Allah:

He who knows himself knows his Lord.

When one understands this, then one knows that there is neither union nor separation. He is the one who knows; He is the one who is known. He is the one who sees; He is the one who is seen. He is the one who joins; He is the one joined. Nothing unites with Him but Him.

Someone who is aware of this is free of the unforgivable sin of attributing partners to Allah. Otherwise he has not breathed a breath that will save him from that sin. For whoever believes that anything other than Allah exists is attributing partners to Him.

When Mahmud finds that he is not Mehmed, nothing is subtracted from him. Mehmed is not annihilated in Mahmud; nor does he become a part of him; nor does he become other than he; nor does Mahmud enter into Mehmed. Mahmud simply knows himself as Mahmud. Thus he knows himself by himself, not by the name Mehmed, for the name Mehmed never existed. How could one know something by means of something that never existed?

Many of those who think they know themselves and their Lord and have freed themselves from the delusion of their own existence say that the only way to the true path is through nothingness and the nothingness of nothingness, and that to know God is only possible for one who annihilates himself.

They have fallen into error because they have not truly understood the Prophet's words: "He who knows himself knows his Lord." He said about them:

> Their delusion is their belief that by annihilating themselves they have annihilated the attributing of partners to Allah.

First, they believe that it is necessary for them to efface their own being in order to avoid setting themselves up as partners to Allah. Second, they feel they must annihilate even the concept of annihilation, so as to achieve the total extinction of all other existence.

However, all these activities are nothing but polytheism, the attributing of partners to Allah! For one must fundamentally believe in the possibility of other existences if one believes their annihilation to be necessary. Without doubt, doing this is trying to affirm that there is another god besides Allah and is thus attributing partners at the core. May Allah guide and lead such people and ourselves to the true path.

If someone asks, "You have demonstrated that if one knew oneself, one would know one's Lord. Yet the one who knows himself is other than Allah. So how can someone other than Allah know Allah?"

Our answer is: The one who knows his Lord through the knowledge of himself knows that his being exists neither by its own existence nor by the existence of anything other than himself. Perhaps his existence is the existence of Allah without his being either within or without, either together with, or from, Allah. But his being is as it always was: nothing—without annihilation or extinction. For a thing to annihilate itself and become nothing presupposes its existing by its own power, not even having been created by the power of Allah, and that is an impossibility.

So the knowledge of oneself is nothing other than Allah's knowledge of Himself, for the self of such a knower is nothing other than the truth. When the Prophet (peace and blessings be upon him) said, "He who knows himself . . ." by the word "self" he meant one's being, and whoever reaches that level does not exist either outwardly or inwardly except by the existence of Allah. His being is Allah's being; his word is Allah's word; his action is Allah's action; his knowledge of himself is Allah's knowledge of Himself. Yet you see him as other than Allah, for you see yourself as other than Allah. "The believer is the mirror of the believer" [hadith].

The Truth is both the eyes and the mirror and the vision in the mirror. For the eyes of the believer are the eyes of Allah and the vision he sees is He, within the mirror of truth. For He is not that which reflects in your eye, nor a knowledge in your mind, nor in your thoughts, nor a figment of your imagination, nor a feeling within you. But He is your eye, your knowledge, your vision.

If someone says, "I am the Truth," do not hear these words from some man, from someone other than He, but hear it from Him, from Allah. For only Allah says, "I am Allah."

You have not attained that which came to the one who uttered these words. If you had reached the state that reached him, you would understand what he means, you would see what he saw, and you would say what he said. For the existence of all and everything is not its own existence but His, without its existing at all.

After all that has been said, beware of falling into doubt and imagining that Allah is created like you and everything else. Know that the one who sees and that which is seen, the believer and that in which he believes, the one who knows and that which is known, the one who understands and that which he understands, the creator and the created—are all one. Without seeing, without knowing, without understanding, without words and without letters, without even His own being, the Lord knows Himself by Himself.

Know that Allah's existence and His knowledge of His existence are without any quantity, quality, seeing, thought, knowledge, or other condition.

When one looks into a mirror one sees oneself. Whatever appears on you appears on the image in the mirror. When you look upon your image in the mirror, your image is looking upon you. Naturally the eye that looks at you from the mirror is your eye. Then, when the image in the mirror looks at you, is it not true that you are looking at yourself with your own eyes? If the name of the one who is looking in the mirror is Ahmad, and if the image in the mirror could speak and say, "I am Ahmad," it would be telling the truth. Yet, as the image is reflected, so would be the words. It would not be the image that calls itself Ahmad, but the one who is looking into the mirror.

So if someone says, "I am the Truth," do not hear it from any other than from the Truth Himself, for it is not a man who says it; it is the word of Allah. That man who utters these words is nothing but an image reflected upon the empty mirror, one of the infinite attributes of Allah. The reflection is the same as that which is being reflected, and the words of the image are the reflected words of the Real One.

The void is a mirror; the creation is the image in it. Man is as the eye of the image reflected in the mirror; the

One who is reflected in the image is hidden in the pupil of that eye; thus He sees Himself. Then:

> He is the One who sees: He is the eye. He is
> the One who is seen.
> (Shaikh Mahmud Shabustari, *Gulsheni-Raz*)

Only the one who has the eyes of his heart open will understand these words.

Is one not to discriminate between the appearance of the beautiful and the ugly, of the good and the bad? Is one to consider a decaying corpse or excrement as God? Allah Most High is beyond and free from such associations. We address those who do not see a corpse as a corpse or excrement as excrement. Our words are for those whose eyes of the heart are not blind, whose ears of the heart are not deaf, and whose tongue of truth is not tied.

For the one who does not know himself is blind, deaf, and tongue tied. The one who is blind and whose tongue is tied can neither see nor understand when the meanings of things are made manifest. These words are for those who are with Allah, not for those who are blind and tongue-tied in believing that things exist without Allah.

The ones who understand are the ones who have resolved to find themselves and to know Allah by knowing themselves and who spend all effort, for they have the divine light of the love and the wish for Allah in their hearts. These are the ones who will know that there is no existence other than He. The one who has neither the wish nor the intention for this will not understand. Allah Most High says in the Holy Qur'an:

> The eyes cannot see Him but He sees all eyes.
> (*An'am, 104*)

In other words, no sight can reach Him, while He is in all that sees. The truth of the matter is in this verse. No eyes can see Him, so no one can perceive Him. He is the only existence, and if no one can see Him, then there is no one besides Him. If there were other existences besides Allah, they should have been able to see Him.

So the meaning of "The eyes cannot see Him..." is that there is no existence other than His. The Truth can only be conceived of by Itself, which has no other identity except the Truth: Allah sees Himself by Himself and by none other than Himself. His Essence sees His Essence.

"The eyes cannot see Him..." because the eyes are created. They came to be after the One who is before the before and after the after. That which is created and temporal and after cannot perceive the Creator who is before the before—permanent—and after the after—eternal.

There are no eyes; there are no things; there is only the One, the Truth. The one who does not reach this conclusion cannot possibly come to know himself. Allah sees Himself by Himself, without any form or quality or eyes or sight.

There is nothing except Allah; all else is nothing. There is only He. Then what are all these things that we see around us? Nothing that is seen is other than He.

The one who sees anything other than He cannot see Him, for one does not see other than what he sees.

The one who does not know himself, who sees himself as other than He, cannot see Allah. Every cup shows what is in it.

No words suffice to describe a thing to the blind. The blind man does not see; the one who does not understand does not understand. The one who sees, sees; the one who understands, understands. These are the signs of the ones who know Allah.

Those who do not know Him will not see Him, whether by teaching or by learning or by thinking. The one who knows only knows though service to a perfect guide. That one will be enlightened by his light and find the path to truth, find oneness and unity... if it be the will of Allah.

May Allah Most High lead us in the straight path— by words and deeds and wisdom and enlightenment which please Him—and to realms and states with which He is pleased.

Amin—and you are the Most Merciful of the Merciful.

May Allah's peace and blessing be upon our Master Muhammad and upon his family and Companions. Peace be unto the Messengers. All praise belongs to Allah, Lord of the Worlds.

AFTERWORD

THE PURPOSE OF THE CREATION OF MAN

In his monumental work *The Meccan Revelations*, Ibn 'Arabi claims that God created humanity in order to make Himself known. He bases his belief on the verse in the Qur'an where God says

> I have only created jinns and men that they
> may worship Me.
>
> (*Zariyat, 56*)

The great commentator Ibn 'Abbas gives the meaning of "to worship" as to *know*, stating that the purpose of man's existence is to know God.

God has created everything in perfect order, connecting everything with everything else, and connecting, also, everything to Himself. He has manifested His attributes upon His creation, and regulates the actions of each thing in relation to the divine attributes bestowed upon it. Speaking through His Prophet, God says, "I was a hidden treasure, I loved to be known, and through this love I created creation." God has honored humanity, His supreme creation, with being a means of His becoming known.

Just as God's essence is incomparable with, and other than, His creation, so the human being has no equal in creation as a manifestation of all His most beautiful names and attributes. God is Most Perfect and has created humanity perfectly. The human being contains all of the potentials necessary for reaching the perfect state. As God is in need of nothing, He has made humanity in need of nothing but Him. Thus God made man to know Him, and man is capable of knowing the truth and finding perfection.

The practical meaning of "worship" in this Qur'anic verse is to abase oneself, to erase oneself in front of the Lord. The reward of that undertaking is a conscious connection between the created and the Creator. It is a means of coming close to Him and knowing Him. The Lord says: "Pray to Me so that I accept your prayers."

In the same divine verse, not only men but also *jinn* are mentioned, because in the whole of creation there are none but men and jinn who, with arrogance, claim to be Lords, themselves, over everything that exists. Nothing else in creation is given the possibility of ownership. Nothing else can inherit. Nothing else can call another of its own kind, its slave. Nothing else can claim to represent God. Nothing else in the world is conscious, claiming to have life, power, and will—the divine qualities of Ever-Living, All-Powerful, and Total-Will, which belong to God.

The possibility of this claim is the meaning of "God has created man in His own image." These manifestations of divine attributes in man, so misused by him, are also the connection and the relationship between him and his Lord, and a means for him to know his Lord.

It is in consideration of man's willfulness and arrogance that "worship" must signify self-abasement before it can mean knowledge of the Lord. For all the knowledge that human beings with their given intelligence can attain, is as nothing before God's infinite greatness. We must bow our heads in cognizance of that fact. It is only through utter humbleness that we will be able to realize the purpose of our creation. But it is also true that someone who does not know his Lord already is incapable of erasing himself in the first place!

HOW TO FIND GOD

The Creator can only be found through His creation. Everything is a witness to His existence. Without knowing the reality of reality, it is impossible to know God.

Avicenna, a contemporary of Ibn 'Arabi, claims that God can be found through rational thinking apart from the knowledge of His creation. Ibn 'Arabi says that the manifestation of God is in His creation and it is impossible to know Him otherwise.

Creation is continuous in the universe. Each event of creation is different; they are not repeated. The endless procession of uniqueness is a proof of the infinite divine power. Every new action is a mirror where divine attributes are manifest, and in every one of them there is a new and special knowledge. This is the only source of divine knowledge.

If we look at the heavens, we see a sign of the manifestation of God's attribute, "The All-Covering Vastness." The seemingly immeasurable ocean suggests the divine attribute of "The All-Comprehending." Were we to contemplate our own life, and the living things around us, we would understand the meaning of "The Ever-Living God." Should we look upon a man of knowledge, we would remember "The All-Knowing God." In a doctor we would see the signs of "The All-Healing God." And if we considered the human being, we would see the evidence of "The All-Uniting God."

The human wish to find our Lord can draw us to see His manifestations in everything around us and within us. Then the whole of life and the universe becomes a book that teaches of the Lord, because every created being is nothing less than a manifestation of the beautiful names of the One who created it.

We will also be aware of things opposite to each other, contradicting each other: the manifestation of the divine attribute of "The Guide" versus the manifestation of "The One Who Hinders"; "The Beneficial One" versus "The One Who Prevents." In some moments of creation, one of these attributes overcomes; and in others, the other. Whenever "The Guide" and "The Beneficial One" are superior in quantity and quality, peace and prosperity are dominant. When that state decreases, difficulty and hindrance manifest themselves, and pain and poverty become dominant. This can occur within a single human being or in the whole of the world.

In this way a creation where good is manifest exists in opposition to a creation where bad is manifest. That is why the people who are bound for Paradise do not like the people who are bound for Hell, and visa-versa. There are animals also, in which beneficial attributes predominate, other animals in which harmful attributes are manifest. Both of these animal qualities are in every human being. Those who are overwhelmed by the nature of wild animals are much worse than the worst of the actual animals, while those in whom beneficence prevails are raised to the level of angels. The saint Mevlana Jelaluddin Rumi says, "O man, you side with the animal in you, and you side with the angel in you. Leave your animal nature behind so that you can rise above the angels!"

Thus humanity must know the manifestation of divine attributes in the continuous creation around us, and find its equivalent in our own nature—for God has taught us all His names. If we do this, we will know our Lord in His infinite qualities. But at the same time that we see the immensity and perfection of the Creator, we will see the minuteness and imperfection of the qualities manifested in us. Then we will realize our nothingness and our total need of Him. That is the beginning of the realization of the human being as the servant and God as the Lord, which is the purpose of the creation.

"HE WHO KNOWS HIMSELF, KNOWS HIS LORD"

The truth of the attributes, the beautiful names of God, is infinite, and manifests in different ways at different times. The proof of Truth is in the realization of the oneness of all creation. Yet multiplicity is a part of the one. Unity manifests itself in multiplicity. With all their differences, and in the infinity of manifestation, the parts interconnect and add up to a whole. Whoever can find this in himself, knows his Lord.

God has created the perfect human being in His own image—in the image of His attributes.

Many Sufis believe that to be able to realize this unity of the self, one must obliterate the manifestation of many "I's" in oneself—in fact, one must deny them existence. Through intensive worship, fasting, meditation, and refusing the desires of the flesh, they attempt to submit their wills to the will of God, and to purify their behavior and habits. All of this discipline and effort is built on the assumption that these many "I's" that one is trying to give up, actually exist. Yet there is no "I" other than God. There is nothing but He. How can one manage to give up something that never was? The only way to know your Lord is by knowing your nonexistence.

Man is nothing but a mirror where God's attributes are reflected. He is the one who sees Himself in that mirror. He is the only one who knows Himself. Neither the prophets, nor the angels, nor a perfect human being can know Him. When we recognize our nothingness and God's totality, we attain the full scope of our knowledge of Him.

THE UNITY OF BEING

Three different approaches are necessary for understanding the unity of being. There is a unity of essence, a unity of attributes, and a unity of action.

The unity of essence is the concept that there is only one existence, one cause—inconceivable, unknowable, yet responsible for the existence of all and everything. The quality, the character, the attributes, the identity of all and everything are the manifestation of this one cause. Every existence is related to it, and every action of every created thing is caused by and connected to it.

Everything is from God, and yet is not God. He is before the before and after the after He is the outer and the inner, the visible and invisible. His outward manifestation is the unity of everything, and still He is hidden in His Oneness. In the beginning, there was nothing but He. Right this moment, there is nothing but He. He is infinite—therefore, He will be when all is gone. His actions are unceasing and change constantly, no two are alike. Therefore there is none like Him, and there is none other than He. Whoever does not see this is blind in this life, and whoever is blind here will be blind in the Hereafter.

Mullah Jami' says, "Look at the whole creation under one single light, so that you will see the truth. There is only one light, but under that light different things are seen. The light unites all. This is the meaning of the unity of being."

That light erases the doubt and ugliness of imagination. The human being whose heart is freed of this ugliness sees the one, the most perfect, the most beautiful existence. There is no more harm, confusion, or deformity; all is right and true and beautiful. Such a one sees his own imaginary existence as a manifestation of the true existence, and thus passes from his existence to the true existence. He sees all humanity and all the created world as faultless, perfect, and beautiful, for truth is beautiful. And all is united in love.

WORSHIP

God says:

> The seven heavens and the earth and all beings therein declare His glory. There is not a thing but celebrates His praise, but you do not understand how they declare His glory!
>
> *(Isra', 44)*

The earth has been entrusted with knowledge by God, as humanity has been entrusted with knowledge. The earth also knows its Creator. The truth is within everything. If man, with heedfulness, looked around himself, he would detect it immediately. God says:

> On that day [the earth] will declare her tidings; for that her Lord will have given her inspiration...
>
> *(Zalzalah, 4-5)*

> Thy Lord has revealed to the bee...
>
> *(Nahl, 68)*

And He revealed to an ant the presence of His
prophet Solomon.
(Naml, 18)

He tells us that a day will come when the earth will
speak of all that has happened upon it. Things we presume
to be without life will be witnesses on the Day of
Judgment; thus, they know. A rock, although it appears
inanimate, has a face turned to its Creator and a face
turned to man. It is filled with the love and fear of God,
while we think that it is senseless. We are senseless ourselves, living and walking upon the face of the world,
believing it to be lifeless!

All creation has a language of its own, but no one,
save those whose ears of the heart are open, can hear it.
How else could the earth evolve into layers of elements—
lead, copper, silver, and gold—into jewels and diamonds?
Seeds grow into plants, into thousands of grains and fruits.
Nothing is lost; everything is kept in the memory of nature.
An ear like Solomon's can hear the words of the winds and
the mountains and the birds.

It is reported by Anas, the Companion and adopted
son of the Prophet, may God's peace and blessings be upon
them, that the Messenger of God took up some pebbles in
his hand. A voice came forth from them, crying, "Allah,
Allah, Allah!" When he gave the pebbles into the hands of
his beloved Companion Abu Bakr, the stones still kept
reciting the name of God. But when Anas was given the
pebbles, no more was heard.

One day the Prophet was ill. The angel Gabriel
came to him in the form of a beautiful human being and
presented him with wonderful grapes and pomegranates.
As he was eating them, a voice proceeded from them,

speaking the name of the Lord. When he gave some to his grandchildren, Hasan and Husayn, the fruits kept reciting the names of God, but when another of the Companions was given the fruit to taste, the sound ceased.

The cognizance of the Creator is within the creation. This is the manifestation of God's name "The All-Powerful."

All that is taken to be lifeless matter—the earth, the water, the air, the fire—is immersed in continuous worship of its Lord. As a stone has neither mind nor thought nor feeling, as it is without emotion or will, it exists naturally in a state of complete submission.

The plants are in a lesser state of submission because they have a will to grow, and in their effort to grow they forget God and lack in worship.

Lesser still is the submission of the animal, the sentient being. Although animals do not have a fully developed mind and will, they have instinct, and that is what prevents them from total submission and full worship and realization of their Creator.

Man is the least apt to submit to God and the most lacking in worship. His mind, his imagination, his lust, the desires of his flesh, his anger, his will are the powers which hold him and keep him in heedlessness. At best, he may intend to know his Lord by his intellect, seeking proofs of His existence, wishing to see Him with his own eyes, and suffering under the influence of the will given to him.

It is only the perfect human being who realizes the limits of the mind and finds the Lord. This comes to a few through the manifestations of the divine to consciousness; through looking at things with the affirmation of unity as a guide; through the opening of divine disclosures; through inspiration. Those few surpass the whole of creation and reach the level of being servants of God.

And then they serve the rest of creation.

MORALS

Ibn 'Arabi says, "No reward that a human being can receive for his achievements can compare with the felicity awarded to whoever shows compassion to humanity." He also says, "God has entrusted animals to men in order to serve them. Treat them gently. When you use them to carry things, do not overload them. When you ride them, do not sit on them proudly." According to Ibn 'Arabi, the essence of morality is compassion.

To help us persevere in treating others with kindness, gentleness, and consideration, he suggests that we be heedful and continuously evaluate, not only our actions, but also our feelings and thoughts.

He says, "May God, who sees everything, open your inner eye, so that you can see and remember what you have done and thought, felt and said, in your daily life. Remember that you must account for it, and that you will be judged for it on the Day of Reckoning. Do not leave your accounting to that day. This is the time and the place to do it. See yourself, close your accounts. The only way to salvation is to go to the Hereafter clear and clean of all debts. Give heed to the advice of the Messenger of God, who said, 'Make your accounting before it is made for you. Weigh your sins before they are weighed for you.' Weigh your transgressions against your good deeds while you still have time.

"While you are alive, you are like a collector of benefits from God's bounties, which come to you from myriads of hands. What you receive is not really yours. You are like a cashier: you must distribute what you have received, but you are responsible for the accounting of it. If you do not do it today, on the Day of Reckoning no one will come to your aid. You will hear the voice of the Absolute Punisher, Who will say, 'Haven't I sent you messengers, haven't I shown you the right way? Haven't I given you time within the day and within the night to follow My orders, to remember Me and to praise Me? Now:

Read your book. Your own soul is sufficient as
a reckoner against you this day.'
(*Bani Isra'il, 14*)

"If you wait until the last minute, you will receive no good from your regret. If you cannot see what you are doing, know that the veils covering the eye of your heart are thick, and you are rejected from God's door of mercy. Go and kneel at the sill of that door; shed tears of repentance and beg for entrance.

"There are three dangers that may keep you from examining yourself. The first is unconsciousness. The next is the imaginary pleasure you take in the deceptions of your ego. The third is being a slave to your habits."

Ibn 'Arabi practiced the continuous contemplation of his daily life. He mentions that one of his teachers wrote down on a piece of paper everything he did and said during the course of the day. At night he would make an accounting of that day's words and actions. If he had done wrong, he would repent; if he had done right he would offer thanks to God. Ibn 'Arabi himself noted not only what he did and said, but also his thoughts and feelings.

He says, "In whatever state you find yourself, even if you are better than everyone else, ask God for, and

265

work for, a better state. In everything you do, do not forget God."

According to Ibn 'Arabi, contemplation and meditation are a means to protect oneself against all evil. In addition, they inspire patience against adversities.

He believed in the value of all human beings, and in interacting with them with the best of intentions. He says, "Treat everyone equally, whether they are kings or paupers, old or young. Know that humankind is one body, and individuals are its members. A body is not a whole without its parts. The right of the man of knowledge is respect, the right of the ignorant one is advice, the right of the heedless one is to be awakened, the right of the child is compassion and love.

"Treat well those who are dependent upon you: your wives and husbands; your children; the people who work for you; animals in your care; plants in your garden. God has given them into your hands to test you, and you are in His care. Treat the ones in your care as you want the One in whose care you are to treat you. The Messenger of God says, 'All creation are God's dependents. God has left a few of His dependents in your hands. Show love, compassion, delicacy, generosity, and protection toward those who depend on you, and in fact to everyone.'

"Teach your children good behavior with the words of God in His Divine Book. Secure for them conditions in which they can exercise what you have taught them. From the very beginning, teach them to bear difficulty, to have patience and consideration. Do not place in their hearts the love of the world. Teach them to dislike the things of this world that will render them proud: beautiful clothes, delicacies, luxuries, excess of ambition; because all these will be subtracted from the good due to them in the Hereafter. Let them not become accustomed to good things—yet beware that this, which may seem austere, should not bring forth in you the ugly character of miserliness toward your children.

"In all the good you do, do not expect any return of favors or of thankfulness. When someone causes you pain, do not retaliate by causing them pain. God considers such response as a sin, while He praises the ones who return kindness to those who have hurt them.

"Consider God's orders and fear His justice in everything you do, in everything you say. He is the All-Seeing, the All-Knowing, the Ever-Present. The essence of all religions is to know that although you may not see Him, He sees you. God's orders are only heard and obeyed by the ones who love and fear Him.

"A miser is a coward because he does not have faith in God the Generous. The accursed Devil whispers in his ear that there is no death, he will live a long time, the world is hostile. If he gives what he has, he will be left destitute, dishonored, and alone. He has to look after himself! If this evil imagination captures the heart, it leads to the edge of Hell-Fire.

"On the other hand, people who give their ears to God will hear Him say:

And whoever is saved from the miserliness of his ego, those it is who find salvation.
(*Hashr, 9*)

Whoever is miserly is miserly to himself.
(*Muhammad, 38*)

"Because God will:

Destroy their riches and harden their hearts.
(Yunus, 88)

"God's Messenger says, "God has next to Him two angels who pray every morning: 'O Lord, increase your bounties upon the generous, and take away from misers what they have.'"

"The one who gives from his sustenance receives more from God than he gave. The miser, in addition to the sin of miserliness, is guilty of distrusting the Ultimate Sustainer, and depends on his miserable goods over the generosity of his Lord. Therefore spend from what God has given you and do not fear poverty. God will give you what is destined for you, whether you ask for it or not. No one who has been generous has ever perished in destitution.

"If you wish to find God's pleasure and support in finding the truth, avoid being negative and control your temper and your anger. If you cannot stop feeling anger, at least do not show it. If you undertake this, you will disappoint the Devil and please God. That is the beginning of the education of your ego.

"Anger is a result and a sign of an ego out of control—left loose like a wild animal, untied and uncaged. When you hold your temper, it is as if you put a bridle on its head and barriers around it. Then you can begin to tame it so that it obeys and behaves, so that it cannot hurt others than itself—because your ego is still a part of you.

"When you can control your temper, your adversary will be calmed, since you are not reacting to his provocations or responding to his negativity. This is more effective than punishing him. He may be led to see the reality of his acts, to realize what is fair, and to confess his fault.

"Give value to your time. Live in the present moment. Do not live in heedlessness and in imagination and throw your time away. God has prescribed a duty, an act, a worship for your every moment. Know what it is and hasten to do it.

"Use your time first to earn your sustenance lawfully. The Messenger of God says, 'The one who earns his sustenance lawfully through his efforts is beloved of God.' And, 'God likes to see the believer working at his profession.' And, 'God likes the person who has a craft.'

"It is related that one day Hadrat 'Umar, beloved Companion of the Prophet, met a group of people who were sitting around lazily doing nothing. He asked them who they were. 'We are of those who put their affairs in the hands of God. We trust in Him,' they replied.

"'Indeed, you do not!' he heatedly responded. 'You are nothing but freeloaders, parasites upon other people's efforts. For someone who truly trusts in God first plants the seed in the belly of this earth, then hopes and puts his affairs in the hands of God the Sustainer.'

"First perform the actions that God has given to you as obligations. Next do what He has given you to do through the example of His prophets. Then take on what He has left you as voluntary, lawful, acceptable good deeds. And work to serve the ones who are in need.

"Distance yourselves from the heedless, for they are the slaves of their egos and of the desires of their flesh. They take hearts away from the light of truth and throw them into the dark hole of heedlessness, as they did with their own hearts. If you are forced to be with them in the same time and space, then face them and advise them. If they turn their backs on you, it is because they do not know their fronts from their backs. Be kind to them whether they turn their faces to you or their backs; then they may like you and respect you, and perchance they may become attached to you and follow you on the path of truth.

"Learn proper behavior. It is the means by which an intention becomes a good deed. Therefore it is the greatest capital in the hand of the seeker. The proof is in the words of the one who was brought with the most beautiful character, the last prophet, Muhammad, peace and blessings be upon him, who said, 'I have been sent to perfect good behavior.'"

THE TRUTH OF ISLAM

Ibn 'Arabi says that the name *Allah* is the proper name of the One and Unique God. It is the name of the essence of God, which contains in itself the beautiful names of all His attributes.

Everything in Islam has generated from the name Allah. It is the cause of the unity of God; the cause of the Holy Qur'an and all other holy books; the cause of worship and prayer. All else is named, but Allah is the Giver of Names. That is why the Messenger of Allah has said, "As long as someone is reciting the Name of Allah, the last day of the world will not come"—because on that day everything named will have ceased to exist. Only Allah, the Namer, will remain.

Ninety-nine beautiful names of Allah have been mentioned in the Holy Qur'an. Some, like "the Ever-Living," "the All-Knowing," are the names of divine attributes. Some, like "the Creator" and "the Sustainer," are the names of divine actions. When one mentions them, one says, "Allah the Ever-Living" and "Allah the Sustainer."

In Islam one declares one's faith by saying *la ilaha illa 'Llah*, there is no god but Allah, signifying that all is from Him, and that there is nothing but He. It is not sufficient as a declaration of belief in Him to say *La ilaha ill' al-khaliq*, "there is no God but the Creator"—although Allah is the Creator. One may say that a *creative* person, a *living* tree, a *sustaining* food, carry the manifestations of His attributes in His creation. However, nothing in His creation may be given the name Allah, for He is other than everything He has created and there is none like Him.

In the Muslim declaration of faith, after "There is no god but Allah," it is necessary to bear witness that "Muhammad is His servant and His Messenger."

The Messenger of Allah is a chosen human being, a perfect man. That he is "servant of Allah" shows us the highest level to which any human being can aspire. That he is "Messenger of Allah" is an indication of his closeness to his Lord. He is a guide and an example to humankind whom Allah has sent as a mercy upon the universe, and who Muslims believe will intercede for the faithful on the Day of Judgment. He is human—but as Shaikh 'Abdul-'Aziz Dabbagh, a contemporary of Ibn 'Arabi, says, "If the strength and valor of forty warriors were put into one man who could drag a male lion by the ear, and if that man saw the truth of the Prophet for a single moment, the awe that he felt would tear his lungs from his chest and his soul would leave him."

None can look upon him except the few saints to whom God has given the strength and the ability to see him. Ibn 'Arabi says that he saw him in an ecstatic state, and that he had no shadow—for the source of light has no shadow. God created the divine light, with which everything may be seen and understood, as his first creation. And He placed this divine light in Muhammad, may God's peace and blessings be upon him.

When this light is reflected in the heart of the believer, that heart sees the truth. That person becomes blind to the cognizance of himself, his ego, his flesh, as well as becoming blind to these characteristics in others. It is like when the ladies of ancient Egypt, invited by Zulaykha to see the beauty of the prophet Joseph, forgot themselves at the sight of him, and cut their fingers while peeling the fruit in their hands.

According to Ibn 'Arabi, the true peace of submission, the truth of Islam, is only possible by passing through that state where one forgets one's self and everything else. The saint Bayazid al-Bistami said: "I was only conscious three times in my life. Once I saw the world. Once I was conscious of the Hereafter. And then one night I saw my Lord, who asked me what I wished, and said He would give it to me. I told Him that I wished for nothing, for He is the Only One."

Thus the truth of Islam cannot be reached without eliminating the worries about this world and the worries about the Hereafter. The ones who can do that are in continuous worship and prayer.

According to Ibn 'Arabi, the way to the truth of Islam is through action and sincerity. The downfall of the ordinary person is to know, but to be unable to act upon that knowledge. For a better person, it is to act upon knowledge but lack sincerity. The danger for the person of higher state is to divulge knowledge without the license of the Lord—for inspired knowledge and the ability to exercise it in sincerity is one of the secrets of the Truth, and can only be shared with others by the permission of the One who gave it.

The confession of faith, "I bear witness that there is no god but Allah and I bear witness that Muhammad is His servant and His Messenger"; daily prayer; fasting during the month of Ramadan; charity; and pilgrimage to Mecca are the five pillars of Islam. Hadrat Ibn 'Arabi adds cleanliness, outer and inner purity, to these five obligations.

He likens Islam to a house with four walls. One wall is the daily prayer, the other is charity, the third is fasting, the fourth is pilgrimage. There is a double door to this house. Upon one leaf of the door is written, "There is no god but Allah," and upon the other, "Muhammad is His servant and His Messenger." The roof of that house is cleanliness—purity of body, mind, and soul. In this metaphor we see that if one of the walls is lacking, the house will not stand; and that prayer, fasting, charity, and pilgrimage offer little shelter without purity of being over all.

Ablution, a symbol of cleanliness, is a prerequisite to prayer. According to Ibn 'Arabi, the water used to clean oneself in ablution is a symbol of knowledge. The heart of a believer is alive only if sustained by knowledge.

When there is no water, one can take ritual ablution with sand or earth. Earth too is a symbol of life, for everything alive comes out of it. While taking ablution with water, one washes one's hands and arms to the elbow, one's mouth, one's nose, one's ears, one's face and eyes, one's feet, and also one puts water on one's head. While taking ablution with sand or earth, one does not put earth on one's head, because worship is an attempt to come close to God, while putting earth on one's head is a sign of mourning, of lamentation, when someone beloved is taken away and one is left alone and far off. God says:

> He it is who has made the earth humble, quiet,
> and submissive to you.
> *(Mulk, 15)*

Earth is the lowest of the four elements. Our need for it to cleanse ourselves is in our need to rid ourselves of the feeling of superiority and arrogance.

Once cleansed, a believer presents himself or herself in front of the Lord five times a day, during the ritual prayers performed at dawn, noon, afternoon, sunset, and night. In the seventeen cycles of obligatory prayer and twenty-three cycles of exemplary prayers, and in other voluntary prayers, we go through certain movements.

First we stand, turning in the direction of the Kaaba. Wherever believers find themselves on the face of the earth they turn toward Mecca, forming concentric circles. Thus, facing the Kaaba, we also face each other, symbolically facing the Lord in the hearts of all believers. For God says in a divine tradition, "I do not fit into the heavens and the earth of My creation but I fit into the heart of my believing servant"; and the Prophet says, "The believer is a mirror to the believer."

The prayer starts in a respectful, standing position. When the faithful raise their hands above their shoulders, palms facing forward, and say *Allahu akbar,* "God is greater than anything He has created," with this gesture they throw the world and their worldly concerns behind them with the backs of their hands. Then they clasp their right hands over

their left hands in a respectful position. In this standing position we are to be aware of the human in us, for only the human
being is vertical and stands erect. We then recite the opening
chapter of the Holy Qur'an:

> In the name of Allah, the Beneficent, the
> Merciful.
> Praise be to Allah, the Lord of the worlds,
> The Beneficent, the Merciful,
> Master of the Day of Requital.
> Thee do we serve and Thee do we beseech for help.
> Guide us on the right path,
> The path of those upon whom Thou hast bestowed
> favors,
> Not those upon whom wrath is brought down, nor
> those who go astray.
> *(Fatihah, 1-7)*

Ibn 'Arabi says that these words are a conversation
between the believer and his Lord. When the servant of God
says: "In the name of Allah, the Beneficent, the Merciful,"
the Lord says: "My servant is calling Me." And when he says:
"Praise be to Allah, the Lord of the worlds, the Beneficent,
the Merciful," the Lord says: "My servant knows Me and he
praises Me, for I love him and I overlook his faults." When
the believer says: "Master of the Day of Requital," the Lord
says: "My servant knows that he will come back to Me, and
depends on My justice and forgiveness."

In the center of the chapter is the key verse: "Thee
do we serve and Thee do we beseech for help," where the
whole of the being, conscious of its exterior actions and
expression and of the inner thought and feeling, promises
to submit to its Lord's will and beg for His help, declaring

that there is nowhere to go but to Him, there is no one from whom to ask for help but from Him. This is the crucial moment in the audience with one's Lord. People who realize this, at this awesome and fearful moment, tremble and shed tears. For the Lord might say: "O tongue, you say that you submit to Me and ask for My help alone, but all the members of that physical body, who have deputized you to talk to Me—your eyes, your mind, your heart—have forgotten Me. Thus, what you say is nothing but a lie." Those who are thus condemned are the people whose minds, eyes, and hearts wander, who look for and see and feel the temptations of this world during prayer.

In the last three verses of the opening chapter of the Holy Qur'an, the Lord speaks to the heart of the servant— for the prayer "Guide us on the right path" calls upon a promise of the Lord, as does "The path of those upon whom Thou hast bestowed favors, not those upon whom wrath is brought down, nor those who go astray."

In the second movement of the ritual prayer, when the believers bow from the waist and repeat thrice *subhana Rabbiy Al-'Azim*, "Glory to my Lord the Most Great," one is conscious of the animal state to which we have been reduced. Most animals roam the earth parallel to the ground. And we plaintively beg our Lord, "Have mercy upon me, O Great One!" Then momentarily we stand up, regaining our human state. With gratitude we throw ourselves into a position of prostration, for realizing our lowliness and the earth from which we are made, we return to the earth.

Then slowly we rise, sitting upon our knees, to remember the Day of Judgment. We turn our heads to the right and then to the left, seeking the help and intercession of those who loved us in this life—our mothers, our fathers, our children—but all in vain; for all will then be concerned with their own fate. The only one immune to the terror of that Day will be the one whom God has sent as His mercy upon the universe, the intercessor for sinners, Muhammad, may God's peace and blessings be upon him.

Before all prayers but one, a formal summons is chanted. The exception is the funeral prayer. And there is no call to prayer which is not followed by worship, except the summons recited into the right ear of a newborn child. The secret is that the call to attend to our departure from this world is issued at the moment we arrive.

The call to prayer consists of reciting four times, "Allah is greater," twice, "I witness that there is no god but Allah," twice, "I witness that Muhammad is the Messenger of Allah," twice, "Come to salvation," twice, "Come to felicity," and again twice, "Allah is greater." Finally, at the end, the reciter says once, "There is no god but Allah."

The reason that these phrases are repeated is that Muslims believe that every human being is born a Muslim—in fact, everything created is created as a Muslim. Some have remembered their original submission to God, while others have not. The first repetition addresses those who realize their state. The second is to remind those who have forgotten.

It is very important that these words be chanted musically and by someone with a most beautiful voice, especially for the congregational prayers in mosques. The Prophet chose Bilal the Abyssinian to perform the call, because his voice was beautiful, although his Arabic was lacking. He said, "When Bilal chants, all the gates of heaven open, up to the throne of God." And when he was asked if that was an honor bestowed on Bilal alone, he answered, "No, this honor belongs to all who call to prayer." In another tradition the Prophet said that the necks of the chanters of the call to prayer are very long—meaning that they will receive blessings as far as their voices reach. He also said that the souls of callers to prayer are together with the souls of martyrs in the Hereafter.

The call to prayer consists of the invitation of God issuing from the lips of a human being. It resembles the revelation of the holy books, which issued from the lips of the prophets. Therefore the real caller to prayer, who invites man to truth and salvation, to peace and felicity, is always the Prophet. As the Lord says in the Holy Qur'an:

> O our Lord, we have heard the call of one call-
> ing to faith "Believe ye in the Lord," and we
> have believed.
> (*Al-i 'Imran, 193*)

Ibn 'Arabi says, "When my Lord made me chant the call to prayer, I saw that each word coming from my lips extended to a distance as far as the eye can see. Then I understood the meaning of the Prophet's words that the necks of the chanters of the call to prayer will be very long, for their Lord's praise for them will be as vast as the area where their voices are heard. The heralds who call the believers to prayer are the best of people, after the prophets, who transmit the truth. The reason that the Prophet of God did not chant the call to prayer himself was because of his compassion for his people. If he himself had called people to prayer, those who couldn't come would have been disobedient to God, and received divine blame for revolting against Him."

FASTING

It is the obligation of every Muslim to fast the whole month of Ramadan, abstaining from eating and drinking and sex from dawn until sunset. During that time it is also important to watch one's emotions, cleansing them from criticism and anger and other negative feelings, as well as protecting oneself from negative impressions, negative thoughts, and negative words. For people at the level of Hadrat Ibn 'Arabi, fasting extends to the whole being. Nothing but God and the godly should enter, not only one's physical being, but also one's heart. Nor should anything leave the being but that which is pure.

Ibn 'Arabi says that the meaning of fasting is self-denial—to deny the evil-commanding ego and the flesh their wishes, which in turn will render the human being pure. No other form of worship or effort to come close to God can equal fasting, for there can be no hypocrisy in it. It is a secret between the Lord and His servant. When one fasts without resentment, sincerely and lovingly, the relation between the fasting servant of God and the Lord becomes selfless, total obedience. One gives up one's will and one's desires, and acts upon the wish of the Lord. That is why God says, "All acts and worship of humankind are for themselves and belong to them. Only fasting is done for Me, and the reward of it is from Me." God also says that the smell of the breath of the one who fasts is sweeter to Him than musk, because what the Lord smells is not the bad odor but the manifestation of His attributes of Patience and Compassion. The one who fasts for God's sake exhales these in each breath.

CHARITY

Almsgiving is one of the five pillars of Islam. Every year

each Muslim is obliged to give one fortieth of his liquid assets to other Muslims in need. As daily prayer and fasting are undertaken for the cleansing of one's soul, almsgiving is the worship proper to one's material belongings. It purifies our possessions and makes them lawful.

As charity is the best of deeds, so stinginess is a grave sin. Hadrat Ibn 'Arabi says, "The one who gives from his sustenance receives more from God than he gave. The miser, in addition to the sin of miserliness, is guilty of distrusting the Ultimate Sustainer, and depends on his miserable goods over the generosity of his Lord. Therefore spend from what God has given you and do not fear poverty. God will give you what is destined for you, whether you ask for it or not. No one who has been generous has ever perished in destitution."

He also relates a story that a saint of the time, misunderstood by the public, was accused of heresy and condemned to be killed. While he was being brought to the place of execution, he passed a baker. He asked the man to give him half a loaf of bread on credit. The baker, having pity on him, gave him the bread. Further ahead on the road there was a beggar. The saint gave the bread to him.

When the procession reached the place of execution, the sentencing judge, following the custom, asked the public gathered there whether they gave their final approval for the execution of the man whom they had declared a heretic and a tyrant. The people cried in unison, "No, this man is a saint, not a heretic! He is the expression of divine justice, not a tyrant!" The judge was shocked to hear this reversal, and had to release him.

The judge asked the saint the reason for the public's favor. "Is your wrath greater, or God's?" the saint inquired. The judge had to admit that God's wrath was greater.

"Is half a loaf of bread larger, or a date?" The judge agreed that half a loaf of bread was larger.

"Haven't you heard the sayings of the Prophet of God?" the saint asked him. "He said, 'Protect yourself from the wrath of God and His punishment by giving to the needy, even if it is half a date.' And also, 'Charity puts out the fire of punishment, and protects from early death.'"

PILGRIMAGE

The fifth principle of Islam is, once in a lifetime, to perform a pilgrimage to the Kaaba in the city of Mecca. This is an enactment of the Day of Judgment. One removes all signs of identity and wraps oneself in a shroud; the king and the beggar are equalized. During this stage, one pretends to be dead, selfless. We are forbidden to step on a blade of living green grass, to kill a biting flea, to pull a scab, or even to comb our hair.

Symbolic acts performed during this pilgrimage include circumambulation of the Kaaba; gathering in millions upon the plains of 'Arafat; and sacrifice of a ram in remembrance of the prophet Abraham's sacrifice for his son. Ibn 'Arabi says that the literal meaning of *Hajj* (Pilgrimage), in Arabic is the conscious intention to do something at a specific time.

When God addressed the prophet Abraham

Sanctify My house for those who compass it round or use it for a place of retreat or bow or prostrate themselves [in prayer],
(*Baqarah, 125*)

He related that house on this planet to Himself. And when He said

The first house appointed for humanity was
that at Bakka,
(*Al-i 'Imran, 96*)

He established it as the first house of worship and
assigned it as a symbol of His Throne upon earth. He
asked humankind to proceed around it, likening this act to
that of the angels who circumambulate His Throne. But
the circling of the Kaaba by people whose words are the
sincere confirmation of what is in their hearts, who have
cleansed their hearts from the temptations of life on this
earth, is a worthier worship than the devotion of the angels
circumambulating God's Throne in Heaven.

God built His temple upon three columns, though
today it appears to us in the shape of a cube. These three
columns are symbolic of the three remembrances of the
heart. The one on the corner where the Black Stone is
placed represents the divine inspirations. The column in
the direction of Yemen represents the angelic characteristics. The third column represents the carnal prompting of
human passions. These three supporting columns are
guardians; they forbid evil suggestions from entering the
house of the Lord. Supported by these three columns, the
four sides of the house of God manifest love—although the
fourth side of the cube, which faces Iraq, represents the
possibility of evil in human beings.

The heart of the believer is the real Kaaba. It also
has the four sides of divine inspirations, angelic attributes, material influences, and diabolic temptations. But the
ones who know their Lord have three sides to their hearts.
The seductions of evil are absent.

As the daily prayer starts with the declaration "God

is greater," so the Pilgrimage begins with the declaration of presence: "O Lord, I am present! I am here now in obedience, ready to receive Your orders! There is none other than You, all praise is due to You, all belongs to You, You have no partners." When the prophet Abraham was ordered to build the Kaaba, God told him to cry out these words—and in the spiritual realm, the Lord made the souls of all believers hear them. In remembrance, the pilgrims recite this cry.

Male pilgrims wear two pieces of white cloth—one wrapped around the waist, reaching to under the knees, and one to be thrown over the shoulder to cover the torso. Female pilgrims, also dressed in white, may not cover the face. This practice erases all difference of rank and social status, and is a symbol of the shroud.

The white Pilgrimage cloth is not sewn—it is as if not fashioned by human hands. It belongs to God, hiding what is reprehensible or lacking in a human being, protecting from everything that God forbids and from the temptations of the flesh. Like Adam, we carry our sins with us upon the Pilgrimage. But if he had not erred, he would not have descended to our world, where he is honored with being the Deputy of God.

The Black Stone embedded in one corner of the Kaaba is like the prophet Adam. It also left the Garden pristine and white. It turned black when it entered the earth's atmosphere. Yet the believers kiss it during the Pilgrimage.

At the end of the Pilgrimage, in a place called Mina, each day for three days the pilgrims throw seven stones at the Devil. Humanity knows its Lord through His three aspects: His actions, His attributes, and His existence. The three days represent these three manifestations. The seven stones represent the seven greater sins: pride in one's spiritual state; common arrogance; hypocrisy; envy; anger and negativity; love of property; love of position. Thus the first day one casts these sins out of one's actions, and the second day, out of one's character. On the third day, with the awe of the mystery of God's essence, one casts them from one's being. Finally cleansed, in the place called Mina, which means "Hope" and "Goal," one finishes the Pilgrimage and returns to the world. And then we try to do what is right, and to be what we are meant to be.

EPILOGUE

O seeker who wishes to find salvation, the first thing you must do is to search out a master who will see your faults and show them to you. You may travel far and wide trying to escape yourself, but it is a master who will save you from slavery under the tyranny of your ego. Do it now, because whatever one has now is better than the best one imagines one will have tomorrow.

When you find him you must behave like a dead body in the hands of the one who gives it its last ablution. You must be ready to accept your master as he is. Never criticize or find any fault in him, even if he acts against religious canons. No man is faultless. All men err and sin and are not safe from wrong. You are not a judge seeking someone guilty; you are someone guilty seeking a judge who is just.

Do not hide anything from your teacher, an idea or an intention, be it bad or good. Do not ever sit where he sat. Do not wear anything he wore. Place yourself across from him with dignity and good manners, like a slave in front of his master.

When he asks you for something or orders you to do something, open your ears and use your mind to understand exactly what he wants. Don't do anything without being absolutely sure that it is what he willed. Don't seek the reasons why he wills what he wills.

If you have to ask something from him, do not expect or insist upon an answer. You must tell him your dreams, but do not insist on an interpretation.

Don't listen to people who talk against him, for it will produce opposition to him within you. If you know people who oppose him, leave them alone: neither fight with them nor keep their company. Leave them to God, who will see to them.

Love those who praise your master and serve their needs as you would your own. If your master divorces his wife, don't ever marry her or have anything to do with her. Even with the best of intentions, never enter his house without his permission.

You must stay as close as possible to him without making yourself noticed. If he wishes to consult with you do not ask any questions or enter into discussion with him. Do not wish anything which he does not wish. If something comes to mind, keep it to yourself; do not exteriorize it. Follow the path he has indicated for you. It is thus that you will keep your noble station, the station achieved by the dignity of good behavior. That is the tie between you and him.

When you consult him about a matter concerning yourself, do it if he approves, do not do it if he disapproves —but if he told you to do it and gets angry at you for doing it, stop doing it. This change of mind is for your good, yet he will regret it. Remembering later that you bore no fault in it, he will find himself responsible and feel pain. He will try to repair what he did to you and at the same time you will keep your dignity and your good conduct. Beware: bad feelings toward the master are only found in students who are lazy, who do not do what they are supposed to do, and had the wrong intentions to begin with.

Don't oppose any of the master's actions or ask his reasons. Always be obedient. Be humble towards students whom your master favors above you. Even in his absence, sit properly, stand properly, and talk properly in accordance with good behavior, as if he were there and looking at you. Do not walk in front of him unless it is dark. Do not look him in the eye—if you do, it will reduce your respect for him and take the beautiful feeling of shame from your heart. Don't sit in front of him unless it is necessary, but wait behind the door, so that you can be there immediately when he wants you. Do not go anywhere, even if it is to visit your father, without his permission.

When you come into his presence the first time, kiss his hand and remain standing until he asks you to sit. Protect his property. If you bring him something to eat, bring what he likes, in the amount he likes, the way he likes it. Don't stare at him while he eats. When he finishes, clear the table immediately. If there is anything left on his plate and he asks you to eat it, do so, for there is blessing in it. Don't be envious of what he eats and don't count his mouthfuls.

Work hard always; that is what will please your master. Always wish good for him and expect good from him. Yet beware that he may trick you, for sometimes masters purposely do this to test their students. Be heedful and very careful when you are with him. If you do something inappropriate in his presence, thinking that he will not see it, know that he sees it very well for he sees everything you do and whatever passes inside you. He merely pretends that he does not, because he does not wish you to be punished. On the other hand, if he chastises you and punishes you and hurts your feelings, accept it without resentment.

As long as he is pleased with you and approves of what you do, your love and respect for him will increase. And as long as your humbleness and obedience toward him increase, your presence will grow in his heart and your state will improve. When your master is on a journey, keep the times when you usually meet him, and at the place where he sits, salute him inwardly as if he were there. It is not for you to ask him where or why he travels. When he consults you about a matter, know that he is not asking your opinion because he needs it, but as a sign of appreciation and kindness. Your answer should be, "You know best." Above all beware of opposing what he wishes to do. Even if you are absolutely sure that what he is doing is wrong, help him to do it and keep your thoughts to yourself.

On the Sufi path one advances only as one's master advances. Your hand is in the hand of your master, and the hand of your master is in the hand of God. Talking, discussing, and interpreting are not going to get you anywhere. The path to truth is to follow instructions without interpreting them, for the understanding of secrets belongs to those who know them. If you say: "I think he means this or I suspect he wants that," trying to interpret your master's orders, you are really only trying to escape from doing what you must: best sit and cry over your failure! All disaster that befalls a student comes from interpreting the indications of the master. This all is the play of the ego. The mind, the true Intellect, does not accept interpretation: it is not either this or that. There is an origin and a reason for every order; the true intelligence is anxious to fulfill it.

Even if you know what should be done next, don't do it or even think about it until your master so instructs you. Accept your master's every action, his whole way of living. The way he eats, drinks, sleeps, and behaves is his business, and you should have no opinions or comments on it. For your own sake, enter your master's life only when invited. Don't say, "Master, shall we eat together at home?" or "If you are not coming to such and such a place, should I go?" You are then trying to make him ask you to eat with him—indeed, to lie down with him! Instead of bringing you together, this will drive you apart, for it will decrease the love and appreciation and respect for you in his heart. If these feelings disappear, the tie is broken and that student will never find salvation or peace. Whoever says otherwise knows neither the path nor himself.

O seeker, see to it that your relations with your master are as I have described: may God so will. Know also that the beginning of this path is repentance. You must try to make even your enemies pleased with you. Forget their tyranny and shed tears for the time that you have spent fighting anything but your ego. Be a friend to knowledge: there is no one who is free from fault and sin. To make public accounting of the wrongs you have done in the attempt to show your master that you are repenting is in itself hypocritical and dangerous. The true sign of repentance is to leave what you have been doing, and from there on to be heedful, sincere, industrious, and pure.

ON WORSHIP

You must offer your five daily ritual prayers in congregation, and additional prayers at home. If you pray somewhere your master has prayed, do not stand at the place where he stood. Make a ritual ablution before each prayer, beginning every action with "In the name of God, the Compassionate and Merciful".

First wash your hands, intending to pull them away

from the affairs of this world. Then wash your mouth, remembering and reciting God's name. Wash your nose wishing to inhale the perfumes of the divine. Wash your face feeling shame, and intending to wipe from it arrogance and hypocrisy. Wash your forearms trusting God to make you do what is good. Wet the top of your head feeling humility and wash your ears wishing to hear the address of your Lord. Wash from your feet the dirt of the world so that you don't stain the sands of Paradise. Then thank and praise the Lord, and send prayers of peace and blessings upon our Master, who brought the canons of Islam and taught them to us.

After you leave the place of your ablution without turning your back to it, perform two cycles of prayer out of hope and thankfulness for cleanliness.

Next stand in the place where you are going to make your prayers as if between the two hands of your Lord. Imagine, without forms and lines, that you are facing the Kaaba, and that there is no one else on the face of this earth but you. Bring yourself to express your servanthood physically. Choose the verses you are going to recite, understanding their meaning within you. With the verses starting "Say: . . ." feel that you are talking to your Lord as he wishes you to do: let every word contain praise. Allow time between the sentences, contemplating what our Master, the Messenger of God, gave us, trying to keep it in your heart. Believing that your destiny is written on your forehead, place it humbly on the floor in prostration. When you finish and give salutations to your right and to your left, keep your eyes on yourself and you connection with your Lord, for you are saluting the One under whose power you are and who is within you.

When you are entering a place, give salutations in the name of God internally and when you have entered it, bless it with two cycles of prayer.

ON EATING

Eat the food a poor person would eat and leave the table without being full. Do not drink while eating and be sparing in the amount of water you drink. Do not accept special treatment while you eat; do not put on airs and affectations. Do not ever show your hunger. Measure the amount of food you eat so that you only partially satisfy your need. Your bites should be neither large nor small. Remember God at each bite, and chew well before you swallow. Each time you swallow, give time for the food to descend in your stomach and praise the Lord.

The practice of the faithful while eating is not to listen to the appetite of the flesh but to eat whatever is in front of one. Eating is a form of worship, so your movements should be controlled. Do not look right and left or think of your errors and shortcomings: be in a state of thankfulness. If there are people sharing the meal with you, avoid looking at them, at what they eat and how they eat, and try to be the last to serve yourself. If someone comments on why you eat so little, be polite but do not respond. If you explain and apologize, beware of being hypocritical. Do not leave the table until it is cleared. Eat only at mealtimes: to eat in between is gluttonous.

ON MAKING A LIVING, SUSTENANCE, AND SATISFACTION WITH ONE'S STATE

Know this: If you forget the truth and do not apply it in your life, you will leave the path sooner or later, for forgetfulness of the truth shows lack of trust in God, and lack of the peace brought by satisfaction with one's lot. Trust in God shows your knowledge that you are unable to do anything by yourself, and that you know very little. Therefore you are humble; you count on Him, the All-Powerful and All-Knowing. That will give you peace of heart.

The evil of your ego may tell you: "So sit where you are, and let Him feed you!" To think this way is unlawful; fear it, for it is a sin. Do not listen to your ego, yet take care of its needs.

In this life you will have to be with others who push you as your ego pushes you, and there will be people of power among them. Try to be with those you know, for in this life it is hard to know who is a foreigner and who is a native. Don't settle in one place. Keep moving. Try not to know anyone or let anyone know you. If you find someone insinuating himself close to you or sneaking up on you, bringing you things, your ego will tell you: "It is God who has made him discover your need and put that generosity in his heart." Do not take what he brings. If you took anything, give it back, for that person has been watching you and is trying to buy you by satisfying the needs of your ego, not your true need. This is not sustenance sent by God. Even if you are about to die, don't accept this kind of gift.

If something unwanted and unexpected is brought to you, examine yourself closely, what you have and what you lack. If you feel pressure or discomfort in acceptance, do not accept that thing. Return it to the one who brought it. If, in addition to the feeling of discomfort, you also suspect that it is unlawful, neither accept what is brought nor the one who brought it.

If you feel no pressing hunger and if what is brought to you comes to you unexpectedly, if you feel no discomfort in taking it and if it is lawful, take the minimum you need and return the rest. However, do not stay in that place anymore. If the one who brought you this gift happens to be among the rich and powerful and insists upon your staying, leave. If he indicates to you places of worship where you could go, in lands where he has connections and influence, you need not refuse.

All these exercises will strengthen the truth in you. Know that if you do not follow this advice, you will be tyrannizing yourself.

Do not listen to the talk of the idle "Sufi," who sits and does nothing and says, " My Lord is sufficient for me," for he has suffered all the things about which I have warned you. Do not be idle, for the best and the most lawful sustenance that comes from God is that which you have gained with your own two hands.

ON FRIENDSHIP

The hardest thing for the one who has taken this path is to keep old friendships. The student aims to leave behind all his old habits and all that his ego desires. Friendship, though, is connection and closeness. Of all things, to leave one's friends behind is the hardest and saddest. The one who wishes to come close to God must indeed distance himself from mankind. Yet when he does that, he is not necessarily with God —but he is necessarily alone. Worse, he may imagine himself to be with God. The best course is to distance oneself from one's habitual friends and tie oneself to one's master. One shouldn't even become too close to the other students of the master, or be with them against the wish of the master. Like a beast in the jungle, a student should stay together with his own species.

Those who wish to be with God and come close to Him should be independent of other people. They should remember, tie themselves to, and count upon God alone. When he is together with the other students, a seeker should feel that he is not with them, but with his master, and if he feels the absence of his master in the company of his friends, he should leave. If he feels no trace of the presence of his master in the conversation, and the conversation is totally secular and flippant, although it may be pleasant, he should escape from there.

The same applies to the clothes you wear. If you like your clothes and feel that they suit you well, sell them or give them away and buy yourself clothes toward which you are neutral. If you like your room or your house, change it. Keep giving things away and changing your place until you have nothing that pleases you, that preoccupies you, that captures your heart—until you feel that you are left all by yourself in this world without anything belonging to you. Know that God will not enter a heart where anything else resides.

A heart devoid of God is sick: if the student did not have his master as a doctor, that sickness would cause his spiritual death. Though the sick at heart cannot be with the doctor always, one must live very close to him, and when in need, seek his help. Still the doctor knows best when to see the patient, and the master, when to see his student. His purpose is to see the student's heart cured and renewed with the medication of remembrance of God and the diet of peace contained in the trust in God.

If you get involved in something without telling your

master and he knows what you are doing from your behavior, it is a sign that your heart has opened to him and you are truly attached to him—for he can read your heart.

Your relations with people should be gentle, generous, and sincere. You should ask nothing from them, knowing that you have no rights over them and that everyone is better than you.

The best thing is to have as little as possible to do with people. In any relationship people have rights over each other. If you have relationships with too many people and if you follow the right course in your relationships by giving them their due, you will not have much left with which to give God His due. If you are bankrupt like this, it is better to run away from the world and its demands.

When you separate yourself from the friendship of this world, if your friends complain about it, admit that you deserve their reproach. If they praise you for it, do not accept their praise; think that they see their own good qualities in you. If you do this, God will hide your real state from them. Woe to the one whose real state becomes visible to others! Remember that he who praises you is your enemy, because he is the friend of your enemy, and he who condemns you is your friend, because he is the enemy of your enemy.

Do not move around much. If you do, let your trips be of short duration. Too much movement is disruptive. It prevents you from advancing toward your real goal.

If you have to go somewhere, do not get distracted by what is on your right and what is on your left. Look where you are going; lower your eyes; watch your steps. Keep your mind on God and remember Him always. Do not stop to talk with this person or that, asking, "How are you?" or "What are you doing?" Idle talk! But if someone gives you salutations, return his salutations. If you see a believing servant of God, offer God's peace and blessings to him as if to all the believers in heaven and earth.

If you come across something that hinders your path, take it and remove it so that it does not hinder others. If you see something good that someone has lost, pick it up so that it is not trampled and put it somewhere visible on the side of the road. Show the right way to anyone who is lost. Help the weak. Share the load of the one who is heavily burdened.

Walk at a fast and steady pace. If you get tired, draw to the side and rest, being careful not to be in anyone's way.

Do not visit other teachers or participate in their meetings without the approval of your master. If your master permits you, you may go there to sit quietly and respectfully. Do not participate in their activities and ceremonies of remembrance, but do your own remembrance inwardly. This is better for you than to get involved in things you do not know. You may be affected by the hymns, the music, and the movements, and you may find yourself swaying. You may hear a hymn about death that casts fear into your heart, saddens you, and brings tears to your eyes so that you feel that life is passing, that the terror of death is near, and that there is a Day of Reckoning and punishment in Hell. All this excitement may seem like an invitation to get up and enter the circle of *dhikr*. Think twice! What is being said? What is being done? Who is saying it, what are his intentions? Is he sincere?

If what you feel is a separation from your senses, and from this world, then get up and participate. That is not a voluntary decision. You are not doing it for yourself; what makes you participate is something else. As soon as you return to your senses, stop and sit, and assume your previous state.

Moving in the ceremony of the Remembrance of God is a break from one's usual temperance and sobriety. Then one either soars above the norm or sinks under it. When you feel your movements and your physical body, you are in descent If your descent continues, you end up under seven layers of the material world and sink into the conditions of Hell. If you lose your sense of yourself, of your movements, and of what is around you, then you leave yourself. Your heart ascends, filled with the might of Truth, to lofty celestial levels.

One is either in Paradise or Hell. Those who see you may think you are in a state of rapture, in communion with God, but that may not be the case at all. So it is best to abstain from participation in the religious services of dervishes of other circles.

If your need for friendship is too pressing, seek out friends who are sincere and righteous. Perchance you will find your master among them or through them. If you do not find such friends in the well-traveled quarters of cities and towns, seek them in lonely places, in ruined little mosques. What such people seek is in those lonely ruins, in deep valleys, or on top of inaccessible mountains. If you find them, try to be with them at the times of prayer.

The most inept seekers are those who miss the times of prayer and come to the congregation late. If you are late, even though you came, you did not come together with the ones who are there. Those who are delayed have been rejected by their guides. When you participate in congregational prayers, do not stand at the same place, or in the same rank, each time; even change mosques from time to time. Ask forgiveness from God for each moment of your life.

Befriend and be close to the poor. Serve them, help them, remember them, and think about them and their needs. Your consideration of them, your thoughts about their needs, are like honorable messengers coming from the One who protects them. How can you refuse to honor such messengers? So do what they need to have done; cook for them, clean for them, be a part of the good that comes to them. Then you will be part of what enters into their hearts.

Only good inspirations enter the hearts of the sincere and faithful who are needy, for their continuous battle with the desires of the flesh prevents them from having unclean thoughts. God Most High rewards them with both worlds for their trust in Him, and when you are with them, He will make you remember what they remember. If you remember and satisfy their needs, they will receive the rewards of their efforts from your hands, and you will be proving your own Trust in Him.

Is that going to be counted as a good deed? Are you to expect a reward? No! Yet do not belittle your action either. Your reward is that you have been brought to this path to truth, while the ones who negate Him are damned.

Whoever has these four attributes will be saved:

1. Service to the needy
2. Purity and peace of heart
3. Good will to the believers
4. Thinking well of everybody and everything

Keep these principles with you at all times. At the beginning, your efforts may not bear fruit. Your good deeds may be thrown back in your face, some by the people involved, some by your Lord.

If you try to do good with an eye toward people's opinion of you, you will consider yourself farsighted, trustworthy, experienced, well respected, and you will end up thinking that others are inferior to you. Then know that the Devil has turned all your good deeds into evil.

The Devil's aim is to tire you, to trip you, to make you fall. He tells you that your lies are truth and that the truth is lies. He rewards you with unexpected gifts for your sins. Repent, take refuge in God, tie your heart to Him and remember Him always. He is the only one who can save you from the accursed Devil.

As long as you are sincere and constant on the path to truth you will keep the Devil at bay.

God knows best. May He keep you safe from the evils of this world and of your own self, and may He guide you on the straight path to truth.

Amin, bi hurmati Sayyid al-mursalin.